Originally published in 1890 by the author, and reprinted by him in 1896.

Reprinted hereinafter in entirety except for cover illustrations, 1985. This reprint is photographically reproduced from a volume printed in 1890. Because the original ink is faded, quality of this reprinting is below standard on some pages. The omission here of the illustration listed *(on page x)* as appearing between pages 112 and 113 replicates an omission in the original publication.

Library of Congress Cataloging-in-Publication Data:

Erskine, Charles.
Twenty years before the mast.

Reprint. Originally published: Boston: C. Erskine, 1890.
1. Erskine, Charles. 2. Voyages around the world.
3. United States Exploring Expedition (1838-42).
I. Title.
G420.E77E77 1985   910.4'1   85-2271
ISBN 0-87474-415-6 (alk. paper)

The paper in this book meets the guidelines for permanence and durability of the Committee on Production Guidelines for Book Longevity of the Council on Library Resources.

This reprint edition is made possible by a generous grant from the Atherton Seidell Endowment Fund.

TWENTY YEARS
BEFORE THE MAST

Charles Erskine

Smithsonian Institution Press
Washington, D.C.

CHARLIE ERSKINE,

Late Coxswain of the United States Brig "Porpoise."

FROM A DAGUERREOTYPE TAKEN BY PLUMB, 75 COURT ST., BOSTON, IN 1842.

MR. CHARLES ERSKINE,

The Author.

Photograph taken by J. W. Black, 333 Washington St., Boston, in 1882.

TWENTY YEARS BEFORE THE MAST

WITH THE MORE THRILLING SCENES AND
INCIDENTS WHILE CIRCUMNAVIGATING
THE GLOBE UNDER THE COMMAND
OF THE LATE ADMIRAL
CHARLES WILKES
1838–1842

BY

CHARLES ERSKINE

With Numerous Illustrations

BOSTON
PUBLISHED BY THE AUTHOR
1890

Morning Star Press,
BOSTON.

To the Crew of the

Ship Universal

THIS BOOK IS

RESPECTFULLY DEDICATED

BY ONE OF THEIR SHIPMATES

THE AUTHOR

Every man is a valuable member of society who, by his observations, researches, and experience, procures knowledge for men. —Sᴍɪᴛʜsᴏɴ.

TO THE READER.

I MUST ask you, as you read the following pages, to bear in mind that I have been only a common sailor before the mast. I trust you will expect from me, therefore, nothing higher in eloquence than a seaman's language. I have stood before no professor's chair, no classic lore has been instilled into my mind, I have received no college or even common school education, nor am I indebted in any way to literary studies for such knowledge of men and things as I may possess. My ideas are my own — not the reflex of another's mind. The world has been my school, and from the book of nature have I taken all my lessons.

For twenty years I sailed the ocean under our country's flag, whose broad stripes and bright stars have floated to the breeze in every clime; and on every shore I visited I found something grand or wonderful, beautiful or sublime, that photographed itself upon my memory. From earliest boyhood my heart went out in admiring love towards those great navigators whose discoveries have caused their names to be inscribed on the scroll of the world's immortals. My heart thrilled at the name of Columbus, whose heroic soul was made to feel the meanness of kings, and whose dauntless courage called into creation a New World which shall yet outrival in glory the greatness of the Old. Of almost equal interest to my boyish imagination were the brothers Cabot; Ponce De Leon, the romantic wanderer after the fountain of perpetual youth; and De Soto, the proud cavalier who discovered the mighty Mississippi, only to find a grave beneath its waters. Men, all these, who were courageous and enterprising, and whose adventures, sometimes tragic, sometimes romantic, have contributed largely to the annals of discovery.

Passing onward through the centuries of maritime adventures, I feel yet, as in the days of my youth, a mighty magic in the names of Drake, Frobisher, and the ill-fated Sir Walter Raleigh. My imagination takes me over the southern seas with Tasman, Cook, and Magellan, over the burning sands of Africa with Mongo Park, Livingstone, and the dauntless Stanley. I visit the ice-bound regions of the Arctic and Antarctic with Perry, Franklin, Ross, Wilkes, and D'Urville, with Hudson, Ringold, De Haven, with Knox, Kane, and De Long; and I drop a tear to the

memory of those intrepid men who, in the realms
of the pitiless ice-king, became martyrs to their
zeal for geographical discovery.

In the world's early days the command of God
to man was, to subdue the earth, to conquer it,
and to civilize and fit it for the habitation of the
human race. Nor did God's command apply to
this portion or that only, or merely to lands where
nature smiles in loveliness; nor yet to the forest
primeval, the cloud-capped hills, the far-stretching
plains, or the regions of eternal ice and snow;
but to the *whole earth* in its completeness. This
should be man's mission. So long as one spot of
this huge globe remains to be subdued, man, the
conqueror, must go forth to battle, and unfurl in
every clime the standard of civilization and Christianity, in obedience to the Divine command.
Such, at least, is my unlearned interpretation of
the Bible language.

I confess myself anxious to inspire you, my
dear friend, with some little enthusiasm in the
cause of geographical science. You cannot, like
Mahomet, go to the mountain, and so the mountain must be made to come to you. We cannot
all be sailors and travelers, and visit foreign lands;
and so I intend that some of these strange places
— the sunny islands of the Pacific and the frozen
regions of the Antarctic — shall visit you. As

you peruse these pages I trust that they will
awaken in your heart an endearing love for the
sublime and beautiful in God's wonderful creation,
and that they will bring you into earnest sympathy with those fearless pioneers of civilization who
go forth in contempt of danger and death, to add
to the sum of man's knowledge of the world, to
widen the boundaries of civilized existence, and to
obey the first and last command of Almighty God,
who has decreed that this earth shall be subdued,
and the Gospel preached to every creature.

I have refreshed my memory by reading the
history of our cruise in the United States exploring expedition, under the command of the late
Admiral Charles Wilkes, and wish to acknowledge
my indebtedness to the same for dates and a few
facts and illustrations.

CHARLES ERSKINE.

LIST OF ILLUSTRATIONS.

FULL–PAGE ILLUSTRATIONS.

TWENTY YEARS BEFORE THE MAST.

CHAPTER I.

I WAS born in the first house on the east side of
Roxbury Street, just over the Boston line, in the his-
toric old town of Roxbury. The hip-roofed old mansion still stands, the front end facing the street. In the
middle of the sidewalk rises a stately elm tree, in front

of which is a stone post some three feet high, bearing
on one side the inscription *R., A. D. 1823*, on the
other, *B., A. D. 1823*.[1] This stone marks the boundary line between the towns of Boston and Roxbury.

[1] In that year (1823) the town of Boston, having twenty-five
thousand inhabitants, was incorporated a city.

As I was born in one of the first houses, I must belong to one of the first families. My father was of Scotch descent. My ancestors came over about the time Miles Standish did. Our family motto is, *"We add honor to that of our ancestors."* I never saw my father until I was over thirty years old, as the sequel will show. My mother was a Sturtevant, of Dutch descent. Ours was a very patriotic family, and fought both in the Revolution and the War of 1812. My mother's brother, Major Thomas Sturtevant, with General Dearborn, Colonel Spooner, and Colonel Wyman, received President Monroe in 1817, and General Lafayette in 1824, on their arrival in the old stage-coach at Taft's Tavern, near the toll-gate at Brush Hill Turnpike. On each occasion my mother served lunch on their arrival at the line, after which the latter, Lafayette, was escorted to the house of Governor Eustis, near the Dorchester line. I have in my possession four of six vases which President Monroe sent to my mother soon after his arrival in Washington.

I was christened in the old wooden meeting-house on the hill opposite the Norfolk House, by Dr. Eliphalet Porter, and was named for an old gray-headed negro who did chores for the folks about town, and went by the name of "Clever Charlie." My father was a well-to-do currier, and possessed some considerable property; but the drawing of a large prize in a lottery ruined him. He became addicted to drink, neglected his business, and finally left for parts unknown.

I was the youngest of five children. When I was quite small, my mother moved to Cambridge, and thence to

Boston. She was not very well or strong, and worked hard to support her little family. I was sent to school, but very seldom went, — in fact, I " hooked Jack " nearly all the time. There were no truant officers or police-men in those days, and only seven constables in all Boston : old Reed, old Jones, old Clapp, the two old Browns, and the two old — I-forget-their-names. I used to run down the harbor in the old sloop *Sal* after paving-stones and sand, and sometimes at noon my feeble voice might have been heard at the head of State Street, crying out, " Here's the *Mail, Bee,* and *Times.*" I also tended dinner-table in old Hunt's cellar on Commercial Street. John B. Gough tended bar there too, and roomed at my mother's. If I was wanted at any other time, I could easily be found down at the wharves, in some ship's jolly-boat, or up in one of her tops, scan-ning the harbor. How I enjoyed listening to the sailors spinning yarns about the foreign countries they had seen and the sunny islands of the Pacific ! I caught the sea-fever badly. It struck to my brain, and I made up my mind to be a sailor anyway. I knew very well that I was not one of the best boys in Boston, though I had one of the very best of mothers. She was so good and loving that I could not harbor the thought of deserting her — I knew it would almost break her poor heart ; but I kept coaxing and teasing, teasing and coax-ing, until I had almost bothered the life out of her. At last I gained her consent, and was made one of the hap-piest boys in all Boston. Without emotion I could say :

> " Farewell to the land of my childhood and youth,
> The land of the Bible, religion, and truth !

Thou bright land of blessings in every form,
I leave thee and fly to the billow and storm."

It was on a bright, sunny morning in the month of
June that we sailed. Old "Sol" never shone brighter, as
he shed his warm rays into the back windows of the old
Spurr house on Commercial Street. Here mother hired
several rooms on the second floor, and it was in one of
these back rooms that I received her blessing. I shall
never forget the time or the place. There was a fond
embrace from a loving mother, a kiss on the forehead,
and a " God bless you, my son ! Be a good boy, obey
your captain, and never forget to say your prayers."
Kind reader, no earthly being can bless you as a loving
mother can. As I looked up and saw the thin, pale face
of my mother, I felt the hot tears roll down my young
cheeks. I was almost choked. I could not look up
again or utter a single word, but I thanked God that I
had her consent to go, and that I was not running
away to sea and leaving mother and home for

" A life on the ocean wave
And a home on the rolling deep."

In less than an hour I was on board the good old
schooner *Longwharf*, Captain Cook of Provincetown,
and standing down the Bay, bound to the Banks for
a fishing cruise.

From this time, I made several trips cod-fishing and
mackerel-catching, and also a number of voyages to the
West Indies and some of the southern ports. As so
much has been written, however, about the slave-ships
and the pirates of the West Indies, I will not go into

the details of any of these short voyages, but, instead,
will give you one of them in the form of a ditty:

A Sailor's Ditty.

'T was on the twenty-first of April, from Hampton Roads we sailed.
Kind heaven did protect us with a sweet and pleasant gale.
'T was on board the *Roving Betsy*, — bold Daniels was his name, —
And we were bound down to Laugarra on the Spanish Main.
When to Laugarra we came, my boys, our orders they were so:
To land a part of our cargo and proceed to Curacoa.
When to Curacoa we came, my boys, our cargo for to unload,
'T was "Get the *Betsy* in readiness for Port Laugarra Roads."
Our captain called all hands aft, and then to us did say,
"Here's money for you all, my lads, for to-morrow we go to sea."
'T was early the next morning all hands appeared on board,
And cheerfully got under way for Port Laugarra Roads.
'T was early the next morning, just at the break of day,
When a man at our foretop-mast-head a sail he did espy,
All hands being called to quarters, our courage for to try, —
All hands being called to quarters, — our enemy draws nigh.
She mounted twelve six-pounders, and fought one hundred men.
And now the action's just begun — it was just half-past ten.
We mounted four six-pounders, and our crew was twenty-two;
But in fifty minutes by the watch we whipped those Spaniards blue.
And now we are repaired, brave boys, bound for Columbia's shore,
And for the famous America and the city of Baltimore.
Now, to conclude my ditty (these lines this world may view),
Success attend brave Daniels and his jovial twenty-two.

Home again! "Home, home, sweet home, — be it
ever so humble, there's no place like home." Never
were there truer words written. So far I have not found
anything homelike, or any sunshine, in the dark, damp,
dingy, dreary forecastle. It does seem sort of jolly,
though, when you pass round the can, and some old

weather-beaten man-of-war's man or privateersman sings lustily :

"Then we'll sling the flowing bowl.
 Fond hopes arise;
 The girls we prize
Shall bless each jovial soul.
 For the can, boys, bring:
 We'll dance and sing,
While the foaming billows roll," —

or " Jack, the Lad," " Black-eyed Susan," or the song Jack likes the best — " The Girl I Left Behind Me."

They were glad to see me home again, — mother, brothers, sisters, and friends, — and we had a jolly time together once more. The very next day, however, I took a cruise on the wharves and visited old Titcomb's shipping office. He told me shipping was very dull and rates low, but offered me a boat-steerer's berth with a very high lay on board a whaler. This almost persuaded me to ship, but while on Constitution Wharf, my eye caught sight of a man-of-war brig lying at anchor in the stream off the Navy Yard, Charlestown. The following day I paid the Yard a visit. While viewing the brig, I saw the boatswain in a boat ahead of her, squaring the yards by the lifts and braces. She proved to be the ten-gun-brig *Porpoise*. She sat like a duck on the water, and looked as trim and neat as a young lady in her Sunday rig. I must confess that I was fairly carried away with her and bewitched with her rakish looks. I was suddenly awakened from my dream by a gentle tap on the shoulder from an officer who proved to be Captain Ramsey, commander of the handsome brig.

He asked me how long I had been at sea, where I was born and brought up, whether I had a father and mother living, and how I would like to sail with him in that man-of-war brig. I told him that was just what I wanted. Calling in at an office near the gate, he wrote and gave me a paper, telling me that if I could get my mother to sign it, I could go. After a great deal of coaxing and many promises I persuaded her to sign the paper. I went on board the brig the next morning, and we sailed in the afternoon.

When a few days at sea, the purser ordered me to sign the ship's articles. I refused. Then, being ordered to sign them by the captain, I made my mark, as I was unable to write at the time. We had on board Commodore Woolseley, Captain Shubrick, and Captain Stringham. We visited the West India Islands and touched at some of the southern ports. On our return we encountered a very heavy gale off Hatteras, and lost two of our bow guns overboard. As I was lashing a hen-coop forward, the brig shipped a heavy sea, and I was washed out overboard through one port-hole, and back, by chance, through another.

On our arrival at Norfolk we were transferred on board the receiving-ship *Java*. The frigate *Brandywine* was being fitted out for the Mediterranean station, and we were told that we must re-enter the service and go on board of her, or be discharged. All hands took their discharge. Mine read as follows : " This is to certify that Charlie Erskine, coxswain, is regularly discharged from the sea service of the United States and from the U. S. ship *Java*." [Signed] E. B. Boutwell, Lieutenant, March, 1837.

In taking my discharge, I was told by Lieutenant Boutwell that my wages amounted to one hundred and sixty-nine dollars, but I was paid only one dollar and seventy-one cents. The lieutenant said that the rest of my wages had been paid to Captain Ramsey three days before, and that he had gone to Washington. Instead of coxswain, I should have been rated on the ship's books as a first-class boy, at eight dollars per month. The duty of the coxswain is to have charge of the captain's gig. It is a petty officer's berth, and belongs to an able-bodied seaman.

The next day I set out for Washington in company with another boy about my age by the name of Martin. He also was rated as a petty officer, and the captain had taken his wages. On arriving in Washington, we soon found the captain's house. He put us at menial service for a time, and then hired us out to work on the Georgetown aqueduct. In the evenings, my chum and I used to visit the Capitol. I remember seeing there John C. Calhoun, R. M. Johnson, John Tyler, Colonel Washington, Judge Bibb, James Bell, James K. Polk, General Cass, Judge Woodbury, Edward Everett, Daniel Webster, John Davies, Colonel Benton, Otis, Hayne, Ticknor, Judge Story, Sumner, General Scott, John Q. Adams, Henry Clay, and other distinguished men. I was very much impressed with their noble looks, and shall never forget them. Most of them had round and very large heads. Calhoun's was long; Clay's was long, but smaller. General Cass had a wart on the side of his nose. Such an array of talent and intellect I have never seen since, although I have visited Washington several times in later years.   It was a grand sight to look upon these great men.

One afternoon the captain paid us a visit, in order to get hold of our wages.   I do not know what he thought of us, for we felt and looked like two drowned rats. We were smeared all over with mud, and were wet through and through to the skin.   We told him that this slinging mud was not sailor's duty.   He told us to seek a better lay.   The next day we went down to Alexandria and shipped in the brig *Joseph*, bound to Philadelphia.   At Philadelphia, while we lay alongside a wharf at the foot of South Street, a fine-looking man came along and gave each man on board a tract.   He spoke very kindly, offering some good advice.   Luckily, he proved to be an uncle of mine, and, getting permission from the captain, I went home with him.   Philadelphia is, I believe, called the " City of Brotherly Love." I found my cousins the pleasantest people I had ever seen.   Philadelphia is, in fact, the most homelike city I was ever in, excepting Boston—of course there is no place like the " Hub" to me.   My cousins lived on either

> " Market, Arch, Race, or Vine,
>   Chestnut, Walnut, Spruce, or Pine "

Street, I do not remember which.

I arrived in Boston after a fifteen-days' passage, all right, and found all glad to see me back home again.

After working a short time in a hook and eye factory, and stubbing my toes against the pavements, I shipped in the navy for the African station.   In a few days, however, I was transferred from the receiving-ship *Colum-*

bus to my old brig *Porpoise*, Captain Charles Wilkes
commander, on the coast survey. After surveying
Georges Banks and Nantucket Shoals, we returned
to Boston. The day after our arrival at the Navy Yard
I was sent over to the city to the office of Mr. Bowditch,
author of the "American Navigator," on State Street.
He said that our charts were the neatest he had ever
seen. He seemed to take quite an interest in me, and
gave me some good advice in a fatherly way, which
came just in time, for I had made up my mind that
I would disappoint every one, and be somebody. From
here I went to the office of the navy agent, where
I received a number of letters, which I put into my
hat — in those days sailors wore tarpaulin hats. I had
been told by the captain to hurry and be quick, and
had obeyed orders in good shape so far; but I could
not go by my home a second time without stopping
to see my mother. She was very glad to see me, and
I shall never forget her fond embrace, and the "God
bless you, my darling boy!" when I left her. As I crossed
the bridge, there was a schooner going through the draw,
and while I was waiting, my hat was knocked overboard. I immediately jumped into the schooner's
boat and recovered it, but of course the letters were
wet. I met the captain near the dry dock, explained
my adventure, and told him how the letters got wet.
He gave me a look dark as a thunder-cloud, and ordered me on board. I went straight to the landing
where the boat was, and the crew told me that the
captain was as "mad as a hornet." As I passed
over the gangway, Lieutenant Boyle ordered the boat-

swain to "introduce me to the gunner's daughter."
I was seized and placed over the breech of a sixty-two-
pound Paxon gun, and whipped with the colt so severely that I could not sit down with any comfort for
several weeks. The colt is a piece of rope about three
feet long and half an inch thick. The boatswain and
his mates always carry one in their hats for immediate
use. I worked my right hand behind me and received
several very painful cuts over the knuckles. All this
time we were lying not more than a quarter of a mile
in a straight line from where my mother lived, and if
she had been at an open window at the front of the
house she could have heard my piercing cries. On
being released, I went forward, and one of the old sailors set me on a bucket of water and put my hand into
another. He said that would take out the soreness.
It was in the fall of the year, and not very warm. I had
on a white under-flannel, — that is, it was white once, —
a blue flannel shirt, and blue dungaree trousers. When
I went below and took off my clothes, I found that my
trousers had been cut through, and threads from them
were sticking to my bruised flesh. When I shipped
this time I had made up my mind to try to be somebody and to get ahead in the world ; but now my hopes
were blasted. My ambition was gone, yes, whipped
out of me, — and for nothing. This has been the case
with many a sailor. Among the letters which I had
received at the agent's were the sailing orders, which
the captain expected, and this was the reason why he
was so anxious for my return. We sailed the next day
for the south.

After surveying Charleston Harbor and those of
Darien, New Brunswick, and Savannah, we sailed for
New York. Our captain had left us at Savannah, having
been ordered to Washington. On our arrival at New
York we were transferred on board the receiving-ship
Fulton, and in a few days the brig's crew were dis-
charged.

After exploring the "Hook" and "Five Points," I
returned to Boston, and found all at home well. My
oldest brother and his friend Gough were supernumer-
aries at the Lyon Theater, where there was a circus.
I shipped in the circus. For a week I was put through
a regular course of training in riding and tumbling. In
trying to turn a double back somerset I came near
breaking my neck. I rather thought that I had better
quit the circus before I did break it. The ring-master—
his name, I think, was Stickney—wanted me to stay,
and so did the old clown ; but after thinking it all over,
I gave up the idea of being a rider and tumbler, and
left the circus.

My brother Thomas, who was a little older than I,
lived on a farm in old Concord. I visited him for a
few days, and had a very lively time, but have always
regretted one thing—that I influenced him to run
away. I planned the whole thing, set the time, and
thought he would run away that night, but he said no,
he wanted to go over to Carlisle the next day. Now
I do not think any one could guess why he wished to
go over to Carlisle. It seems he had heard that there
was an Irishman in that town, and, as he had never
seen one, thought he would improve the opportunity,

for he would probably see nothing of the kind in Boston. No one in those days was spoken of as an Irishman, a Frenchman, a Norwegian, or an Italian, but simply as " a foreigner." Almost every one who wore whiskers wore a pair, one on each side of the face, or a full beard all around. The mustache, imperial, and goatee are foreign importations. A young Boston dandy who wanted to appear outlandish raised a mustache. When next he visited a country village, a good farmer's wife laid her hands carefully on his clothes to see if they were homespun. Finding that they were not, she asked him if he was a " furriner." He told her that he was no foreigner, but a Boston boy. " What on airth do you wear that bunch of hair on your upper lip for?" inquired the good woman.

In those days we burned whale oil in our lamps, and built fires in good old-fashioned open fireplaces. There were no stoves or coal oil. We made our own matches, and struck fire with flint and steel in the old-fashioned tinder-box. A familiar byword was, " A smoking chimney, a scolding wife, and green wood to burn." Most men wore leather straps to keep their trousers down, and leather stocks to keep their dickies up. The women used to wear moccasin hoods and calashes. Almost every man wore boots, up to the time of the Rebellion ; now nearly all wear shoes. In the good old days gone by, when people paid their grocery bills a glass of black strap was given to the old man, a couple of nutmegs to the old lady, and a stick of peppermint candy was added for the baby.

CHAPTER II.

WITH the characteristic restlessness of a sailor, I could not remain long at home, and in a few days I had shipped again in the navy, this time for the Mediterranean station.

> "How I love the blue waters! Their deep, maddening roar
> Is food for the spirit unbounded by shore.
> Thy whirlwinds may shriek, thy lightnings may flash,
> Yet safe o'er thy bosom, old Ocean, I'll dash."

I was first sent to New York with a draft of men to join the receiving-ship *Fulton*. In a few days, however, I was transferred to the brig *Porpoise*, Captain C. Ringold commander, and we sailed the next week for Norfolk, Va. Here we joined the exploring expedition just setting out on a voyage of discovery round the world. This was the first and only expedition sent out by the United States, and such a chance to visit the various quarters of this huge globe was never offered before or since. I liked our captain very much. He treated the crew like men; and as for the brig, she looked more rakish than ever, and I must acknowledge that I was more than ever in love with her. The squadron consisted of the sloop-of-war *Vincennes*, the flag-ship, Charles Wilkes commander; the sloop-of-war

Peacock, Captain William L. Hudson; the ship *Relief,* Captain A. K. Long; the brig *Porpoise,* Captain C. Ringold; the schooner *Sea Gull,* Captain Reed; the schooner *Flying Fish,* Captain Samuel R. Knox; together with a full corps of scientific men, consisting of philologists, naturalists, mineralogists, conchologists, botanists, horticulturists, taxidermists, draughtsmen, etc., and a complement of six hundred and eighty-seven men. The entire equipment of the squadron was generous

DEPARTURE OF THE EXPEDITION.

erous and complete, and could not but reflect honor upon the nation whose public spirit could thus plan and execute a noble project the value of which to the cause of science could not easily be estimated.

Everything being ready, we dropped down to Hampton Roads. Commodore Wilkes inspected all the vessels and their crews. As he passed me at muster, "old Adam" came up, and I could not raise my eyes from the deck, for it was Commodore Wilkes at whose command I had been flogged. The following day we were honored by a visit from the President of the United States, Martin Van Buren, and his cabinet. All the vessels had their yards manned, and a national salute was fired. The next day, the 17th of August, 1838, a gun was fired, and signals were made that the squadron was under sailing orders. Soon after, the commodore's gig came alongside, bringing orders for me with my bag and hammock. It seemed to me that I should sink through the deck. I felt more like jumping overboard than sailing with my worst enemy, and one on whom I had sworn to be revenged. I begged Captain Ringold to let me remain on board the brig. He said he wanted me to stay, but that he must obey orders, and told me to get into the boat. As we neared the ship, another gun was fired, and signals were made for the squadron to get under way. Shortly after we arrived on board, the capstan was manned, the anchor catted, and we were soon off, with an ebb tide and a light air from the sou'west. At five P. M. we anchored at the Horseshoe, in consequence of its falling calm, but at nine A. M. the wind freshened, and we tripped and stood down the bay. At four P. M. on the 19th we passed Cape Henry Light, and at nine A. M. we discharged our pilot and took our departure. This being Sunday, at six bells A. M. all hands were called to muster, and Divine service was performed by our chaplain, Mr. Elliot. He preached earnestly about the dangers and length of the voyage, and the probability that all of us might not live to return to our native land, then sinking from view. He spoke of God and his goodness, and reminded us that his all-seeing eye was ever upon us, whether at sea or on dry land. Every one looked solemn. Thoughtless as I was at that time, I yet felt great reverence for the Supreme Being, and always doffed my hat before eating my meals. At the end of the service, each mess was given a Bible and a Prayer Book.

The day was indeed beautiful, with a light breeze, and the squadron was in company. I said that the crew looked sober. I know that many of them felt sad. Some of them had shipped for this expedition soon after the act was passed by Congress authorizing it to be fitted out, in the year 1836. Others had shipped for various stations, and had been for over a year on board the frigate *Macedonian*, under Commodore Jones and other commanders, to take off the rough. A few days before we left Norfolk the commodore had given all hands a day's liberty on shore ; still, many felt very sad at having laid at anchor a year without visiting home or seeing any of their dear ones. Though Jack is a hand before the mast, he is a fellow-man with rights and feelings, and they should be respected by a generous government such as ours.

This was the first full-rigged ship I had ever sailed in, and it appeared different from all my other sea homes, which had been sloops, schooners, and brigs. In the first place, we had three decks — the spar deck, gun deck, and berth deck. Then, too, the crew was so large — two hundred. We were divided into sixteen messes, twelve men in a mess. I was in one of the petty officer's messes. Each mess was provided with a piece of canvas, — which, when spread on deck, served as a table-cloth, — a large tin pail and pan, and two wooden kids or little tubs, with brass hoops. We each furnished ourselves with a tin pot, pan, and spoon, likewise our small stores, such as tea, sugar, pepper, soap, etc., not forgetting our tobacco, all our clothing, with needle, thread, and wax. We drew on the purser for these things, and they were charged to our accounts. We were also divided into watches — starboard and larboard — and stationed in different parts of the ship, — some on the forecastle, some in the fore, main, and mizzen tops, and some.in the waist and after-guard. I was one of the forties, that is, the " never-sweats," — a mizzen-top man. I liked my station, the ship's officers, and the crew ; but the captain ! — when I saw him, it made me revengeful, and I felt as if the evil one had taken possession of me. I only wished I could forget the past, and that it might not so constantly haunt me.

It was now the 22d of August. We were in the Gulf Stream, —

> " Where the lightnings gleam
> And Boreas blows his blast."

For several days the weather had been lovely. The squadron sailing in line, free communication was had between the ships. In case of separation, we were to rendezvous at Madeira. On the eve of the 22d we had a most beautiful sunset and moonrise. It was a glorious sight to see the sun dipping beneath the waves of the ocean in the west, and to see at the same time the moon rise out of the waters in the east. Try to picture the scene, kind reader, I cannot describe it. The sea is indeed a fit place for contemplating the majesty and power of the Almighty,—" Where the air is calm, where sleep the deep waters." The scenery of the heavens and of the sea was magnificent, the former covered with those peculiar clouds called

> " Mackerel skies and mares' tails,
> The signs of sweet and pleasant gales."

The sea was as smooth as a mirror through the night. Nothing seemed to disturb its peaceful bosom, except now and then some huge monster of the deep or the gleaming of a shark's fin.

On the 25th we set our course towards Madeira. For several days the weather was fine. On the 29th we crossed the Tropic of Cancer, longitude 4° west, at eight bells — twelve o'clock midnight. I had just relieved the lookout on the lee quarter. Except for a slight roll of the ship, silence reigned supreme. I am now about to reveal a secret that has been smothered in my breast for fifty long years. Would to God I could blot it from my memory ! Through all these years it has been known to none save myself and to Him whose all-seeing eye is ever upon us. As I was looking down the cabin skylight, I saw Commodore Wilkes, the man who had ordered me to be flogged, sitting at a table tracing out a chart. I remembered my oath, and even then felt the sting of the boatswain's colt. I realized the situation, and the devil took possession of me. I watched my opportunity, and as the officer of the deck walked forward I grabbed an iron belaying-pin from the rack. In an instant it was suspended over the commodore's head, while I paused a moment, waiting for the ship's weather

roll. At that instant I saw, or fancied I saw, the up-
turned face of my mother. " My God ! what does this
mean ? " I gasped under my breath. The belaying-pin
was soon replaced in the rack, but it seemed to me that
I had a death grip upon it. It was some time before I
could take my hand from it. I felt as if I had committed the act, and were a criminal in thought, if not in
deed. If I looked down into the blue sea or up into
the depths of blue above, there I saw the face of my
mother. I was only consoled by knowing that I had a
forgiving Father. The awful suspense was broken by the
officer of the deck singing out through his speaking-
trumpet, " A bright lookout fore and aft ! " " Ay, ay,
sir ! " was responded by the lookout from the fore-yard
forecastle, weather and lee bows, gangway, and quarters.

At eight bells — four A. M. — the watch was relieved
and I went below, but not to sleep. My mind was in
a terrible turmoil. At sunrise the lookout from the
fore-topsail yard reported a wreck.

" Where away ? " was the cry.

" Two points on the weather bow," came the answer,
which created considerable excitement on board.

We stood for what we supposed to be a wreck with
the mast gone. It proved, however, to be a large cot-
tonwood tree, one hundred and twenty feet long and
fourteen feet in circumference. It had been in the
water a long time and was covered with barnacles, and
a large number of dolphins and deep-sea sharks were
swimming about it. It was probably thousands of miles
from the spot where it grew on the banks of the Mississippi. In rough weather it might easily have been

mistaken for rocks. There is little doubt that many of the numerous reefs on our charts have as little reality as our supposed wreck. I recall that a few days before we sailed for Georges Banks, the Banks were reported to be out of water by several inward-bound vessels. While surveying them we ran afoul of one of the largest dead whales I ever saw. It measured ninety-three feet in length, and was covered with barnacles. It had drifted in a tide-rip about a mile long, and in a storm it might easily have been mistaken for a sand-bar or a reef. Probably this whale and the seaweed had been thought to be the exposed Bank ; but the Bank was not exposed, for the shoalest water we obtained on the Banks at that time was three fathoms.

September the 9th being Sunday, all hands were called to Divine service. The sermon from our chaplain was a discourse upon profane language. Such services called to mind scenes of the past, and awakened the better feelings of our natures. On the afternoon of the 10th the man at the mast-head reported land, which proved to be the Peak of Pico, one of the Western Islands. On the following day we made the northern coast of St. Michael's, belonging to the same group, a high and mountainous island, but exceedingly fertile, and dotted with valleys, groves, and cultivated fields, which could be seen from the ship's deck. For several days we were favored with fine weather and fair breezes, and were making rapid progress toward the place of destination. On the 15th, while he was setting the mainto'-gallant-sail over a single reef topsail, George Porter, one of the maintop men, met with an accident. In loosing

the sail, the buntline in some way got a couple of half
hitches around his neck, and when we hoisted the sail
we dragged him over the yard. Here he was seen to
hang nearly lifeless, his tongue protruding from his mouth.
As he swung there by the neck, two men ran aloft to
his assistance, and it became doubtful on deck whether
all three would not be dragged over by the weight of
his body. A breathless anxiety held us all, as we stood
in momentary expectation of seeing a fellow-being dashed
to the deck. Finally others gave assistance, and he was
lowered and brought to the deck still alive. He soon recovered his senses, and recollecting that the drum had
rolled to grog just before his accident, he asked, sailor-
like, for his share of it. This was truly a narrow escape,
but, however, poor George was not destined to live out
the voyage. He died on our way home, in the China
Seas, from the black vomit.

On the 16th of September the tall cliffs and jagged
outlines of the island of Madeira were discerned loom-
ing up above the water to the south. We soon doubled
Estrouga Pass, a prominent landmark for mariners while
making the island. It is nearly sixteen hundred feet
above the sea-level, and can be seen at a great distance.
It is the home of the osprey and the sea-gull. At six
o'clock we dropped anchor in Funchal Roads, near the
town. We were soon visited by the American consul,
who often came on board.

While lying here, we went on shore with the surveying party and witnessed the method of manufacturing
the famous Madeira wine. Although a description may
not add a relish to one's cup, I will give it here as

I saw it. A rude box or vat, about twelve feet square and two feet deep, was filled with grapes. Then an old man, an old woman, two dirty looking boys and girls, and two black boys stepped into the tub, the latter having the blackest faces I ever saw, and I have seen a great many. There was a striking contrast between their faces and their large, handsome ivory teeth and the whites of their eyes. While stamping the juice out of the grapes, they would sing and thrust their hands into their hair, scratching their heads furiously. From their appearance I do not imagine that they knew what a comb was. It was a very warm day, and they exerted themselves so violently that the perspiration fairly streamed from them. Their only articles of clothing were dirty, ragged shirts. I was astonished and disgusted, especially at the appearance of the two black boys, who looked as if they had been parboiled. After the grapes had been sufficiently trodden out, the tired laborers sat down, one after another, on the edge of the vat, while the old man scraped their legs and feet, commencing with the old lady. It takes about two bushels of grapes to produce one gallon of wine. Madeira wine, once shipped, can never again be introduced into the islands. This recalls one of my early voyages to the West Indies. We went out with a cargo of New England rum, and returned with the same rum, which was sold at a high price as real old Jamaica.

The Madeira Islands belong to Portugal, and have a population of about one hundred thousand inhabitants, including the blacks. The houses of the working people would here be called huts. They are composed of walls of stone about five feet high, with the roof rising from all sides to a pole. They are thatched with broom, and contain only one room. There is no need of a chimney, as a fire is seldom required. The women wear bodices and very short petticoats. They have shoes and stockings, but only put them on when they wish to appear fine, usually going barefoot. The children are poorly clad. They have but one garment, and that is often ragged and dirty. The men wear trousers that reach to the knees, with a shirt or jacket of gaudy colors. For a head-dress, both sexes wear funnel-shaped caps of cloth, tied under the chin with a string.

Here in this delightful climate grow all varieties of fruits, such as oranges, citrons, lemons, bananas, plantains, figs, pomegranates, apples, currants, pears, plums, peaches, melons, tomatoes, and the egg-plant. Here, on the summit of the mountains, flourishes the potato, solitary and alone. While anchored here, our ship was well supplied with plenty of fresh beef, vegetables and fruits of all kinds. I suppose there is no place in the known world which produces finer beef, fruit, and vegetables than this island. While here, some of the officers, scientific men, and some of the crew were busily engaged surveying the island and learning the manners and customs of the natives. This was done in all the places that we visited. The mountain paths we traveled in our surveying expeditions were almost impassable. In many places our mountain ponies were compelled to leap from rock to rock, frequently at an angle of forty-five degrees with the horizon. In passing through Machico we visited a small church, said to have been erected over the graves of two lovers, Anne d'Arfet and Robert Machim. The story of their love and suffering has long since been classed among legends, though it is still credited in Madeira. As the adventures of this hero and heroine are supposed to have led to the discovery of the islands, it may be well to give them a place here.

During the reign of King Edward III. of England, Robert Machim, an English gentleman, became the lover of the beautiful Anne d'Arfet. It was long before their mutual attachment was discovered ; but when at length it became known, Machim's imprisonment was procured by the influence of Anne's family, to punish him for his presumption in aspiring to the hand of one so much above his rank. During his confinement, Anne d'Arfet had been forced into a marriage with a nobleman who imprisoned her in his castle near Bristow. By the assistance of a friend, Machim escaped, and induced Anne to elope with him to seek an asylum in France. They sailed during a storm which prevented them from gaining their intended port. After many days of anxiety and suffering, they were cheered by the sight of land that was clothed with the richest vegetation and with flowers in profusion. They determined to disembark, and found a beautiful climate, while birds of the gayest plumage tenanted the island. After wandering a few days in this paradise, there came on a violent storm which drove the vessel from the island. This was too great a blow for the unfortunate Anne, and she died soon after of a broken heart. Robert did not long survive her, and his dying request was that he might be laid in the same grave with her whom he had loved "not wisely, but too well," in a chapel which they had erected to commemorate their deliverance from shipwreck. This story is said to be derived from the account given by the other survivors of the wreck, who left the island and after many adventures returned to their native land with an account of the discovery of Madeira.

On the 25th we weighed anchor and bade adieu to the beautiful island. The weather was all that one could wish, with a sweet and balmy breeze. At two bells — nine o'clock — all hands were called to muster, and many of the crew were rated : John Black, seaman, to be a boatswain's mate ; Jack Bowlin, seaman, to be captain of the forecastle ; Tom Coffin, seaman, to be captain of the maintop ; Thomas Piner, signal quartermaster ; Samuel Williams, gunner's mate ; Samuel Stretch, seaman, quarter gunner ; James H. Gibbon, seaman, to be coxswain ; Daniel Banks, ordinary seaman, to be seaman ; and so on. Your humble servant, the writer, was raised from a first-class boy to an ordinary seaman, from eight to ten dollars a month, and that, too, from the day that I shipped. I recollect once arriving at Long Wharf, Boston, in an old molasses drogher from Bermuda. The captain, who was very tyrannical, abused us terribly, and provoked one of the crew so that the man swore he would give him a good sound thrashing as soon as we were made fast head and stern. We had gone below to pack our clothing, when the captain put his head over the companion-way and sang out in a soft, feminine tone of voice : " My men, I want you all to come down into my cabin, I have something for you all." We all went except old Jack, the man who had been so angry. The captain sent the cook after him. When the cook returned, he was ordered by the captain to get half-a-dozen bottles of old Jamaica out of the locker. After we had " spliced the mainbrace " several times, the captain addressed us in the following words : " You are the best sailor-men that ever lived in a ship's forecastle, and I want you all to go with me on my next voyage." We all left the brig together, and were soon at the head of the wharf, when we missed old Jack. He soon hove in sight, however, with his head hanging down, looking very serious and pale. We asked him what the matter was with him. He said that he had been seriously thinking about the old man. " What of him ? " we asked. " Well, now, my shipmates, he is not so bad, after all, is he ? " Just so, to be raised from a boy to a man — from eight dollars to ten — is not so bad, after all, is it?

I never saw the sea more alive with its inhabitants. Its surface seemed to be covered with schools of whales, sharks, flying fish, bonitoes, dolphins, and porpoises. We caught several of the latter, and made a fish or porpoise dinner.

Weather fair, with a light wind from the north, and a few fleecy clouds overhead. A very large water-spout was seen on the lee quarter, and another forming close aboard. About half a mile to leeward we saw what looked like a school of fish, fifty or sixty feet broad, on the surface of the water. It soon became much disturbed, and looked as if boiling. A bluish vapor or steam arose from it, and directly over it was a heavy black cloud resembling a huge balloon.

The lower part or nozzle of the balloon cloud was seen to descend and unite with a whirlwind which had caught up the agitated waters. It assumed a trumpet shape, with the broad end downwards. Its narrowest part between the whirlwind and the cloud was about twenty feet broad. The sun, which looked like a huge ball of fire, was rising at the time. There was quite an upper current of wind, which drove the balloon-shaped cloud onward and dragged the whirlwind or lower part of the water-spout over the surface of the water. The sun shining through the spout gave it the appearance of being on fire. Vivid flashes of lightning frequently issued from the black cloud, which continued from the commencement of the first ripple upon the surface of the waters until the bursting of the spout half an hour later. This was immediately followed by a heavy shower of the largest raindrops I ever saw. Scarcely a breath of air stirred to ripple the mirror-like expanse of the ocean, and the big drops falling upon its surface sparkled like diamonds in the sun. The morning display was followed that night by an exhibition of old ocean's fireworks that far excelled the most brilliant ever given on Boston Common on Fourth of July.

I had often seen what seemed to be tiny sparks in the wake of the ship, but that night the whole surface of the sea was bespangled with what seemed like lightning-bugs or fireflies of mammoth size. There was a considerable swell, and the sea, sparkling as it did in every part with light, was truly grand. It seemed as if the sky had dropped to a level with the ship, and its bright, glittering stars were rolling about over the billows. The smaller fishes could be traced by running lines ; while now and then the movement of some monster caused the gleaming light to extend many fathoms in every direction.

After passing the Canary Islands, we cruised for reefs and sunken rocks, reported as being in this quarter, the squadron sailing in open line. Good lookouts were kept at the mast-heads, and soundings were taken with three hundred fathoms of line every half-hour, but no bottom was discovered. There was sufficient swell to cause breakers on any shoal which rose to within fifteen feet of the surface of the water. We sailed over the locality without perceiving anything that looked like shoal, rocks, or reefs. On the morning of the 7th of October we came to anchor off the town of San Jago, on one of the Cape Verde Islands. They were discovered in 1460 by the Portuguese, and are still subject to Portugal. They form a group of twenty islands, and are sparsely inhabited. The land is all mountainous, with scarcely enough vegetation to support the people and their cattle. The inhabitants, isolated as they are, with nearly all channels of communication between them and other countries cut off, are dependent for their chief means of sustenance upon vessels stopping there for wood and water. All trade is carried on by barter. From the time of their discovery, these islands have been subject at intervals to severe drought and famine. The rain of heaven is often withheld for several years in succession, and at such times all the sources of fertility are dried up, and the people and cattle perish for want of water and food. The most fatal of these famines occurred in the year 1832, when half the population lost their lives and all the cattle died. Liberal assistance was rendered by other countries as well as by our own, and the generous conduct of our nation is still remembered among them with the liveliest emotions of gratitude.

In a valley west of the town, about half a mile distant by the path, is the marketplace. Here there is a beautiful spring surrounded by tropical trees, such as the cocoanut, date, banana, papaya, and lime, with grapes and other fruits. Over the spring is a thatched roof. It is always surrounded by a group of the most remarkable objects in human shape that can well be conceived. Looking on one side you see blind beggars, dirty soldiers, and naked children ; on the other, lepers, boys with monkeys, others with parrots and fowls, half-dressed women, donkeys no larger than sheep, driven by very large boys, to say nothing of numerous persons suffering from loathsome diseases who are performing their ablutions. Here were sailors washing, chatting, singing, and laughing ; there a group of natives of all sizes, sexes, colors, and ages, with turbaned heads and gay-colored handkerchiefs. These latter are worn in a fashion different from what we are accustomed to. They are arranged like a shawl reversed, the ends hanging down behind, while the point is in front, and the breast and part of the face are covered by it. Market is held daily in the morning when any shipping is in port. We witnessed a morning drill of the recruits, which was amusing. The men were cleanly dressed, but the rattan was freely used by the sergeant. During the drill he ordered one of the men out of the line to light his pipe.

We weighed anchor on the 11th of October and stood for Patty's Overfalls, as laid down on the chart. In the afternoon we spoke the Danish brig *Lion*, Rio de Janeiro. We also spoke the ship *Crusader*, seventy-five days from Bombay. She was in need of medical aid, and we sent a surgeon on board. It also afforded us no small pleasure to supply them with fruit and vegetables. On the 9th we reached the supposed position of Patty's Overfalls. We saw nothing of them, although we sailed over several tide-rips. We sounded every half-hour with our deep-sea line, but did not touch bottom. We now cruised for the Warleys. The English, French, and other vessels had reported shoals off the African coast. The squadron was spread as before in open order, covering as much space as possible, and we passed over the locality mentioned, but saw no appearance of shallow water or danger of any kind. While here we witnessed a brilliant display of falling stars, some sixty or eighty falling in a minute. They were large and brilliant, and seemed to shoot in all directions from the constellations of Gemini, Taurus, Orion, Leo, and Pleiades. It was a wonderful sight.

Nothing more of importance occurred until near the close of November, when land was reported from the lookout aloft. In a few hours we caught sight of the richly variegated tints resting like a halo over the tall summit of Cape Frio, forty miles north of Rio de Janeiro. Favored by a light wind from the sou'east, we entered the harbor under full press of canvas. As we proceeded, we saw our own flag floating to the breeze from the mizzen peak of that magnificent specimen of naval architec-

ture, the frigate *Independence*, Commodore Downs ; and
as we passed her our hearts beat to the tune of " Hail
Columbia," played by her band.   I shall have little to say
of Brazil and the Brazilians, Peru and the Peruvians,
Chili and the Chilians, as I did of the slave-ships and
the pirates of the West Indies, which are so familiar to
the general reader.   I shall prefer to dwell more on the
sunny islands of the Pacific and the frozen regions of
the Antarctic.

CHAPTER III.

RIO DE JANEIRO is built at the entrance of a bay one hundred miles in circumference, sprinkled here and there with ever green islands. There the flags of all nations may be seen, each floating from a man-of-war. Among other vessels there was the English line-of-battle-ship *Thunderer*, of ninety guns and a crew of one thousand men. They usually sang on board of her every night, and always wound up at eight bells by singing the first or second part of " The Chesapeake and Shannon," which was very aggravating to American patriotism.

THE CHESAPEAKE AND SHANNON;

OR,

The Glorious Fight Off Boston Lighthouse.

I.

" She comes, she comes, in glorious style.
　　To quarters fly, ye hearts of oak !
Success shall soon reward our toil,"
　　Exclaimed the gallant Captain Broke.
　　　　" Three cheers, my brave boys, let your ardor bespeak,
　　　　　　And give them a round from your cannon,
　　　　　　And soon they shall find that the proud *Chesapeake*
　　　　　　Shall lower her flag to the *Shannon*."

Lawrence, Columbia's pride and boast,
    Of conquest counted sure as fate.
He thus address'd his haughty host,
        With form erect and heart elate :
            "Three cheers, my brave boys, let your courage bespeak
                And give them a taste of your cannon;
            And soon they shall know that the proud *Chesapeake*
                Shall ne'er lower a flag to the *Shannon.*"

Silent as death each foe drew nigh.
    While lock'd in hostile, close embrace
Brave Broke, with British seaman's eye,
        The signs of terror soon could trace.
            He exclaim'd, while his looks did his ardor bespeak :
                " Brave boys, they all flinch from their cannon;
            Board, board, my brave messmates; the proud *Chesa-
                peake*
            Shall soon be a prize for the *Shannon.*"

Swift flew the word — Britannia's sons
    Spread death and terror where they came;
The trembling foe forsook their guns,
        And called aloud on Mary's name.
            Brave Broke led the way, but fell, wounded and weak,
                But exclaim'd : "They have fled from their cannon;
            Three cheers, my brave seamen, the proud *Chesapeake*
                Has lower'd her flag to the *Shannon.*"

The day was won, but Lawrence fell;
    He closed his eyes in endless night;
And oft Columbia's sons will tell
        Of hopes all blighted in that fight.
            But brave Captain Broke, though wounded and weak,
                Survived, again to play his cannon;
            And his name from the shores of the wide Chesapeake
                Shall resound to the banks of the Shannon.

II.

At Boston, one day,
As the *Chesapeake* lay,
The captain and crew thus began on:
" See that ship out at sea!
She our prize soon shall be,
'Tis the tight little frigate, the *Shannon.*
How I long to be drubbing the *Shannon,*
Oh! 'twill be a good joke
To take Commodore Broke,
And add to our navy the *Shannon.*"

Then he made a great bluster,
Calling all hands to muster,
And said: "Now, boys, stand firm to your cannon;
Let us get under way,
Without further delay,
And capture the insolent *Shannon.*
We shall soon bear down on the *Shannon;*
The *Chesapeake's* prize is the *Shannon;*
Within two hours' space,
We'll return to this place,
And bring into harbor the *Shannon!*"

Now alongside they range
And broadsides they exchange,
But the Yankees soon flinch from their cannon;
When captain and crew,
Without further to-do,
Are attacked sword in hand from the *Shannon;*
And the tight little tars of the *Shannon*
Fir'd a friendly salute,
Just to end the dispute,
And the *Chesapeake* struck to the *Shannon.*

> Let America know
> The respect she should show
> To our national flag and our cannon;
> And let her take heed,
> That the Thames and the Tweed
> Give us tars just as brave as the Shannon.
> Here's to Commodore Broke of the *Shannon*,
> To the sons of Thames, Tweed, and Shannon :
> May the olive of peace
> Soon bid enmity cease,
> From the Chesapeake's shores to the Shannon !

One night Commander Wilkes happened to appear on deck just as they were singing the obnoxious song, which seemed to annoy him extremely. I will do him the justice to say that, with all his faults, he was a true American, and loved dearly the old flag. One of the crew went aft and asked him if we might return that song next Saturday evening by giving them " The Parliaments of England." " Yes, my man," was the reply, " and give it to them in thunderous tones, with plenty of Yankee lightning." Fifty of the best singers began to practice, and on the next Saturday evening, just as the crew on board of the *Thunderer* had finished singing their usual song, our chorus commenced :

THE PARLIAMENTS OF ENGLAND.

Ye Parliaments of England, ye Lords and Commons too,
Consider well what you're about and what you mean to do.
For you're now at war with Yankees, and I'm sure you'll rue the day
You first roused the Sons of Liberty in North America.
You thought our frigates were but few, and Yankees could not fight.
Until bold Hull the *Guerriere* took, and banished her from sight.
The *Wasp* next took your *Frolic*. You nothing said to that.

The *Protectress* being off the line, of course you took her back.
Oh, then your *Macedonian!* No finer ship could swim, —
Decatur knocked her gilt work off, and then he towed her in.
Then you sent your *Boxer*, to box us all about,
But we had an enterprising brig that beat your boxer out,
And boxed her up to Portland, and moored her off the town
To show the Sons of Liberty the *Boxer* of renown.
Then upon Lake Erie brave Perry had some fun, —
You owned he beat your naval force and caused them all to run.
Then upon Lake Champlain, the like ne'er known before,
A British squadron beat complete, some took, some run ashore.
Then your Indian allies, — you styled them by the name
Until they turned the tomahawk, then savages they became, —
Your mean insinuations despising from their hearts,
They joined the Sons of Liberty and acted well their parts.
Go tell your king and parliament — by all the world 'tis known —
That what you gained by British force the Yankees have o'erthrown.

It was sung with such a will that it re-echoed throughout the silent bay and made the welkin ring. We soon heard the call of the boatswain followed by his mates, calling all hands to cheer ship, and then we were given three times three, from the one thousand voices on board the ninety-gun ship.

While on shore one day with one of my messmates, an old privateersman, we were taken in tow by a mighty clever man, who treated us several times, and finally coaxed us on board his brig. He tried to persuade us to desert our ship, and go with him to the coast of Africa to trade for gold dust and ivory. He took us down into his cabin and showed us many tricks of the trade. Arriving on deck and seeing the coast clear, I told him all the gold dust was in his eye and the ivory in the negroes' mouths. My old messmate gave me such a slap on the back that it came very near shivering my timbers. "Well!" said he, "what sort of a craft have you not sailed in, my lad?"

After our arrival at this place, two slavers were brought into port by an English man-of-war brig. I was on board of one of them when they took off the hatches. Though quite a small brig, she had confined in her hold three hundred negroes. When the hatches were opened, such a cloud of steam and such a horrible smell issued that it staggered everybody on deck. They found only thirty living human· beings out of three hundred. This was only one of the many horrors of the African slave-trade.

Sugarloaf Hill is so called from its shape. It is one immense, isolated rock, and lifts its almost perpendicular sides to the clouds. It is about one thousand feet above the level of the sea. It is said that its summit has been reached by only one person, and he an Englishman, who in triumph planted his country's flag and left it there, but was never seen afterwards. We ascended the mountain for the purpose of taking observations. We did not reach its summit till after dark, so had to remain there all night. We had with us several fathoms of lead line with which we lashed ourselves together, so that none of us could roll off while asleep. I have heard it said that a Scotch mist wets an Englishman through to the skin, and that a Peruvian dew wets a true-blue through as well. Sure enough, in the morning we found ourselves wet through with the Sugarloaf dew. Up there we found the pitcher plant growing. It bore a small flower that looked just like a pitcher. It was the color of a purple morning-glory, only much handsomer. It hung from the stem of the plant as if from a little handle, while drop after drop fell from its mouth.

While in this port we received a letter-bag from home by a ship just from New York. Bill Roberts, a Boston boy, got two letters and read them to me. It made me feel badly to hear them, and I asked him if he could write. "Why, I wrote home just before we sailed from Old Point Comfort, and then again from Madeira," said he. Without saying another word, I went down to the berth deck into the yeoman's storeroom, and told him that I wanted to learn to write. He made some straight marks and some that were not straight on a piece of paper, and told me to copy them in ship-shape fashion. I did copy them every chance I got. Finally I began to think it very silly to continue making those straight marks, so I asked the yeoman one day to write as plainly as he could the word "mother," which he did. I went to work copying, and covered many fathoms of paper with that precious name.

The palace of the Emperor Dom Pedro was in full view from our ship. The fact that it was a palace was the only thing that recommended it to passing notice. It was opposite the only landing for boats on the beach. On the emperor's birthday all the ships in the harbor were decorated with flags, and at twelve o'clock, noon, twenty-one guns were fired in honor of his attained majority.

The streets of Rio Janeiro are long and very narrow. Like those of all Spanish and Portuguese towns, they are also very filthy. The poorer classes are indeed poor, while the condition of the slaves is pitiable. They are

driven about the streets, yoked together with heavy necklaces of iron and urged on by a driver.   They are the

SLAVES SLEEPING.

only burden-bearers, and outnumber the whites five to
one.

On the 6th of January, all our repairs being finished,
we dropped down the harbor.   On passing the frigate
Independence we were saluted with six rousing cheers,
which were returned with a will.   We were favored with
fine weather, and the squadron sailed in company.   The
bleak and lofty mountains fast receded from our view,
and in a short time were swallowed up in the distance.
The first part of this month was very pleasant, but we
were destined to experience some little change.   The
morning of the 15th set in cloudy.   At five bells it commenced to rain smartly, with all the wind we wanted.
The wind soon increased to a gale, and at ten o'clock all
hands were called to close-reef topsails.   There was a
pelting rain, and the drops, as they struck on the backs
of our hands and in our faces, felt like shot.

At daylight on the 25th " Land ho ! " was sung out
from the mast-head, and at five o'clock we came to anchor in five fathoms of water off Rio Negro, on the coast

of Patagonia.   Our scientific men went ashore in quest
of objects in their different departments, and to see what

GROUP OF PATAGONIANS.

curiosities could be found.   The other officers were busily engaged in surveying, etc.   There is a considerable
Spanish settlement on this coast, about twenty miles from
the mouth of the river, and also a village of about two thou-
sand·inhabitants, consisting mostly of women and soldiers.
When they saw the squadron standing in, they fled into
the country, mistaking us for a French fleet, as they were
at war with France at the time.   They soon found out
their mistake, however, and returned, some of them
minus their dinner, which they had left on their tables
in their hurry to escape.   This district of Patagonia
abounds in all kinds of game, while fine horses and horned
cattle are numerous   We brought off some armadillos

and some young ostriches and ostrich eggs. The Patagonians are a fine race of people, unusually tall and well-
formed.

PATAGONIAN BEAUTY.

On the 30th of January a strong land-breeze began to
blow, which obliged us to get under way and beat out to
sea. The weather now began to grow cold, the thermometer ranging from 50° to 45°. Our ship glided
through the water like a thing of life. For several days
many whales, seals, and porpoises showed themselves on
the surface of the water. The porpoises differed from
any I had ever seen before, in having a stripe around

their necks. We captured several of them, and this made a fresh mess for all hands round. The next night at midnight we had a view of the rugged peaks of Terra del Fuego, and at twelve o'clock we entered the Straits of La Maire. The land here presents rather a dreary appearance. The high peaks on either hand are covered with snow, even in midsummer.

At sunset we passed the straits and again entered the open sea. We doubled Cape Horn in our shirt-sleeves, with studding sails set on both sides, below and aloft, and left it under close-reefed top-sails, with our pea-jackets on. We had but just rounded the cape and arrived in the South Pacific, or summer seas, when the wind suddenly shifted to the south, blowing a perfect gale from the regions of perpetual ice and snow. The change of temperature was sudden and keenly felt, and made us hug our pea-jackets closely about us. Such is the life of a sailor — from one extreme to another. Cape Horn is in latitude 55° 48′ south, and sometimes vessels are driven as far as 60°, in order to get round into the Pacific. Cape Horn is called the "stormy cape." It takes its name from the peculiar hornlike shape of its rocky mountain heights, which terminate the land. Be it fair or foul, rain or shine, in all weather and at all seasons, Cape Horn is a terror to the sailor, and many a long yarn is spun in the forecastle by poor Jack as this much-dreaded point is approached.

On the 18th of February we came to anchor in Orange Harbor, Terra del Fuego, or, as the name implies, the "land of fire." This is the first harbor on the western side of Cape Horn. The cape was discovered by Ma-

gellan in the year 1519. It was at this spot that the
celebrated circumnavigators, Captains Cook, King, Fitz-
roy, Laplace, d'Urville, and others used to make their
rendezvous and lay in a supply of wood and water. The
harbor is land-locked, and is the safest on the coast. It
has many small bays, the best of which is Dingy Cove.
Here boats may enter to obtain wood, and from its banks
game and fish may be taken in great abundance. Everything about has a bleak and wintry appearance and is in
keeping with the climate, yet the scenery is pleasing to
the eye.

The 22d of February was duly observed by the hoist-
ing of flags and " splicing the mainbrace." We had not
time to make a holiday of it. While here we saw many
of the native Fuegians. They are not more than five
feet high, and are of a light copper-color, but their original hue is almost obscured by smut and dirt. Their
faces are short, with narrow foreheads and high cheek-
bones, eyes small and black, noses broad and flat, with
wide-spread nostrils, and mouths extremely large. As
one old sailor said : "They could not open them any
wider, unless the Almighty set their ears back." Their
hair is long and black, hanging straight over the face,
and is covered with ashes. The whole face is compressed.
Their bodies are remarkable for the great development
of the chest. Their arms are long and slim ; but their
lower limbs are small and ill-shaped. There is, in fact,
no difference between the size of the ankle and leg.
This want of development is owing to their constant
sitting posture, both in their huts and canoes. It is impossible to imagine anything in human shape more filthy.

The climate is always at freezing point here, even in summer, which lasts through January and February. Notwithstanding the severe cold, their only article of dress is a piece of sealskin worn over the shoulders, and this they change according to the way the wind blows. They are very much pleased at receiving pieces of red flannel, which they prefer torn into strips rather than in the whole piece. These they wind around their heads in turban style, and it is amusing to see their satisfaction at this small addition to their wardrobe. The home of the Fuegian is in his small, frail canoe, or in his miserable hut, built from limbs of trees. The ends of these are bent together in the form cf a cone and covered well with seaweed. The floor is mother earth, and is carpeted with some of the same seaweed as that upon the roof. Their food consists of snails, limpets, wild berries, roots, and shell-fish. Sometimes they find a dead whale that has drifted into the kelp ; then they enjoy a Thanksgiving dinner. While we were on shore one of the natives seemed anxious to talk with us. He pointed to the sou'west and then again to the ship, after which, clasping his hands in the attitude of prayer, he said, " Eloh, eloh," as though he thought we had come from God. One day a party of natives came on board. They were highly delighted and surprised at everything they saw. When they left the ship most of them were dressed in sailor rig. Jack was bound to make everything fit: If a jacket was found to be too small, a slit was made down the back. If a pair of trousers proved to be too small around the waist, a piece of spun yarn remedied the defect. If the legs were too long, the

sheath knife was resorted to. Most difficult to fit was
an old uniform coat given to an old woman. This she
concluded belonged to her nether limbs. Her feet were
thrust through the armholes, and after a hard squeeze

TERRA DEL FUEGIAN.

she succeeded in getting the sleeves on. The tails were
then brought up in front, and she took her place in the
canoe with pride and satisfaction amid roars of laughter
from the crew.

One bean-soup day a canoe came alongside, full of natives, and I handed them my tin pan half full of soup, through one of the port-holes. It was so hot that they dipped it in the sea, and it was then so salt they could not eat it. They poured it overboard and kept the pan, and no signs or threats would induce them to return it; so I was a quarter out, besides my regular beans. If any one on board had advanced the idea that some day they would become civilized, he would have been thrown overboard for a Jonah. It was here that Father Coyne first began his missionary labors. Finding his efforts useless, he went to the Sandwich Islands. The Terra del Fuegians seem but little above the brute creation, and are the lowest in the scale of humanity. Well might we ask ourselves, " Who are these so haggard, and so wild in their attire, who look not like the inhabitants of earth, and still dwell on it?"

Having made preparations for an Antarctic cruise, we weighed anchor on the 25th and put out to sea. For several days it had been blowing furiously, with a high sea running. This was a good time to measure the height

DIAGRAM OF WAVE.

of the wave, for seldom will the sea be observed to run higher than off Cape Horn, where two oceans meet. To get the height of the wave, we sighted the schooner while in the trough of the sea, and cut the mast to the horizon with our eye from the *Porpoise*, as in the illustration. This measurement gave as a result thirty-two feet. Spray can dash up over a hundred feet, but the waves seldom run over thirty odd feet, and are never "mountains high."

On the 1st of March we encountered our first icebergs. They were much worn by the action of the sea and frequent storms. The albatross, gray pigeon, and petrel hovered around, and could be seen at times resting, as it were, on the waves. At noon we made Ridley's Islands, and in the dog-watch sighted Cape Melville. Bearing south by east, the north foreland of King George's Island could be seen. After cruising for several weeks in these cold, bleak, icy regions, and visiting Aspland's, Burgman's, Elephant, Cornwallis's, and O'Brien's Islands, the Seal Rocks, the South Shetlands, and Palmer's Land, we found ourselves in latitude 70° south, the highest ever made up to that time, and south of the *ne plus ultra* of Captain Cook. On the 7th William Stuart, captain of the maintop on board tbe *Peacock*, fell from aloft overboard. He was seen to float feet upward. A bow-line was thrown over his exploring boots and he was drawn on board ; but it was a narrow escape, for a boat could not have lived in such a sea. Poor William died soon afterward and his body was committed to a watery grave.

Finding no passage through the icy barrier to the pole, and being nearly hemmed in by those frozen bulwarks which extended east and west as far as the eye could see, it was decided, as the season was growing late, to turn the ship's head to the north. Although the sun set bright and clear at fifteen minutes past ten, everything about looked dark, dreary, and cheerless. It was bitterly cold, — a cold which, at this extremity of the earth, seemed almost to freeze the words spoken before they could reach the ear. As we worked our passage through the field and drift ice, huge floes, and lofty icebergs, the wild sea-birds, which were very plenty, and the inhabitants of the briny deep flocked about us and viewed us with their small, round eyes in wonder and astonishment. After much suffering and many narrow escapes, we returned to Orange Harbor, Terra del Fuego. I shall give a fuller account of this frozen region in my description of our second Antarctic cruise, which we made from New Holland in the year 1840. We had no sooner come to anchor than we were visited by the natives. They are great mimics and are very fond of music. Our fifer played for them " My Bonny Lad," " Sweet Home," and " The Girl I Left Behind Me." They did not understand these songs, but when he struck up " The Bonnets of Blue" they were all immediately in motion, keeping time to the music. They were entirely naked, except the small piece of sealskin which they wore over the weather shoulder. The only word they spoke was " Yammurscunar." They appeared to be very fond of their children. Nothing would induce the women to come on board. They sat in their canoes with their feet under them, tending the fire which may always be seen in the bottom of the canoes on a pile of stones and ashes, surrounded by water. How they manage to make a fire, I cannot imagine, unless it is by rubbing two dry sticks together. Drake tells us that they live in and paddle the same canoes to-day that they did two hundred years ago. These vessels are made of bark sewed together with shreds of sealskin. They are very frail and require constant bailing. I have read in *The Missionary Herald* that since our visit the Fuegians have become civili.ed, and that many of them have been converted to the Christian religion ; and now they live in houses, sit at the table, and eat with knives and forks.

Directly overhead are the celebrated Magellan Clouds, three in number, two large and one smaller. They are of a dusky, leaden gray color, and look like three burnt holes in the sky. They are separate from each other, though close together, but when they become one, look out for squalls and take in all your canvas. We took our final leave of these dreary regions on the 20th. The land had but just disappeared from our view, when we were struck by a terrible gale, in which probably the *Sea Gull* was foundered, and twenty as noble lads as ever trod a ship's deck found a watery grave. The *Sea Gull* was never seen or heard of afterwards. The next day we passed the island of Diego Ramieres.

" Sail, ho ! " cried the lookout from aloft.

" Where away ? " sang out the officer of the deck.

" Right ahead," was the response.

In a short time a vessel was seen from the deck. She looked like a very large ship, broadside on, with her foretop-gallant-mast gone. The captain sent below for his speaking-trumpet to hail her, but by the time it arrived the stranger had vanished from sight. This is an illusion very common in these latitudes. It is called by the sailors the " Flying Dutchman." This day might

be called a nautical show-day, for we had not only seen
the crew of the " Flying Dutchman " walking her deck,
but had been favored with mock suns and a mirage.
The upper is the true sun, while the left-hand and right-
hand appearances are the mock suns ; but all these were
equally bright, and it was hard to tell which was the true
one.   These illusions continued for nearly half an hour.
Mock suns, mock moons, halos, circles and half-circles,

MOCK SUNS.

zodiacal lights, the mirage, shooting stars, solar eclipses,
gorgeous rainbows, the *aurora australis*, and other rare
and beautiful appearances are often to be seen in these
latitudes, and some of them are considered by the ignorant and superstitious natives the forerunners of war,
famine, or pestilence.

Some little time after we had a mirage of the ship or a
reflection of the *Peacock* presented to us.   There were
three images of the ship in the air, one inverted, the

other two right side up, while a fourth, in the horizon,
showed nothing but the hull and the stumps of the lower

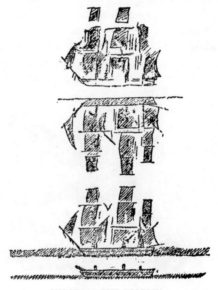

MIRAGE. — THE PEACOCK.

mast, as in the sketch. On board the *Peacock*, at the
same time, they had three reflections of our ship. Science tells us that these reflections are caused by concave
surfaces of the atmosphere when it consists of warmer
and colder strata. The ship *Relief* came through the
Straits of Magellan and surveyed them. In doing so
she came near being wrecked off Nor Island, at which
place she lost all her anchors.

On the 12th of May, at daylight, we made the coast

of Chili. It was a sublime sight at sunrise to view the
lofty peaks of the Andes Mountains, not more than sixty
miles distant. The highest peak is Tupongati, 23,200
feet high, which is at times an active volcano. They
are unlike any mountains I ever saw. They do not rise
gradually from the base, but shoot right up out of the
earth. The fact is, you can stand with one foot on the

MIRAGE. — THE VINCENNES.

level plain, the other on the side of the mountain. On
the 14th we sighted the Point of Angels, and before sundown we dropped anchor in the harbor of Valparaiso, or
" Valley of Paradise," as the name implies. The letter-
bag was soon brought on board, and its contents emptied
on the quarter-deck All the officers received letters,
but only a dog-watch of the crew, while all the rest of
us were left out in the cold. Willie got his usual number, and read them to me. One of them said that Long

Wharf had not sunk, and that Chelsea was not dead. While here all hands had liberty on shore. Of course we visited the fore, main, and mizzen tops, named after the well-known hills on the south side of the fort, where the sailors resort. The valley between the hills is the resort of the abandoned and the roughs of Chili. Valparaiso has twenty thousand inhabitants. There are many Spaniards, Dutch, French, English, and Indians, and a few Americans. The native Chilians are very patriotic. The young ladies have very black, piercing eyes, and are quite fond of music. When passing the houses, one can nearly always hear them singing. Then up will come a little Chilian girl, with her field-pike in her hand, singing, "When Callao is taken, our sea-coast will be free." The houses are mostly one story, built of sun-dried bricks. These bricks are about two feet long, and one wide, and are very rough. They look like the surface of a corn-ball. The walls are from two to six feet thick, plastered outside, and are anything but neat inside.

June 5th we bade farewell to "Paradise Lost" and stood out to sea.

CHAPTER IV.

NOTHING of importance occurred during our passage of fifteen days, when we dropped anchor close in under the island of San Lorenzo, Bay of Callao. Here we found all the missing squadron, except the *Sea Gull*. The island of San Lorenzo is of volcanic origin. There is a legend that an old Peruvian was fishing in his boat, when suddenly he missed the weight of his sinker. Thinking some ravenous sea monster had stolen both his bait and sinker, he commenced hauling in his line. On looking over the gunwale of his boat into the water, he saw the bottom of the sea coming up. The island is said to have sprung forth at this time, and was named for him, San Lorenzo. This happened in the year 1740, and was caused by an earthquake which destroyed the whole city of old Callao. San Lorenzo is nothing but a range of tremendously high sand-hills. Nigh abreast of where our ship lay is a small valley between two mountains, where poor Jack finds a resting-place after the toils and troubles of this life are o'er. Many a sailor, cut off in the bloom of youth and prime of life, has been laid to rest here peacefully and undisturbed; and many a rough board, ay, and rougher inscription, testifies to the kind regard of their former shipmates, and to the good character of those who sleep beneath the drifting sands of this dreary-looking spot. I have often wished that, if I were sick unto death, some kind

ISLAND OF SAN LORENZO — THE SAILORS' BURYING-GROUND.

friend or shipmate would see that I was laid in my last hammock in some peaceful vale like this. A few of the inscriptions are as follows :

IN MEMORY OF WILLIAM PEARCE,
A SAILOR BOY ON BOARD THE U. S. BRIG BOXER,
WHO DIED SEPTEMBER THE 25TH, 1838,
AGED 16 YEARS.

A mother's eye will look, but look in vain,
For her loved son, returning from the main.

He left his home to tempt the fickle wave,
And now reposes in a foreign grave.
Peace to his soul, ay, everlasting peace,
Where tortures come not,—pleasures never cease.

IN MEMORY OF JON. M. DUBLOIS,
SEAMAN OF THE U. S. SHIP NORTH CAROLINA,
WHO DIED AUGUST, 1837,
AGED 40 YEARS.

IN MEMORY OF JAMES TAYLOR,
SEAMAN ON BOARD THE U. S. SHIP PEACOCK,
WHO DEPARTED THIS LIFE JUNE 19, 1832,
AGED 51 YEARS.

SACRED TO THE MEMORY OF JAMES LAURENCE,
LATE SEAMAN ON H. M. S. PRESIDENT,
WHO DEPARTED THIS LIFE SEPT. 1, 1836,
AGED 33 YEARS.

A worthy shipmate and a friend sincere,
In the cold, silent grave now sleeps he here.
His warning was but short,—think of his fate,
And prepare for death before it is too late.

SACRED TO THE MEMORY OF WILLIAM EDWARDS,
LATE ROYAL MARINE OF H. M. S. HARRIS,
WHO DEPARTED THIS LIFE NOV. 29, 1837,
AGED 26 YEARS.

I am here at rest from busy scenes,
I once belonged to the Royal Marines.
I am now confined within these borders,
Remaining here for further orders.

Ci Git Meace Francois Marie-Nele,
April, 1810, a etables mort le Sept., 1833;
Ci Git Guine Joseph Marie-Nele,
20 Sept., 1814, a plein mort a board de la
Frigate Andromede le 2 Juin, 1828.

Sacred to the memory of three seamen,
Who departed this life on board of H. B. M. S. Blond,
In the month of May, 1835:
John Bowdon, aged 26 years;
Edwin Pean, aged 23 years;
James Oldridge, aged 29 years.
Also Benj. Beecroft, who died in June, aged 15 years.

Tremendous God! Thy sovereign power
Has severed from us like a flower
These seamen in their bloom.
In tribute to their memory dear
Their shipmates have interred them here,
And reared this humble tomb.

Daniel Dickson, landsman,
of the U. S. ship North Carolina,
Died in June, 1837,
Aged 19 years.

In memory of Blyth Gayle,
Who departed this life July 28, 1838,
Aged 20 years.

Swift was the summons to the dreary tomb
To him who lies beneath this sod.
The friend he trusted crushed his early bloom,
And sent him unprepared to meet his God.

No kindred weep above his youthful bier,
And stranger hands, his shipmates, placed this tribute here.

IN MEMORY OF THOMAS HENDRICK,
LATE SEAMAN OF THE U. S. SHIP NORTH CAROLINA,
WHO DEPARTED THIS LIFE MAY 31, 1838,
AGED 16 YEARS.

In vain had youth his flight impeded,
And hope his passage had delayed;
Death's mandate all has superseded,
His final order Tom 's obeyed.

IN MEMORY OF HUGH MCKENZIE,
WHO WAS DROWNED ON THE 25TH OF DEC., 1838,
AGED 27 YEARS.

Weep not for me, my shipmates kind,
Nor mourn at my untimely end:
In heaven I trust we all shall find
A kind Redeemer, still our friend.

Jack's signal of distress is a red flannel shirt tied in the fore rigging. Two of these signals of distress were made here in this port from two American whalers, both full of oil, and homeward bound. Our commodore answered the signals in person, and made the two captains promise that they would treat the men better and give them better rations. While lying here the U. S. ship *Falmouth*, Captain M. Keever, arrived from Valparaiso. She had on board three deserters from our ship. The ship *Relief* was discharged of all her cargo, for she was just alive with big rats and swarming with cockroaches. I should think the latter must have been from two to

three inches long. There was a lot of whisky on
board of her for the squadron, on which most of the
crew and the marines got drunk. Next morning at sunrise all hands were called to witness punishment. Every
man who had been intoxicated received one dozen lashes
on the bare back with the cats, with the exception of
the deserters, who received, one thirty-six lashes, the
others forty-one each.

The commodore was very busy at this place. Among
other things he overhauled the officers and crews of the
squadron, and sent all invalids and idlers on board the
Relief, which ship was ordered to the Sandwich Islands,
and thence to Sydney, New South Wales, to land stores
for the squadron, thence to sail for the United States by
the way of Cape Horn. All hands wanted to go in her.
We had a fine view of the famous Andes Mountains,
which tower in lofty grandeur above the surrounding
country. When the sun sets, and sheds his golden
rays upon their numerous summits, they seem to move,
as though they were having a frolic, and look like the
waves of the ocean running after one another. We lay
here until our repairs were nearly completed, when we
up anchor one fine afternoon and ran over to the port.
We came to in the evening, outside of the rest of the
shipping, by the starboard anchor. Callao presents a
poor appearance from the bay. The fort and castles on
the right are by no means handsome, and in front of
them is a dirty, sandy beach. To the left is the dirtiest
of all dirty places, Callao. When you land, the first
discomforts you feel are the fleas making acquaintance
with your dainty flesh,—and the Lord help a greenhorn

on his first landing, for there is no peace for him ! I have seen the officers go ashore in white trousers, and in less than thirty minutes after landing they were black with fleas and spotted nearly all over with blood.

As a general thing the houses are eighteen or twenty feet high, built of mud and reeds, some of sun-dried bricks, and usually have but one room, with a veranda in front. The yard and cellar are on the roof, where you will find all the cooking utensils, rubbish, etc. There is always a large guyaquil, or hammock, swung from one corner of the room to the other.

The dress of the Peruvian ladies is the *tapada saya*, or petticoat, made in plaits, containing thirty yards of costly silk. It is drawn very close at the bottom, so that the wearer cannot take a step of more than eight or ten inches. A costly mantilla, or cloak,—and for the poorer women one of cheaper material,—is drawn over the head, concealing all the face but one eye. The dress of the men is the *poncho*, some of which are very costly and richly trimmed. The poorer ones are like a blanket with a slit in the middle, through which the wearer thrusts his head, and the garment falls on all sides. The ladies are very fond of sitting in the veranda to see and be seen, and, if pretty, to be admired. They walk very prettily and gracefully, and have very small hands and feet. The color of their hair is black, and it is very soft. They wash it in water in which Peruvian bark has been steeped. They seem to look through you with their piercing black eyes.

The tide at Callao is small, at three feet only. The situation of old Callao, which was destroyed by an earthquake in 1687, can be seen under water, and at times, when fishing, you may haul up the skull of some old Peruvian patriot. It is said that it never rains in Peru, and it is true, I think ; for it is full of dust, dirt, and fleas. The shops are very poor. As for the inhabitants, they are a miserable set, a dirty, lazy gang of loafers. The country is full of soldiers, badly clad and worse fed, and dirty, wretched looking objects, but with their old cry of " *Vive la Perarano!* " still in their mouths. Conquered as they are, they still have thoughts of liberty and freedom. May they never forget them ! The fort and castle here are strong enough to resist almost any force, if properly handled ; but treachery was at work, and the Peruvians lost the day.

Lima, the capital of Peru, is some six or seven miles from here. It is situated in a valley of the Andes. While we were here the Chilian troops were in possession of the country and Lima was garrisoned by them. There was a big celebration while we were here. It was held in the valley of the Amancaes, two miles from the town. Several nationalities were present — Peruvians, Chilians, Indians, Negroes, half-breeds, and others of both sexes. They danced the fandango to the tunes played on the guitar, while others were drinking their orgedent, singing, gambling, swearing, laughing, fighting, and begging. It was the 24th of June, the celebration of St. John's day by the Peruvians. It carried me back to the days of my youth, in those good old times when Boston Common was inclosed by a wooden fence, and the cows grazed thereon, and Independence Day was celebrated in the good, old-fashioned way. Even the

Glorious Fourth is not forgotten here, for our ship was dressed in many and gay colors, from stem to stern, and from the main truck to the water's edge.   At twelve o'clock, noon, a national salute was fired from the sloop-of-war *Falmouth* and immediately answered by H. B. M. ship *Samorang.*   Such exchanges of international cour-

THE SOUTHERN CROSS.

tesy do much to keep up the kindly feeling between the two countries.

On the 8th Benjamin Olden, a marine who had died the day before on board the ship *Peacock,* was laid at rest in the quiet graveyard on the little island of San Lorenzo.   His body was escorted to the grave by a corps of marines.   The "Southern Cross" was directly over our heads, and when on shore we could hear the *gen-*

darmes cry out, " Midnight is past ; the cross begins to
bend."

> " While overhead the holy sign,
>   The Southern Cross, is in the sky :
>   Assurance that an eye Divine
>   Watches the exile from on high."

The cross consists of four large, bright stars, two perpendicular and two horizontal, to which fancy gives a
cruciform shape. The two perpendicular are the lode
or magnet, and point us to the south pole. They are
the emblem of peace to the sailor. Humboldt refers to
his first view of this constellation with much emotion,
and Mrs. Hemans gives vent to her feelings in the
following verses :

> " But to thee, as thy lodestars resplendently burn
>   In their clear depths of blue, with devotion I turn,
>   Bright Cross of the South ! and beholding thee shine
>   Scarce regret the loved land of the olive and vine.

> " Thou recallest the ages when first o'er the main
>   My fathers unfolded the ensign of Spain,
>   And planted their faith in the regions that see
>   Its unperishing symbol emblazoned in thee.

> " Shine on — my own land is a far distant spot,
>   And the stars of thy sphere can enlighten it not;
>   And the eyes that I love, though e'en now they may be
>   O'er the firmament wandering, can gaze not on thee !

> " But thou to my thoughts art a pure-blazing shrine,
>   A fount of bright hopes, and of visions divine;
>   And my soul, as an eagle exulting and free,
>   Soars high o'er the Andes to mingle with thee."

CHAPTER V.

On the 13th of July we got under way and stood out to sea, all the squadron in company except the *Sea Gull*. The ship *Relief* directed her course towards the Sandwich Islands, and the rest of the squadron towards the South Pacific, or summer seas. Next day we fell in with a Peruvian brig very much in need of water. We were most happy to be able to supply them with the necessary article. On this day the following order was read from the quarter-deck : " The undersigned, commanding the U. S. expedition, informs the officers and crews under his command that, as they are now about to visit the islands of the Pacific and to have intercourse with their inhabitants, he wishes to inculcate on all in the squadron that courtesy and kindness towards the natives which are well understood and felt by all classes of mankind ; and trusts that neither contempt of nor interference with their customs, habits, manners, and prejudices, nor arrogance over them will be shown by any one belonging to the squadron, always bearing in mind that savage natives have but vague ideas of the rights of property, and that theft committed by them has been the great cause of collision between them and civilized nations. He would therefore enjoin upon them all great moderation in everything respecting their intercourse with them, that no act of hostility will be committed, and that an appeal will be made rather to their good-will than to their fears. That the manner of trading established in the squadron will be most strictly adhered to by all, and that in event of difficulties or collision all acts of force will be avoided, unless for self-protection. In short, our aim will be peace and good-will and proper decorum to every class, constantly bearing in mind that the future intercourse of our countrymen with the natives of the islands we may visit, will very much depend on the impressions made on their minds by us, and recollecting that it is in the nature of the savage long to remember benefits and never to forget injuries. It therefore behooves us, wherever we go, to leave behind us, whether among civilized or savage nations, favorable impressions, not only as respects this national expedition, but for our flag and countrymen. The commander-in-chief feels confidence in relying on the officers and crews to carry out these views from their good, exemplary conduct, and trusts that he will not have to regret the confidence he reposes in them. Any acts inconsistent with these views will meet with the most exemplary punishment."

August 1st Alexander Ogle, one of our marines, died. He had been sick but a few days. In the afternoon all hands were called to bury the dead, and his body was committed to the deep.

We had very fine weather after leaving Callao. For days and nights together not a cloud was to be seen, and the air was refreshingly clear. This is one of the loveliest climates in the world. I never saw the sea look so smooth as here — not a ripple to be seen on its surface ; and if not for the long swell, or heaving of its mighty bosom, it might be taken for a sea of glass.

On the 29th we had a moderate breeze from the west. In the evening we witnessed a grand display of the zodiacal light. It was very bright. Many shooting stars from each quarter of the heaven were also seen. Several of the following days and nights were very cloudy, with much lightning, thunder, and rain, and sudden squalls from the sou'west. We were now making our way very rapidly towards the fairy islands of the Pacific. There are three classes of them, — the low coral, the high coral, and the mountainous islands. The squadron sailed in line, still we sailed over several reported islands and reefs set down on the charts. On the 13th we made the island of Minerva, one of the Paumotu group, or Cloud of Islands. This is one of the low coral or lagoon islands. It proved by our surveying to be only twelve feet above the level of the sea, ten miles long, and six hundred feet to its lagoon. These islands are composed of coral and vegetable matter. We landed, and got some shells, plants, and coral, but the natives soon drove us off. John Sac, a New Zealander, one of our crew, spoke the Tahitian language, which they understand. John swam to the shore and talked to them, but the only answer was several of them crying out at the same time : " Go to your own island. This belongs to us, and we do not want to have anything to do with you." It was impossible to land again and have a peaceful chat with them. It is no wonder that they do not want anything to do with so-called civilized men, after having been so

shamefully treated, especially their women, by whalers
and traders in these seas.   It is a disgrace to civilization.
In the center of many of these islands is a beautiful basin
of water, called a lagoon.   It is of a rich blue tint, and
generally has an opening through which the tide ebbs
and flows.   The pearl oyster is very abundant in these
lagoons.   The plants and shrubs upon these islands are
few, and the cocoanut, growing above them all, is the
only fruit or vegetable the islands produce.   After lying
to all night under the lee of the island, at daylight we
bore away for Serle Island, which we surveyed.   On the
19th we made Hennake or Honden Island.   Here we
caught several large turtles, and all hands had turtle
soup.   There are no natives on this island.   The sharks
near the shore and in the lagoon were ravenously hungry,
and would bite at anything they could reach, so it was
not very pleasant to swim to the shore and back again to
the boat.

This island was swarming with a variety of birds.
They were so tame that we pushed them off their nests
to get at their eggs.   Among them were the frigate-bird,
gannet, sooty tern, and other beautiful tropical birds in
large numbers.   One could capture any number of them
without the least resistance.   Some of the curious sights
to be seen were crabs walking off with snakes, and then
both being themselves borne away by some monster
bird.   Armies of piratical crabs were seen in all directions, and as for spiders, spider-webs, and snails, there
seemed to be no end to them.   There were no cocoanuts or fruit of any kind on this island.   On the 23d we
made the two Disappointment Islands of Byron.   This

day George Reynolds, ordinary seaman, died on board the brig *Porpoise*. Our chaplain went on board in the afternoon and performed the burial service.

On the 24th we made the nor'west end of Wytoohee, which island lies in latitude 14° south. The natives seemed greatly astonished to see us, and after rubbing noses with us — their mode of salutation — they would lay their hands on us to satisfy themselves that we were really human. The younger ones were the first to show any freedom, and were disposed to joke with us. While on shore we inquired for their huts. They seemed to be taken all aback. When we had made them understand that they had nothing to fear, they led the way through the bushes of palms to an open space surrounded by cocoanut and pandanus trees. This was their village. On looking into their huts and seeing no one, we inquired for their women and children, when they burst out in great laughter and gave us to understand that they lived on an island where there were none. Their huts are so small they hardly deserve the name. They are six to eight feet long, four feet high, and five feet wide.

We discovered, on the 28th, an island not laid down on any chart. It was named King's Island, for the man at the mast-head who first discovered it. It was only six feet above the level of the sea. It was a lagoon island, and was eight miles long. After surveying it we bore away for Raraka, and made it soon after. As we neared it another island was discovered to the northward, which was named for our ship, Vincennes. After visiting Dean's Island, Aratica, and Waterlandt, and dis-

covering Peacock Island, we bore away for Metia, or
Aurora Island, and made it on the 9th of September.
This was one of the high coral islands, and was totally
different from any we had fallen in with. It looked as
if it had risen up out of the sea. By our survey we found
it to be two hundred and fifty feet high. We took a
cast of the lead one hundred and fifty feet from its perpendicular cliffs, and found no bottom with one hundred
and fifty fathoms of line. On landing we were soon
surrounded by the natives, men, women, and children,
of all ages, and dressed after the fashion of all nations.
They seemed delighted to see us. They gathered round
and stared at us just the same as we would at a tribe of
Indians walking on our public streets. The young ladies
seemed to be dressed in their holiday attire. They had
oiled themselves with stale cocoanut oil, which gave
them a bright orange look. This oiling process is to
keep off the numerous flies, for they dislike the smell of
rancid oil. The young women's heads were adorned
with many and gay flowers. On the island we found
several refreshing springs. There were also plenty of
pigs and hens. Here grow the yam, the taro, the bread-
fruit, and the cocoanut. The coral reefs are alive with
a variety of pan fish and crabs. There was an abundance
of large, green " bottle " flies, whose bite is very poison-
ous. Seeing that the natives had no war-clubs, we
inquired for them. They said it used to be all war, but
now it was all peace, "*mittionari mai-tai, mai-tai,*"
meaning " missionary, good, good " ; and that they had
no use for clubs or spears now.

At six o'clock, the surveying boats having returned,

TAHITI, THE GEM OF THE PACIFIC.

we bore away for the Society Islands. There are eight large and several small islands in this group. They were first discovered by that distinguished circumnavigator, Captain James Cook, in the year 1769. On the 10th of September we came to anchor in Matavai Bay, off Point Venus, Island of Otaheite. This is one of the mountainous islands. Aorai is about 7,000 feet high, and to the summit of Orohena is 10,000 feet. We ascended these mountians for the purpose of taking observations. While here we saw many wild hogs, and groves of the banana sometimes called hog banana. This fruit is twice as large as the common banana. It is over a foot long and from two to three inches thick, of a rich golden hue and a very delicious flavor. For several days our decks were crowded with natives. At last orders were given that none but big chiefs would be allowed on board. Finally a stop had to be put to their coming on board at all, for every native, no matter how small, was a big chief. In fact, they were as thick as colonels and majors in the Southern States after the Rebellion.

The sick of the squadron were taken on shore, and our observatory was put up at Point Venus. This is the place where Captain Cook took the transit of that planet over one hundred years ago. The natives here seemed to be very happy, gay, and cheerful. They are very honest, but are great beggars. The ladies — may God bless them all, old and young ! — are pretty ; that is, I mean to say, they have handsome, round, full faces, jet-black hair, dark, round, piercing eyes, and large, white teeth. They are of a light olive complexion. But their

forms! they are either round-shouldered, knock-kneed,
bow-legged, or parrot-toed; some are also badly cross-
eyed.   It seems as if they can see two different ways
at the same time.   In fact, Jack says they are lop-sided
and out of kilter altogether.   Those who wore any head-
gear had on high, flaring chip bonnets of their own
make, which looked like baskets, minus bottoms and a

TAHITIAN GIRL.

portion of the rims, and tied on their heads edgewise.
Their frocks were made of silk and of other kinds of
cloth, the same width around the neck as around the
bottom, drawn in around the neck with a showy handkerchief.   The hat worn by ladies is something like a
wreath of flowers, made from the pandanus, or cape
jessamine.   A rose is often stuck through the lobe of
the ear, and is a pleasing contrast to their glossy, black

hair. The dress of the men is the *pareu*, a piece of cloth tied round the waist, extending down the leg to the calf, and a gay-colored shirt. Often the shirt without the *pareu* is seen, and some dress in sailor rig.

They live on yams, taro, bread-fruit, vi-apple, bananas, oranges, cocoanuts, sugar-cane, fowls, and fish. The latter they eat raw. They use neither chairs, tables, nor salt, but instead of the latter they use sea-water. It is very amusing to see them eat. They sit upon mats spread on the earth-floor, both sexes cross-legged, and "sail right in." Each article of food is dipped into the sea-water, and they munch away with their mouths full. Such a smacking of their lips ! it is jolly to see and hear them. They are, in fact, perfect gormands. They eat, eat, and eat, until they can scarcely breathe : and then those who are so full that they cannot get up, roll over and go to sleep, and don't eat again until they get hungry. Their huts are of an oval shape, sixty by twenty feet, and from twenty to twenty-five feet high, built of bread-fruit and cocoanut trees. The walls are of bamboo, the roofs are thatched with pandanus. They contain one large room, which is screened off at night with various mats. They are generally built in a grove of cocoanut or bread-fruit trees. A native can live wherever he likes, for food is to be found everywhere in abundance. As for lodging, it never enters his mind, for the Tahitian can sleep just as well on the beach at high-water mark, or under a banana tree, as in his own hut. They are very fond of the water, and when in it are as happy as ducks. They are very graceful swimmers. They tie a line to the top of a cocoanut tree, and on it swing across the water, and sometimes they let go and drop in. They are beautiful singers and are always humming. Nearly every night, about three bells, we were roused from our peaceful slumbers by the fair Tahitian mermaids, who would launch forth from their coral caves with comb and glass in hand, their long hair floating in the breeze. When they reached the beach just ahead of the ship, they would commence to sing. Richer, clearer, softer, or sweeter voices I never listened to in any part of the world. That we might understand and join with them they would now and then sing in our own language "Old Hundred" or "Coronation." They always wound up by singing some familiar sailor songs, which they had learned from the whalers, such as "The Bay of Biscay," "Black-eyed Susan," "When will my Sailor Boy Come Home?" "Bonny Bunch of Roses, O,"

> "Off Japan, and wide awake,
> Plenty of whales, and no mistake,"

and "We Won't Go Home till Morning." These Tahitian operas usually lasted till two or three o'clock in the morning, when many of the singers would swim to the ship and beg to come on board. Being refused, they would go back to their coral caves.

This group of islands was the first discovered in the South Pacific, and has been oftener visited than any other islands. Their language was the first native language reduced to writing.

The first missionary society ever formed was in Scotland, and it was called the "Missionary Society," afterwards the "London Missionary Society." This society sent out the first mission-ship, called the *Duff*. She sailed from Cadwell, England, August 10, 1796, with thirty missionaries on board, a number of whom were accompanied by their wives. Then the first missionary-flag — three doves on a purple field, bearing olive branches in their beaks — floated to the breeze from her mizzen peak. The directors of the society received the missionaries of different denominations. Simply as Christians they sent them to the isles of the sea, putting into their hands the Bible, with this brief and simple charge : " Go, beloved brothers. Live agreeably to this blessed Word, and publish the Gospel to the heathen according to your gifts and abilities." The mission-ship was hailed a few days out by a man-of-war.

" Ship ahoy ! "

" Ay, ay, sir ! "

" What ship is that ? "

" The *Duff*."

" Where bound ? "

" Otaheite."

" What cargo ? "

" Missionaries and provisions."

Eighteen of these men were left on this island. They must have done a great work, for now they have quite a number of churches and schoolhouses in this group, and many of the natives can read and write.

Saturday, September 14th, arriving on their Sunday, by our reckoning, all labor was stopped, and all hands except the first part of the starboard watch went on shore to meeting. There were two missionaries, Mr. Wilson and Mr. Pratt. The former, a very old man, preached. He came here in the ship *Duff*. The audience, all native except our crew, listened attentively to the preaching. Sitting cross-legged upon the ground and listening to preaching which we did not understand, was something to which we were not accustomed. The next day, the 15th, being our Sunday, we went on shore again to meeting in the mission chapel. Our chaplain preached. It seemed odd to have two Sundays so near together. Sunday is very much respected here. No labor or games of any kind are allowed ; no, not even the picking of a cocoanut, or the paddling of your own canoe, is permitted on that day. In fact, it is more quiet and Sunday-like on the civilized islands of the Pacific than in our cities and towns. There, it is truly the Lord's Day, and the people not only recognize it as such, but keep it sacred.

The penalty for breaking the Sabbath is making so many " fathoms " of road ; for the second offense the number of " fathoms " is doubled. The walk to Papara over Broom Road is lovely, and reminds one somewhat of the shell-road leading from New Orleans to Lake Pontchartrain. It leads around the island, and is about one hundred miles long. It is sometimes called Pomars, or the Queen's Road. At certain distances there are groves of cocoanut trees planted by Queen Pomars. They form a delightful shade, and travelers are at liberty to help themselves to the fruit. Almost every house has its garden of luscious bananas, tempting oranges, delicious pine-apples, etc. Whenever one of the trees has a piece of tapa tied around it, it is tabooed. This law, the taboo, is always respected under all circumstances

by the heathen. Here in our civilized and Christianized
land you may see those little signs,—"No trespassing on
these grounds," "Beware of the bulldog and the shot-
gun," etc., but the fruit is stolen all the same.

NATIVE WITH COCOANUTS.

This island, Tahiti, is enchanting, and well deserves
the name, "The brightest gem of the Pacific."

> " Where the pale citron blows,
> And golden fruit through dark green foliage glows."

Several of our men deserted here, and a reward of
thirty dollars was offered for each man arrested. They

were captured in the mountains and brought down to
the reef by the natives. Their wrists and ankles had
been tied each to the other, and a limb of a tree run
through, the ends resting on the shoulders of the natives.
This is their mode of carrying burdens. As soon as the
deserters had been brought on board they were ordered
to take from the capstan the reward of thirty dollars and
place it in the hands of those natives who captured them,
after which each deserter received thirty-six lashes with
the cat on his bare back.

Having finished the survey of this group of islands we
bade adieu to the fair Tahitians and their fairy islands.
Then we up anchor and stood out of the bay. It was
beautiful indeed to sail along these shores and see the
villages, in the coves and valleys, surrounded by cocoanut and bread-fruit trees. The day, as all days in Tahiti,
was lovely. The night was as fine and clear as the day,
although we had much lightning with no thunder.

A day or two afterward we had a sailor's tea-party.
Through the oversight of our purser, his steward, or
some one else, our tea, which was not of extra quality,
ran short, and the purser took this opportunity to double
the price. In consequence, the crew held a council of
war. After some debate we left the matter in the hands
of a committee, composed of the petty officers, who were
to decide our course of action. It was amusing to hear
them laying down the law, and talking seriously about
mutiny. Jack Kennison, whose father was in the Boston
Tea-party, argued the case first, then Sam Williams, one
of our gunner's mates, then many another " old salt."
Finally, the committee gave the following verdict : " We

will buy no more of the tea at any price, let this be
called mutiny, a tea-party, or whatever they choose to
name it." Our mess bill, which we received at the end
of each month, read as follows: " Tea, sugar, tobacco,
mustard, pepper, bees-wax, soap, white and black thread,
thimbles, scissors, palms, large and small needles, dead-
eye buttons, tin pots, tin pans, tin spoons." Our division
bill: " Pea-jackets, blankets, mattresses, blue jackets,
blue trousers, blue flannel shirts, yards of sheeting, yards
of dungaree, black silk neckerchiefs, yards of black rib-
bon, stockings, shoes." Whatever of these articles we
wanted, we would sign for, and they would be charged
to our account. We now signed for everything we
wanted, except tea and sugar, and then, with intense
anxiety, awaited the result, expecting every minute to
hear the drum beat to quarters, or the boatswain and
his mate calling all hands to witness punishment. The
commodore and the purser were walking the quarter-
deck, next morning, talking very seriously. The former's
face, which was always hard, this morning looked as
genial as if he had discovered a new planet. We did
not hear any more about tea until we arrived at Sydney.
In the meantime our breakfast and supper consisted of
a scouse made of yams and taro, and salt junk, with our
usual ship-bread and water.

After visiting the islands of Huaheine, Tahaa, Bora-
bora, and Maufili, we made Bellinghausen's Island.
This is one of the low coral islands. Here we landed,
and made magnetic observations. On the 7th of October
we made Rose Island, the most eastern of the Samoan
or Navigator group. This is also one of the low coral

islands. The tide rises here but two feet, and at high water the island is overflowed. In the center of its lagoon is a most remarkable sight. It is nothing less than a large submerged coral tree, thirty feet in diameter across its top. We sounded, and found over six fathoms of water all around it. Fishes of various colors, shapes, and sizes were playing among its coral branches, presenting a beautiful sight. We captured several turtles, but their flesh was very rank and coarse. The Samoan Islands were discovered in 1678 by Bougainville, a French navigator.

CHAPTER VI.

On the 10th of October we came to anchor in Pago Pago Bay, on the south side of the island of Tutuila. This is another rendezvous of our whalers and South Pacific traders. Ships seldom enter or leave Pago Pago Bay without a great deal of " going about," " tacking," "wearing," " luffing," " letting go," and " hauling." Then one must be very careful, or the ship will get " in stays or irons." If this happens, the alternative will be to " box her off " or to " wear her round on her heel." Entering this harbor is something like beating up the Straits of Balambangan, when the ship's yards have to be braced chock up in the wind's eye to keep the monkey's tails from getting squeezed in the brace blocks.

This bay, Pago Pago, is very deep, penetrating so far into the island as to cut it nearly in two. Its shores are rugged rocks, of a volcanic nature, from eight hundred to a thousand feet high. The bay reminds one of a huge extinct crater half full of water. There is a coral bank about a mile long, near the entrance, and the sea breaks over it when there is any wind. As soon as we had dropped anchor we were surrounded by numerous canoes filled with natives, bringing fruit of all kinds. These savages were highly delighted with the ships, and the

number of men on board. On many of the islands of the
Pacific there were runaway convicts from Hobart Town
and Sydney, the Botany Bay of Great Britain. There
were also many runaway sailors and many who had not
run away, but who had been driven off by bad usage.
The next morning after our arrival, an American whaler,
hailing from New Bedford, came into port with a red
shirt fluttering to the breeze from her fore-rigging.

PAGO PAGO BAY.

When a man-of-war's man sees that signal he well knows
that there is difficulty between Jack before the mast
and the officers of that ship. Our commodore was soon
on board the whaler and listening to Jack's yarn. He
was told that they were two years out; that they were
full of oil, had plenty of provisions, and were homeward
bound; that they had been put on short allowance;
were short-handed, five of the crew having died, and
three being sick in their bunks from ill-treatment; and

that they were so tyrannically abused that they had taken charge of the ship, confining the officers below in the cabin, and had steered for the nearest port. Our commodore, who acted as arbitrator, soon settled matters, and the whaler sailed for the United States a week afterward, with several of our invalids on board of her.

The Samoan group of islands is situated in the South Pacific Ocean, between latitudes 13° and 15° south, longitude 168° west. There are about twelve islands, large and small, Savaii being the largest, then Apolima. Tutuila is about one hundred miles in circumference. The entire area of the group is about three thousand square miles. The population was at that time nearly sixty thousand. The people are divided into two parties, — the Christians, who follow the missionaries, and the "Devils," who do not. The latter were so named by the former. While exploring the interior, we discovered several extinct craters, on Mt. Malata, over two thousand feet above the level of the sea. One on the summit was two miles in circumference and three hundred feet deep. Its bottom was a beautiful sight. It was thickly covered with a forest of lofty palm trees. We also found several mountain streamlets, beautiful waterfalls, and fairy lakes. The various vines, and rattans almost a hundred feet long, were so thick that we could with difficulty make our way through them. The warbling of beautiful birds was enchanting. Our botanist seemed at a loss for words with which to name the unknown blossoms that adorned these woods and filled the air with their fragrance. The wild orange was very plentiful, and in places the ground was literally covered with it. I think they are of a richer flavor than the cultivated ones,—at any rate, they are larger.

On our way back to the ship we came to one of the "Devils'" villages. Near it was a fine, stately tree. It had been stripped of its branches except at its top. It was timbered in at its base after the fashion of the hull of a ship. This tree served as a mast; a small cocoanut tree made a bowsprit; another, a rudder; blocks of coral answered for ballast, while vines, creepers, and rattans served as her rigging. This Papalangi ship, as the natives called her, afforded them a great deal of amusement and pastime. There were a great number of young natives, heathen or devils, as you choose to call them, playing and having a jolly time with her.

After our return to the ship, on going down to the berth deck, Elijah King, a Boston boy, called me by name. On looking round I saw him and another man whom I took for a native. The latter had very long hair and whiskers and was tattooed from head to foot. He had nothing on but the *mora*, or girdle. He looked wild and savage, though very intelligent. They were sitting on a mess-chest talking, others of the crew round them listening. King asked me where I was born. I said on Roxbury Neck. At once the stranger seized me and set me on his knee, while the big tears rolled down his cheeks. He said that I had sat upon his knee when a child, before my father left home. I told him I had no remembrance of my father. It was always mother, mother, mother with me. This man's name was Daniel French, and he was born in Roxbury. He said his relatives lived in the western part of the town, and that he was in ill health when he shipped on board of a whaler. They had had extraordinarily good luck, for in twenty months they were full of oil; but their rations and treatment were so bad that he, with several others, left the ship, and he had been on this island ever since — sixteen years. He had married a "Devil" chief's daughter, and had thirteen little ones. In 1875 I heard that Mr. French was still living.

A whaler's crew are not paid by the month, but have a lay; that is to say, the captain has one barrel out of every thirty, and Jack before the mast one out of about every five hundred. At the end of a voyage, through much abuse and tyrannical treatment by the officers of the ship, Jack before the mast is often fairly driven from the ship. This is called desertion. Then his lay falls to the owners, if the captain does not contrive some way or other to secure it.

In the Christian villages we saw their churches and schoolhouses. The missionaries here have their printing-press, and had translated and printed most of the Bible into the native language. Many of the native women dress in loose gingham or calico frocks, and the men wear a shirt or a pair of trousers, and sometimes both. Both sexes wear their hair short and sprinkle it with coral lime to destroy the vermin. This causes their hair to turn a carroty red. Sunday is strictly observed here. A native will not so much as get you a cocoanut upon that day. I do not remember ever having been in a meeting where the people were more quiet and attentive to the preaching than here among the missionaries. Here was the old pioneer, the Rev. John Williams, the author of *The Missionary Enterprise.*   All hands used to like his preaching.   He was truly one of God's noblemen.

We found no churches or schoolhouses in the " Devils' " villages.   They live altogether differently from the Christians.   They dress in the old heathen style, wearing only the *titi*, that is, a girdle of leaves that gives them

A "DEVIL" MAN.

a most graceful appearance.   The leaves are slit, and the dress has the appearance of a short striped petticoat. They wear their hair long, usually tied in a bunch on one side of the head, which gives them a wild look.

We witnessed some of their war dances.   The "Devils' " dance was only indulged in by the young ladies.   The audience would lie down on mats, and three or four of the old women would beat time with small sticks on a short log.   The dancers kept excellent time to the music,

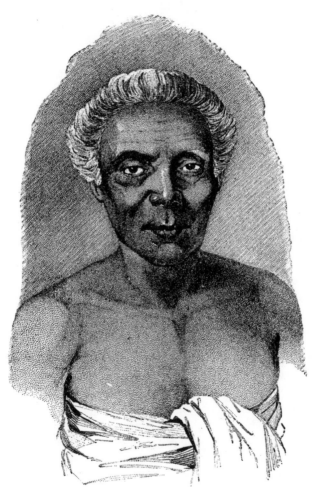

MALIETOA, THE CHRISTIAN CHIEF.

with contortions of the body, throwing around the arms and legs like one of our pasteboard jumping-jacks. This dance is something like the Spanish fandango, only more immoral. It is held in the *fale-tele* where strangers are entertained. The dance is kept up till sunrise, and ends with a loud shout and a clap of the hands. Many of the nights are spent in this way, and most of the day is passed in sleeping, eating, and swimming.

There was no king over these islands, but there were several chiefs, each of whom ruled over a district, village, or bay. The Ten Commandments were the common law of the islands. I will give the "Devils" their due, and say that they entertained us hospitably while we were in their villages, although they were duly compensated through our traffic with them. Their mode of salutation is to take one's hand and rub the back of it over their noses. The first pigs were brought here by Captain Cook. The natives decorated the largest hogs with wreaths of flowers, and tied necklaces of shells around their necks ; in fact, they were fairly carried away with this, to them, new species of animal. The missionaries have introduced many cattle, horses, and fowls. The first mule that was imported was a "Jumbo" to them. He also was decorated with many gay flowers and wreaths and was marched around the island to gratify the natives with a sight of him. There are many specimens of manly beauty among the Samoans. As for the women, they are stout and ill-formed. The girls are lively, have expressive countenances, and, what is rare among the islands of the Pacific, have a degree of bashfulness unlike their sisters of Tahiti. They have not very musical voices, but are wonderfully correct in beating time. When a native wishes to take a wife he gets the consent of the chief. Then he takes a basket of bread-fruit and offers it to the girl of his choice. If she accepts, his suit is gained. He then must pay to her parents a certain price for her. A chief's daughter is valued as high as a musket, a half-dozen hatchets or plane-irons, or as many yards of sheeting. Tattooing is called "*ta-ta-tau.*" The natives are very fond of it, and it is not uncommon to see the whole body covered. It is performed by persons who make it a regular business.

Having finished the survey of Tutuila, we up anchor and stood for the island of Upolu about forty miles to the westward. Next morning we dropped anchor in the harbor of Apia. We were soon visited by the big chief of the Christian party, his wife, two daughters, and a number of small chiefs. Pea, the big chief, wore a sailor's jacket, trousers, a white vest, a tall beaver hat, and shoes. His wife wore a short calico jacket and a straw bonnet, but no shoes. He looked like a grandson beside her, for he was a very small man, while she was an extremely large woman. Their two daughters were very gayly dressed. They wore short gingham frocks, flashy waist-ribbons, and morocco shoes. The small chiefs wore nothing but their native *tapa* tied round their waists so as to cover the lower part of the body. After visiting the different parts of the ship, refreshments were served in the wardroom, where they ate and ate until they could eat no more.

During our surveying trip across the island we visited many of the "Devils'" towns, or those not yet Christian-

EMMA, DAUGHTER OF MALEITOA.

ized, and were always treated with much respect. At Sagana, a Christian village, we saw the old chief, Malietoa, whose hair was white with age. He was in his domestic circle taking a siesta. One of his daughters was fanning him. She was the prettiest young lady we had seen in this group. Her name was Emma, and she was as intelligent as she was pretty.

The native canoes are finely built, and have a deck both forward and aft. They are long and narrow, with an out-rigger, and are elegantly modeled. The seat of honor is the forward deck, in the center of which a row of pegs is placed, to which a large oval shell is attached by way of ornament. A native finds no difficulty in sitting there, but a stranger is painfully impressed before many minutes are over, and will long remember the honor he there enjoyed. Nor will he soon forget the canoe song : " *Lilei tusilava le tan mau, leango tusilava le tan mau,*" " Good above all is the part before, bad above all is the part behind."

During our stay here the missionary brig *Camden* arrived with missionaries for this station. A few days before we sailed, all hands but a quarter watch went on shore to the mission house, armed with bowie-knives and pistols, to drill. There we met several thousand natives who were waiting to witness the performance. Greatly astonished and wild with fear they watched our cutlass-exercises. But at the close, when, all together, we discharged our pistols into the air, they fell flat on the ground and kissed the earth. Before we went on board Mr. Williams was appointed American consul for the Samoan group, and the American flag was hoisted at his house.

When these islands were first discovered, in 1678, they were estimated to have a population of about one hundred thousand. It is a most singular fact that the group was not again visited, as far as known, by any ship from the civilized world, until 1778, a hundred years afterward, when the *Astrolabe* and *La Perduse* touched there and the captain and part of the crew of the former were barbarously massacred by the natives. When visited by the missionaries, in 1830, from frequent wars among themselves, the population had decreased to less than sixty thousand. The missionaries found two white men here. One of them was Mr. Daniel French, who remembered me when a child, to whom I have previously referred. The Rev. John Williams revisited them in 1836, in the *Messenger of Peace*, a small vessel of about ninety tons, built by him at the Society Islands out of cocoanut and bread-fruit trees. He was accompanied by a number of missionaries for this station, among them Mr. Harris.

The constellation of the Pleiades, though small its stars and pale their light, is of wide fame. They are called by Jack before the mast "The Seven Sisters," though there are really fourteen of them. Their appearance on the horizon in December is hailed with shell-music and rejoicing by the natives in these latitudes.

Having completed our survey of all the islands of this group, on the 10th signal was made for the squadron to get under way. Our anchor was soon catted, and sails hoisted to catch the gentle breezes of the Pacific. In a short time the beautiful port of Upolu was far in the distance. On the 12th we made Uea or Wallis Island.

NATIVES HAILING THE RE-APPEARANCE OF THE PLEIADES.

Instead of one island, as laid down on the chart, there are nine separate islands, ranging from one to ten miles in circumference. We made a running survey of them. Next day we made Hoorn Island, discovered in 1616 by Le Maire. The highest part of Wallis Island is two thousand five hundred feet above the level of the sea. Leaving Hoorn Island, we made all sail for the Southern Passage, passing within fifty miles of the Fiji group. On the 15th we were in the Eastern Hemisphere. Since leaving the United States we had gained a day, by our reckoning, which is always the case in doubling Cape Horn, going westward. When coming round the Cape of Good Hope, eastward, sailors always lose a day.

On the 18th we made Matthew's Rock. It is about a mile in circumference, and over a thousand feet high. On the 24th we had a very serious storm of thunder and lightning. Our conductors, from the royal-mast-truck down to the night-heads, yard-arms, and mast-heads, were all illuminated with *corpo santos*. All hands felt the electric shocks more or less. The wind blew furiously all night. It was more sublime than anything I ever experienced in the Gulf Stream. On the 26th we made Ball's Pyramid, which is a large, barren rock uprisen from the sea. At sunset we made Port Jackson Light, and lay to off the light-house for some time waiting for a pilot. None answering our signal, our commodore acted as pilot and brought the squadron up to the city. About eleven o'clock we quietly dropped anchor in the midst of the shipping, without any of the pilots or the authorities knowing anything about our arrival. The good people of Sydney were much surprised in the morning, and indeed frightened, at seeing an American squadron, lying in their harbor, which had come up in the night, unknown to any of the city authorities. Their fears were soon allayed when they learned that we were merely on a scientific expedition.

The morning was beautiful, and the scene which met our eyes was unlike anything we had hitherto witnessed during our voyage. The familiar language spoken, and the strong resemblance which everything bore to our own homes, gave us an indescribable feeling of pleasure. Not long before our arrival it had been debated whether more effectual means of fortification were not necessary for the harbor. The idea of this being needed was ridiculed by the majority, but the entrance of our ships by night seemed to change their opinion, for we might, after firing their shipping and reducing the greater part of their city to ashes, have effected a retreat before daylight in perfect safety. Since then they have built several new forts.

The Australian Club House was thrown open to our officers, and balls and parties were given in their honor. A few days after our arrival, the brig *Camden* arrived from the New Hebrides, when we learned the melancholy intelligence of the death of the Rev. John Williams, who, it appears, preached his last sermon on board our ship, so short a time before, at the Samoan group. Mr. Cunningham related the following : " After leaving Pago Pago, they placed native missionaries at Rotuma and Totoona. Mr. Williams landed at Tanna, which they found in a high state of cultivation, and were hospitably received by the natives. These were Papuans,

and spoke a language very much like that of the Hervey
Islanders.   At Tanna Samoan missionaries were also left,
and they then proceeded to Erromango.   Here they
found a barren country and a different race of men—
black, with woolly hair—who did not comprehend a
word of any language known to the missionaries.   The
natives, though apparently suspicious, exhibited no signs
of actual attack.   Mr. Williams with Mr. Harris, Mr.
Cunningham, and the captain of the brig landed and
were strolling about and amusing themselves picking up
shells.   While thus engaged they had separated from
each other.   Mr. Harris and Mr. Williams were in
advance of the others.   Suddenly the war shout was
heard, and Mr. Harris was seen running, pursued by a
crowd of natives.   He was soon overtaken by them and
clubbed to death.   Mr. Williams then turned and ran
for the boat ; but he had delayed too long, and, although
he had reached the water, was followed into it and slain
also." Mr. Cunningham and the captain escaped with
great difficulty, and, after some fruitless attempts to
recover the bodies, left the island.   Mr. Cunningham
was of the opinion that the attack was not premeditated,
but arose from a desire to obtain possession of the
clothes of the persons massacred.   The missionary cause
sustained a great loss in Mr. Williams's death.

Portions of the island of Australia were visited by the
Spaniards as early as the year 1520.   The Dutch, when
they captured it in the year 1606, named it New Holland.
When the English took possession of it they named it
New South Wales.   It is now called Australia.   It was to
this place that England used to transport her convicts,

and from this fact it was named the pickpockets' quarter of the globe. Sydney is its capital and seat of government. George Street is the Broadway of Sydney. The Cove — God save the name ! — is the old Ann Street of Boston ; South Street of Philadelphia ; River of Styx, Norfolk ; Sausage Row, Cincinnati ; Five Points or the Hook of New York ; Hog Lane of Canton. In fact, it is more than the Ratcliffe Highway of London. There are plenty of old Fagins and old Fagin's pupils living here. Here you will find all nations mixed up together, eating, drinking, singing, dancing, gambling, quarreling, and fighting. Inns abound here, for which the English, you know, are celebrated. Here is the Sailors' Inn, the Soldiers' Inn, the Ladies' Inn, Punch-Bowl Inn, Shamrock Inn, Thistle Inn, the Ship's Inn, King's Arms Inn, and others too numerous to mention, not forgetting the Dew Drop Inn.

One day a boat's crew of us dropped into the Jolly Sailors' Inn. It was a large square room. On either side were a number of tables, over which hung various national flags. Under the Russian Bear were seated a boat's crew, singing the Russian national song. It was given with a will. When they had finished, an English boat's crew, sitting under the Union Jack, sang :

> " When Britain first at Heaven's command
>   Arose from out the azure main,
> This was the charter of the land,
>   And guardian angels sang the strain :
>   Rule, Britannia ! Britannia rules the waves !
>   Britons never, never shall be slaves ! "

This was sung several times in true-blue style.

At the French table, sitting under the Tri-color of France, the French boat's crew sang the Marseillaise Hymn:

> "Ye sons of France, awake to glory!
> Hark, hark! what myriads bid you rise!
> Your children, wives, and grandsires hoary;
> Behold their tears, and hear their cries!
> Behold their tears, and hear their cries!
> Shall hateful tyrants, mischief breeding,
> With hireling hosts, a ruffian band,
> Affright and desolate the land,
> While peace and liberty lie bleeding?
> To arms, to arms, ye brave!
> Th' avenging sword unsheathe!
> March on, march on, all hearts resolved
> On liberty or death!
>
> "O Liberty! can man resign thee,
> Once having felt thy generous flame?
> Can dungeons, bolts, and bars confine thee?
> Or whips thy noble spirit tame?
> Or whips thy noble spirit tame?
> Too long the world has wept, bewailing
> That Falsehood's dagger tyrants wield;
> But Freedom is our sword and shield,
> And all their arts are unavailing."

This was grand. When the French had finished singing, our boat's crew, sitting under the Stars and Stripes, gave them

YANKEE DOODLE.

Ye gallant sons of liberty, you bravely have defended
Your country's rights by land and sea, and to her cause attended.
With Yankee Doodle, doodle, doo, Yankee Doodle dandy,
Our tars will show the haughty foe Columbia's sons are handy.

Upon the ocean's wide domain our tars are firm and true, sirs,
And Freedom's cause they well maintain, with Yankee Doodle doo,
sirs.

The Fourth day of July, 't is said,—that day will Britain rue, sirs,—
An independent tune we played, called Yankee Doodle doo, sirs.

Columbia's sons then did declare they would be independent,
And for King George they would not care, nor yet for his descend-
ant.

The regent thought he 'd send a fleet of ships to take our few, sirs,
But then to sea our sailors went, playing Yankee Doodle doo, sirs.

The British tars think that they can whip Yankees two to one, sirs,
But only give us man for man,—they 'll see what we can do, sirs.

That our tars care no more for France than Britain is most true, sirs,
They can make any nation dance to Yankee Doodle doo, sirs.

After this we "spliced the mainbrace" all together, the
English drinking their 'alf and 'alf out of pewter mugs,
the French drinking their claret out of very thin glasses,
while our Russian shipmates and ourselves drank something harder out of thick glasses which were very small
at the bottom. Although the Russians had sweet, soft
voices, their national song is, like "Rule, Britannia,"
very tame, and extraordinarily short. The Marseillaise
Hymn, however, made up for both. It was inspiring.

I have never been in a place where there existed such
a low state of society, and where so much drunkenness
was to be seen. There were not only half-dressed, dirty
soldiers, but dirty and drunken women, staggering along
the public streets, brawling and fighting, or being carried
off by the police, who, by the way, were the proprietors

of many of the rum shops. It was a curious, but not an uncommon sight, to see a big, burly, thick-lipped negro, black as a coal, walking on the street, arm in arm, with a beautiful English lady, both neatly dressed. Although seeming to be rude, one could not help stopping and staring at such sights and noticing the great contrast.

The convicts, on their arrival, were let out to contractors, and might be seen on the streets with iron chains attached to their ankles, and dragging after them, or with large, heavy, iron shackles on their legs. The chain-gang was composed of a number of convicts, who were chained together, two and two. These were driven in gangs aggregating from fifty to a hundred. The government was compelled to keep several regiments of soldiers and a large force of mounted police at this place to keep the convicts in subjection. Many of them were hired out to the settlers, to work during their terms of transportation, or until they were pardoned. Then a ticket of leave was granted them. Some of them went to work for themselves, others sought the bush and there robbed and murdered all who came within their reach. The latter were called bushrangers or outlaws, and might be shot wherever found. Quite a number were hanged after our arrival in port. A very few became good citizens. One died recently who was worth a thousand pounds sterling.

I once heard a lecturer, who had spent several weeks in Australia, say that her cities were far ahead of Boston in morals. It is not many years since complaint was made to the government against Governor McQuarrie. In reply to the complaint the governor stated that there were two distinct classes of people in Australia,—those who had been convicted, and those who ought to be. The lecturer's remarks, considering his short residence in the cities of Australia, remind one of a certain English lord who visited this country. While walking down Broadway with a friend, he inquired if there was not such a place in town as the Bowery.

"There is, and we will take a walk down there," was the reply.

Arrived there, the noble lord made known his wish, which was to see a Bowery boy. Mr. Seward pointed out Mose, on the other side of the way, leaning against a lamp-post, with his right foot flat on the sidewalk, his left resting over the right, his trousers rolled up to show his red-topped boots. He wore a red flannel shirt, and on his head was perched a tall, black, beaver hat nearly covered with crape. His hair hung in soap-locks down his cheeks, and a long-nine cigar was in his mouth. After eyeing him some little time, his lordship said :

" I will go over and speak with him."

" You had better not," replied his friend.

He went, however, while Mr. Seward walked slowly up the Bowery. When he came abreast of Mose, the Bowery boy, he scanned him from head to foot ; then, very politely raising his hat, he said :

" I am looking for Broadway, governor."

Carelessly withdrawing his cigar, and puffing a volume of smoke in his lordship's face, Mose said :

" Why in —— do n't you find it, then ? "

On his return to England, my lord published a book entitled " The Bowery and Bowery Boys."

While on a short expedition in the country with a surveying party we saw many of the natives, the Corroborys.
They were of medium height.   The color of their skin
was a dark chocolate without any cream in it — a sort
of reddish black.   Their hair was fine, black, and silky,
and inclined to curl.   They were more hairy than the
whites.   They were slender in form, and had long legs
and arms.   Their foreheads were narrow ;   their eyes
deep-set, small, and black ;   their noses much flattened
at the upper part, between the eyes, and broad at the
nostrils.   The forming of the latter feature was done by
the mothers during infancy.   Their features were uglier
than those of the Terra del Fuegians, but they had much
more manly forms.   They were very haughty and independent, having no masters or chiefs over them.   They
considered one man among them as good as another, as
long as he behaved himself.   Their huts were more simple and exposed than those of the Terra del Fuegians.
Two forked sticks were driven into the ground, and on
these was laid horizontally the limb of a tree, as a ridge-
pole.   The sides of the roof were composed of strips of
thick bark, extending from the ridge-pole to the ground,
covered first with leaves, and then with the skins of the
kangaroo and other animals.   The scanty clothing which
they wore was made from the skins of animals.   They
lived on herbs, fowls, and the flesh of the kangaroo,
which they killed with spears, and sometimes with the
boomerang.

Their spears were about ten feet long, very slender,
made of hard wood, and barbed at the end.   The
boomerang is a flat stick about three feet long, two inches

wide, and half an inch thick, crooked or bent in the
middle. It was a very formidable weapon in the hands
of a native. They could throw it and hit an object
behind a tree which was behind the thrower. An attempt
to throw it by any one unaccustomed to its use might
result injuriously. It was used both in war and the

NATIVE THROWING THE BOOMERANG.

chase, and was peculiar to the natives of Australia, no
other tribe or nation having anything bearing the
slightest resemblance to it.

We witnessed one of their Corrobory dances. It was
held in a little clearing near the woods, close to their
huts, and near a fire. About twenty natives, in quick
succession, came out of the woods, their dark bodies
marked with pipe clay to represent skeletons, with white

CORROBORY DANCE.

lines drawn across the ribs, legs, arms, and head. They
looked hideous, frightful, and ugly. It was an awful
spectacle to look upon when they stood in line, with the
dark green foliage behind and a bright fire before, and
strangely suggestive of Hades.

Before beginning the dance they stood still and mo-
tionless for a long time, staring very wildly at us ; then all

NATIVE DANCE.

of a sudden they jumped up and yelled like so many hyenas. They kept on jumping up and down, throwing their
whole arms and legs about as if they had no ankle or
knee joints or elbows. There was no balance to partners,
up and down the center, all hands round, or fore and
aft with them ; but they would suddenly, one after the
other, vanish from sight, which was done simply by their
turning around, when their dusky forms would become

invisible. The dance ended with a very loud " Ho-ho-ho !" way down in their throats.

The woods here are charming. There is very little underbrush, and the trees grow straight up. There are many gum trees among them. Their tops are alive with parrots and paroquets, and other birds of rich plumage may be seen winging their graceful forms in the air or flying from one tree to another. There are many humming-birds here, and bell-birds whose notes sound like the clink of a stone hammer. It is generally believed that all Indians are very fond of dogs, but these natives never have any, though there are many wild dogs here.

A great variety of entertainments — balls, parties, dinners, and late suppers — was given our officers by the governor and other officials. They and the American consul often visited our ships. They were greatly surprised when they learned that we were bound to the south polar regions. They said that our ships were too frail to cruise among icebergs ; but that we were young Americans, foolhardy and reckless, and they supposed that we would go on. In fact, our ships were not built, like the Russian and the English ships, for the express purpose of cruising among the ice, but we had been ordered to go, and we obeyed orders. All the ships of the squadron having undergone the necessary repairs, such as calking, overhauling, setting up our standing rigging, reefing new running gear, etc., all hands put in a hard day's work on Christmas, and then we were ready.

CHAPTER VII.

On the morning of the 26th of December all hands were called to weigh anchor, when we made sail and stood out to sea. In passing the English ship *Druid*, Lord John Russell commander, we were greeted with three hearty cheers, which were returned just as heartily from all our ships' crews. After breakfast all hands were called to muster, when the commodore thanked us for our good behavior while lying in port. He then told us that we must look forward to a dangerous cruise, and said a few words as to what our country and he himself expected of us in aiding him in the endeavor to promote health and comfort, and as to the necessity of economy in our rations and clothing.

When we were piped down, we took advantage of the fine weather by sending up our stump to'-gallant-mast, bending new sails, and building little hurricane houses of rough boards over the companion-ways for the exclusion of the cold air. Drying stoves were slung between decks to make it more comfortable, and several barometers were put up in various places with orders given to keep the temperature at 60°. By the 1st of January all the decks had been cleared of all loose and useless articles, and everything snugly stowed away.

Our battery was made doubly secure, and everything put in good order for housekeeping or rough and cold weather.

This was one of those days familiarly known on sea and land as a "weather breeder." The sea was placid, but the sky lowering, and had a wintry appearance to which we had been strangers for a long time. We had been sailing rapidly in a due south course for several days with a rising sea, and the weather had been misty.

January 5. At muster this morning three stowaways made their appearance aft at the mainmast, and surrendered themselves. They looked anything but convict-like, for they were dressed in the rig of our crew, with blue trousers, blue flannel shirts, black silk neckerchiefs, and black tarpaulin hats. The commodore was much surprised at their appearance, and informed us that we were mistaken if we expected that they would be harbored on board of his ship, and declared that if the ship was so fortunate as to weather the southern cruise, he should do his duty by sending them back to Sydney to be given over to the authorities. The stowaways were then entered on the ship's rolls for rations only, and stationed on the afterguard.

January 6. We were favored with a view of the sun and found our latitude to be 53° south. This day we rigged up our crow's nest at the foretop-mast-head. During the night we double reefed our topsails.

January 7. Weather misty and squally, with a heavy sea running.

January 8. The air very raw and chilly. None of the rest of the squadron in sight.

January 9. Weather more moderate, and set to'-gallant sails.

January 10. By observation found our latitude to be 61°. This day we made the first iceberg. We sailed close to it and found it to be a mile long and one hundred and fifty feet out of the water. It was much worn by the action of the sea and by frequent storms, and resembled the ruins of some Gothic church or ancient castle. A second berg was met some thirty miles and a

THE FIRST ICEBERGS.

third some fifty miles south of the first. After these we passed many of various sizes and shapes, some inclined to the horizon, others square with flat tops.

January 11. Wind from the nor'west, with a light mist. As the icebergs increased in numbers the sea became smooth and we were often compelled to change our course to steer clear of them.

January 12. This morning entered a deep bay. At six o'clock in the afternoon we had reached its extreme limits and found that our further progress was checked by a compact barrier of ice, inclosing large, square ice-bergs. This barrier consisted of masses, closely packed, and of all varieties, shapes, and sizes. We hove to until daylight. The night was fine, and everything seemed wrapped in slumber. Ay, everything was silent but the distant swash, swash of the waters against the ice. Our latitude was 63 ° south. There was every appearance of land at the south. It took all day to beat out of the bay. For several days the weather had been foggy.

January 16. *Peacock* and *Porpoise* in sight. High mountains were plainly seen at the south from all the ships.

January 17. Weather fair. At twelve o'clock we were in 66° south. Many whales were playing around the ship, and some large seals and penguins were on the ice. Land in sight.

January 18. Weather variable. Occasional snow-squalls and mists. Water of an olive green.

January 19. Found ourselves in a deep bay this morning. Land could be plainly seen from the ship's deck. It bore sou'east and sou'west. It averaged from two to three thousand feet high. The mountain ridges looked dark and gray. Two volumes of smoke were seen rising from the mountains.

January 20. At two o'clock this morning the sun and moon appeared above the horizon at the same time, but in opposite directions. The moon was full. The effect of the sun shedding his deep golden rays on the distant icy mountains and the surrounding icebergs was beautiful beyond description. We witnessed a sea-fight between

THE VINCENNES IN DISAPPOINTMENT BAY.

a whale and one of his many enemies, a killer. The sea was quite smooth. A short distance from the ship was seen a large whale, lashing the smooth sea into a perfect foam, and trying to disengage himself from his enemy. As they drew near the ship the struggle became more violent. The killer, which was about twenty feet long, held the whale by the lower jaw. The huge monster seemed to be in great agony, and spouted blood. Suddenly the whale threw himself out of the water, at full length, the killer hanging to his jaw ; but all his flounderings and turning flukes were useless, as the killer still maintained his hold and was getting the advantage. He soon worried the whale to death. After the battle, the ship appeared to be floating in a sea of blood. During the last few days we saw many beautiful snow-white petrels either up in the freezing air or on the ice-floes.

January 22. Weather foggy. This morning we found bottom with eight hundred fathoms of line. The arming was covered with slate-colored mud. In the afternoon we took a second cast of the lead and found bottom at three hundred and twenty fathoms. The bottom same as before — slate-colored mud. The *Peacock*, while boxing off the ship from some ice under her bows, made a stern board which brought her in contact with an iceberg with such force as to crush her stern and larboard quarter boats, and carry away her bulwarks to the gangways. While getting out the ice anchor to heave the ship off, she gave a rebound which carried away her rudder and all the stanchions to the gangway. This second shock caused the ship to cant to starboard, when both jibs were given to her just in time to carry her clear of the iceberg. She had not moved more than a dozen lengths before a huge mass of ice fell from the iceberg in her wake. If this had happened twenty minutes before, it would have crushed the ship to atoms. As soon as we gained the open sea, Captain Hudson very wisely put the ship's head for Sydney, where she arrived in a shattered and sinking condition. For several days the weather had been foggy.

January 26. Hove to alongside of an iceberg, lowered a boat, and took in a supply of ice. Filled several of our tanks with it.

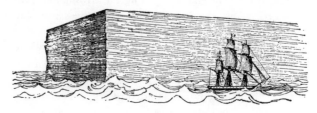

TABULAR ICEBERG.

January 27. Weather fair. Wind from the sou'-sou'-west. All day working the ship out of an ice-floe. A long row of tabular icebergs were in sight from the south. Latitude 64° 1′ south.

January 28. Weather fair. We were now surrounded by many tabular icebergs, from half a mile to three miles in length. We had run some forty miles through them, when we made high land ahead, eighteen or twenty miles to the other side of the ice barrier. We hove the lead and found bottom at thirty fathoms. Coarse black sand covered the arming.

At twelve o'clock the weather began to thicken, and the breeze to freshen, when we stood out of the bay.

At five o'clock all hands were called to close-reef topsails. The reef points were frozen so stiff that we could not knot them. In getting spinning-lines around the sails several of the crew were so chilled and benumbed

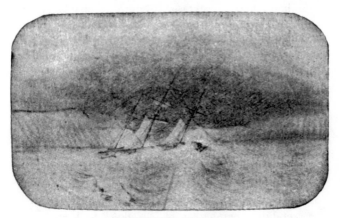

THE VINCENNES IN A GALE.

by the bitter cold that we had to sling them in bowlines, drag them from the yard, and lower them on deck.

At eight o'clock the ship was under her storm sails. It was bitterly cold, and every spray that touched the ship was converted into ice. At four bells all hands were called to work ship. We were in a high southern latitude, on an unknown coast, a terrific gale blowing from the south, accompanied by a blinding snow-storm, a narrow channel to navigate, and surrounded by icebergs. Such was our situation ; and all that we could do was to be ready for any emergency, and to have all hands at their regular stations, while the good ship was being driven by the fury of the gale. Suddenly many voices cried out from the to'-gallant forecastle, "Icebergs on the weather bow!" then, "On the lee bow, and abeam!" Destruction seemed certain as we dashed on, expecting the almost inevitable crash. Return we could not, for we had just passed large bergs to leeward. The ship was kept on her course. Louder and more furious raged the gale. Now the lee guns were under water; the next instant the ship rose upright on an even keel.

At last we entered a narrow passage between two monster icebergs that were gradually closing together. Every officer and man was at his station with bated breath and blanched face; yet true to discipline there they stood like specters. We felt that we were death-doomed. One thought of the dear ones at home, a brief prayer to our God, then we nerved our hearts to meet our fate. But you know the song tells us that "there's a sweet little cherub that sits up aloft" to keep watch over poor Jack; and on this occasion of extreme danger, Providence was indeed kind. As our gallant ship sailed onward a glimmer of hope arose, and our hearts grew lighter and lighter as we heard the whistling of the gale grow louder and louder over our heads, while we gradually emerged from the passage. The suspense we endured while making our way between those two icebergs can be better imagined than described. It was something terrible, and, as we dashed along in clear water, we felt that we had escaped an awful death, and thanked God in our hearts for our preservation.

The mean temperature between decks was about 40°. In severe weather hot coffee was served out to the crew. We had watch and watch, but it was mostly, "All hands reef topsails," "Shorten sail," "Make sail," or "Work ship," the whole twenty-four hours. The commodore seemed to be on deck all the time, and how he managed to sleep was a mystery.

January 30. The sun rose in great brilliancy this morning, and all was quiet save a brisk breeze blowing from the eastward. All sail was set, making for a bay bearing sou'west. By noon we had reached its extreme limits. A barrier of ice one hundred and fifty feet high prevented our further progress south. Thirty or forty miles inland, behind the barrier, mountains could be seen from two to three thousand feet high ; also smoke as from a volcano. Rocks were also seen several feet out of the water, with seals basking on them. This bay was named for our signal quartermaster, Piner's Bay. It is situated in latitude 66° south, longitude 140° east. The wind had been freshening and there was too much at this time to tack, so we luffed the ship up into the wind and wore her short round on her heel. At noon the wind had increased to a gale, and by one o'clock we were reduced to storm sails, with our to'-gallant yards on deck. This, like the last gale, was an old-fashioned blinding snow-storm, and the sea we experienced short and disagreeable, but nothing to be compared with the first gale. The snow had the same steely or cutting quality as in the first gale, and seemed as if armed with icicles or needles.

January 31. No moderation of the weather. At one

o'clock a field of ice close under our lee. Wore ship instantly and just in time to avoid coming into contact with it. After lasting nearly thirty hours the gale abated, and then we made sail.

February 2. Found ourselves sixty miles to the westward of Piner's Bay.

February 3, 4, and 5. Foggy, chilly, and uncomfortable. Our sick list increasing rapidly.

February 6. The same thick weather. The sailors are much afflicted, here in these cold regions, with saltwater boils.

February 7. Weather much pleasanter. Sailed all day along a perpendicular, icy barrier, one hundred and fifty to two hundred feet high, with high land behind it.

February 8. Weather the same as yesterday. The night very unpleasant.

February 9. Another fair and pleasant day. At midnight we had a splendid display of the *aurora australis*. It extended around the northern horizon and was very brilliant, glowing with all the colors of the rainbow. This continued about half an hour.

February 10. Weather fair, with glorious sunshine. This gave us a chance to air the ship and dry our wet clothes.

February 11. Fair and pleasant.

February 12. Sailed through a great deal of floe ice. Came up with a solid barrier which prevented our further progress. Land could be seen twenty or thirty miles distant. The air was very clear and the water smooth. We landed on an iceberg ; and in a valley at the foot of a knoll, by cutting through a thin skim of ice, we found a pond of delicious water. We were provided with leather bags for the purpose of watering the ship. We filled these with water, and, carrying them on board, filled several of our tanks. This iceberg was three miles in circumference. Imagine an iceberg three times larger than Boston Common, afloat, and drifting in the water. Such was the fact, however, and some icebergs are much larger. This one had at some time been aground, and had turned over, for we found on it heaps of stones, pebbles, gravel, and mud, where we landed. We saw several large boulders or rocks imbedded in it. What was exposed to view of one of them would probably weigh eight or ten tons. We obtained many specimens of the stones and pebbles. They were of basalt and red sandstone. These specimens from the Antarctic Continent were in great demand during the remainder of our cruise. We had a jolly time while on this iceberg, sliding, snowballing one another, and playing with the penguins and seals. As we had not got our "shore legs" on we received many a fall on the ice, which, we found, was very hard and flinty, and caused us to see a great many stars. I never saw wild sea-animals so tame and innocent-looking as these seals. Three or four of us caught hold of an old sea-horse's tail, and he dragged us quite a distance. When we reached the edge of the berg we let go and he tumbled into the water. He soon came up again with two or three others, looked all about, and seemed much surprised at not finding us in the water with him. We captured several of these seals, called sea-lions, sea-elephants, or sea-tigers, and they form part of our collection at the Smithsonian Institute, at Washington, D. C.   They are about ten feet long, and nearly as large round as a horse.

There were many fine fur seals in the Antarctic Ocean. It is, however, a singular fact that there are no walruses or auks seen in the Antarctic seas.   On many of the icebergs were armies of penguins.   They are about twenty-four inches high.   Some of them are dark gray, nearly black, with orange or light-gray breasts.   On each side of their heads is a bunch of bright-yellow feathers.   They stand erect and appear very dignified and soldier-like.   They march in companies or regiments, following after the drum-major or king-penguin, who turns around at times to take a view of his old comrades. They reminded me of a little incident which I will relate.

At the commencement of the Mexican War, as shipping was dull, and I felt very patriotic, I shipped in one of the soldiers' companies.   The following is one of the notices which I received :   "You, being enrolled as a soldier in the company of volunteers to be annexed to the first regiment of light infantry, are hereby ordered to appear at the usual place of parade of said company in Fanueil Hall, on Wednesday, the 17th of June, at nine o'clock in the forenoon, as the law directs, for military duty. By order of Alonzo Coy, commanding officer of said company.   Dated at Boston this 8th day of June, 1846." We were playing soldier finely, when the commanding officer ordered us to "ground arms."   Instantly a great, clumsy soldier on my "larboard side" grounded his big, heavy gun right on my toes.   I gave an awful shriek that frightened the whole regiment.   There were no herdics in those days, so they sent me home in a cab. I quit the army the next day.

These birds, the penguins, keep excellent time with their file leader. It was very amusing to see them walk, they were so very awkward. If we annoyed them, they squawked furiously, flapped their wings, and showed fight. They would nip and bite so severely that even our thick clothing was poor protection from their attacks. On our return to the boat we captured several of them, the old king-penguin and a number of his followers, and, tying their legs, put them in the boat. When about half-way to the ship, they set up such a squalling and cack-ling that their comrades swimming about in the water would leap into our boat and sometimes completely over it, knocking our hats off, striking our heads and faces, and nipping us at every turn. They came in such num-bers as to very nearly swamp our boat, and, to make the matter worse, the king and two or three others escaped, and then how they did lacerate us with their nippers ! Just then, three big sea-lions came up alongside the boat and looked in. One of them boldly rested his head on the gunwale. I never saw such innocence pictured in a face as was in his. We expected that he would leap into the boat, or, by his weight on the gunwale, would swamp us, and thus give us all a chance to swim to the ship. Suddenly the old king-penguin, which we had again secured, made a desperate effort and regained his liberty, and, followed by two others, escaped from the boat. This seemed to pacify their comrades at large, and also the seals, for they all disappeared under water. A few strokes of our oars brought us alongside the ship.

When we went below to change our clothes, we found our bodies and limbs covered with bruises. Several days afterward we captured a number of the king-penguins. One of them measured forty-eight inches from the tip of his tail to the end of his beak, and weighed thirty-two pounds. They are now in the National Museum at Washington, D. C.

In cruising among the icebergs we found many *crustacea* and shrimps. These are believed to be the food of the numerous whales in these seas. They are also food for the penguins and other birds.

For several days nearly all the icebergs we saw were discolored with earth. Many seals were seen on them, basking in the sun. These seals were of different kinds and ages, from the small fur and hooded varieties to the big sea-elephant. There were also many cape pigeons, white and gray, and large and small petrels.

February 16. The weather fair, and wind sou'east. To-day we discovered one of the largest sea-elephants we had ever seen. Two boats were lowered and sent to capture him. Many balls were fired at him, but he scarcely noticed them, simply raising his head and looking round. The two boats' crews surrounded him, and then he commenced to flounder about, knocking them helter-skelter on the ice. He soon reached the water, his native element, and so escaped. There was a large pond of muddy water on this iceberg, not frozen over, though the weather was several degrees below freezing point.

February 17. To-day began with snow squalls. The snow, instead of being in flakes, was in grains, very hard and dry, and large as buckshot, though not at all like hail-stones. They were pure white. We were surrounded all day by a very large number of huge sperm whales, whose curiosity seemed to be greatly excited by our presence. They would come up close aboard, puffing and blowing like locomotives. They were covered with so many great barnacles that they looked like large rocks alongside the ship. When coming up to blow, the

AURORA AUSTRALIS.

little whales, or calves, were as spry and active in their native element as kittens. It was not pleasant to have them so close aboard, and it was convincing proof that they knew not the enmity of man.

This night we had a splendid display of the *aurora australis.* It excelled everything of the kind we had ever witnessed, and appeared like some enchanted vision. Across the whole horizon, overhead, and all around were seen flashes of light showing all the prismatic colors. At the same time, or in quick succession, it flashed in all directions, and streamed up and down like the lightning's fitful glare. It would thicken at times like fog, and shut out from view the brilliant stars. Canopus and the Southern Cross were in the zenith at the time. While lying on our backs on the deck and looking up, we could command the entire magnificent view.

February 18. Wind easterly, sea smooth. During the day had several snow squalls. The snow that fell was in the form of a regular, six-pointed star.

February 19. Weather fair, sea very smooth ; ship surrounded by many icebergs. Much anxiety existed among the officers lest the ship should be hemmed in by these frozen bulwarks.

February 20. This morning our hearts were made glad by feeling a slight swell of the sea with a little breeze from the sou'east. By nine P. M. we had worked the ship through many narrow passages between the icebergs into clear water, latitude 63° south, longitude 101° east.

February 21. Weather moderate with light westerly winds. At eight bells every appearance of bad weather. At two bells all hands called to muster, when the commodore thanked us for our exertions and good behavior during the trying scenes we had passed through, and congratulated us on the success that had attended us. He said that he should represent our conduct in the most favorable light to the government, and that he had no doubt that the government would grant us a suitable reward for our past services. He also informed us that he had determined to bear up and return north ; so the ship's head was pointed towards New Zealand, three thousand miles distant. After giving three cheers for

the Antarctic Continent, all hands were called to " splice
the mainbrace." Up to this time we had had only
hot coffee.

January 30. On board the *Porpoise*. At four P. M.
a ship was discovered ahead, and shortly after another,
both standing to the south. The brig hauled up nor'-
west, intending to speak them, being sure they were the
Vincennes and the *Peacock*. Shortly after, seeing that
they were strangers, Captain Ringold hoisted his colors.
It was known that the English squadron under Sir James
Ross was about to visit these seas, and he was preparing
to cheer the great English navigator, when the stranger
showed the French colors. One of the ships displayed
a broad pennant. Captain Ringold concluded that they
must be the French discovery ships under Captain
d'Urville. While closing with the strangers — for he
desired to pass within hail under the flagship's stern —
he saw to his surprise that they were making all sail.
Without a moment's delay Captain Ringold hauled down
his colors and bore upon his course before the wind.

It is with regret that I mention the above occurrence,
and it can but excite the surprise of all that such a cold
repulse should come from a French commander, and
that the vessels of two friendly powers should meet in
such an untraversed and dangerous quarter of the globe
and not even exchange the common civilities of life, and
should exhibit none of the kinder feelings that the situation would awaken, but refuse to allow any communication. It showed that the commander was devoid of all
manly feeling and brotherly love, to commit such a
breach of the courtesy due from one nation to another.

He knew not but that the brig was in need of medical aid or had important communications to make. It was truly surprising what could prompt him to pursue such a course, for during my twenty years' experience before the mast—and I have cruised among pretty nearly all nations—I have found the French people to be the most courteous and polite of any whom I have met.

This distinguished French navigator, Commodore Dumont d'Urville, had discovered land eleven days previous, in the evening of the 19th of February, in latitude 65° south, longitude 142° east. He said it averaged over a thousand feet high, and was entirely covered with ice and snow. He cruised along its shore to the westward about one hundred and fifty miles, where it suddenly turned to the south, and here he met our brig *Porpoise*. Land was then in sight. He named this land La Terre Adélie, for his wife. The next day, the 1st of February, he bore away for Hobart Town, where he arrived after an absence of forty-nine days.

The next year, 1849, Captain Sir James Ross of the British navy visited these seas. How far he was guided by the copy of our chart and log, sent him by Commodore Wilkes, and which he never acknowledged, can only be surmised. The English admiral's ships, the *Erebus* and *Terror*, were unlike the Frenchman's and our ships. They were so strongly built that they were forced through a thick belt of ice two hundred miles into an open sea beyond. Our ships would have been completely destroyed before they could have penetrated one-quarter of the distance. Sir James Ross left Hobart Town on the 12th of November, 1841. Entering the

Antarctic Circle, he stood farther to the east than we did, and penetrated as high as latitude 78° south, where he discovered land. Coasting many weary miles along its frozen shores, on the 28th he discovered two mountains, the highest of which is 12,400 feet, having on its summit an active volcano, which the admiral named Mt. Erebus. The other, which is 10,000 feet high, he named Mt. Terror. These mountains are situated in latitude 76° south, longitude 168° east. Well might the discoverer of the north magnetic pole feel proud of his discoveries in these unknown and untraversed regions. The English admiral named it Victoria Land. The ceremony of taking possession was in the name of Her Most Gracious Sovereign Majesty, Queen Victoria. He made two subsequent voyages in these seas, but they did not prove as successful as the first. In 1845 Lieutenant Moore of the British navy sailed in the bark *Pagoda* from Cape Town on a scientific cruise to the Antarctic regions. He penetrated a little farther south than Ross, and thus completed the observations left by him, and confirmed the discovery of an Antarctic Continent by our squadron. As our discovery of some portions of the Antarctic Continent has been called in question by a few Englishmen, who have rendered a verdict not proved, it would probably be wiser for me, as I am the only known survivor of the six hundred and eighty-seven men who served in the expedition under Commodore Wilkes, to keep silent, but my American pride will not allow me to do so.

In tracing the English maps of to-day, I find no mention on many of them of our discovery of the Antarctic

Continent. That continent is laid down as South Victoria Land, from latitude 64° to 79° south, and from longitude 162° to 97° east.   This long line of coast includes not only our fifteen hundred miles of the Antarctic Continent, but also the one hundred and fifty miles of coast discovered by D' Urville, the French navigator.   These lands are named Victoria Land, Mt. Erebus, Mt. Terror, Mt. Sabine, North Cape, Terre Adélie, Cotta Clara Land, and Enderby Land.

All of the above are, no doubt, detached portions of the Antarctic Continent, which were discovered from three of our vessels on the 16th of January, 1840. The land was frequently in sight in fair weather, while we cruised along its shores for fifteen hundred miles.   We occasionally obtained soundings from twenty-five to eight hundred fathoms, the arming being covered in places with black sand, dead coral, clay, and gravel. Commodore Wilkes very appropriately named the land discovered the Antarctic Continent.   Our discovery was also confirmed by Lieutenant Moore in 1845.

CHAPTER VIII.

THE following will be read, I am sure, with much interest by every American. It is the address of the President of the Geographical Society of London.

Gentlemen : You have just heard the announcement that the council has awarded the Founder's medal to Captain Wilkes of the United States Navy, for the zeal and intelligence with which he carried out the Scientific Exploring Expedition intrusted to him by the Government of the United States in the years 1838 and 1842, and for the volumes which he has published, detailing the narrative of that expedition. It therefore becomes my duty to endeavor to give you some account of the performances of the gallant officer, and of the services which he has rendered to the progress of geography. It must be remembered that this was the first expedition ever fitted out by the Government of the United States for scientific purposes. Greater difficulties must therefore be supposed to have attended its organization than would have been the case with more experience. On the other hand, merit of the success is proportionately increased.

The expedition left Hampton Roads on the 17th of August, 1838, and its first scientific operation was the establishment of an observatory at Orange Harbor, in Terra del Fuego. Here some of the vessels remained, while others detached to the westward, and Captain Wilkes himself proceeded, on the 25th of February, to the south, for the purpose of exploring the southeast side of Palmer's Land. After reaching latitude 63° 25′ south, finding the season too far advanced to make any progress against the ice, he turned his ship's head to the north, and the whole squadron was soon collected at Valparaiso. Here another observatory was established. A scientific party visited the bank of snow from which the city is supplied with water, on one of the outlying ranges of the Cordilleras, the principal heights of which rose nearly four thousand feet above them. Others visited the mines of Chili. They then proceeded to the coasts of Peru, and thence, after a visit to the interior and to the ruins of Pachacamac, commenced their explorations in the Pacific.

On the 26th of December, 1839, they left Sydney, and first fell in with the ice on the 10th of January, 1840, in latitude 61° 8′ south, and longitude 163° 32′ east; and on the 11th some of the officers were confident they saw indications of land. Captain Wilkes does not rely much on this, but on the 16th those evidences became more positive, and on the 19th they distinctly saw land in longitude 154° 30′ east, and latitude 66° 20′ south. Captain Wilkes, however, only dates the discovery which he claims for his expedition, from the land seen on the 16th. I mention this the more anxiously on this occasion on account of the controversy which has arisen between him and Sir James Ross, who sailed over the spot where land was supposed to have been seen on the 11th. To this, however, I wish to allude as lightly as possible, convinced as I am that both these gallant officers have only been anxious to establish the truth, and to advance the cause of science. Undoubtedly, on the tracing which Captain Wilkes furnished to Sir James Ross the land supposed to have been seen on the 11th is sketched in, and, as a measure of precaution, it was, perhaps, prudent in Captain Wilkes so to do. It would have been more satisfactory if he could have stated to Sir James Ross, as he had done in his published account, on what slight and imperfect evidence its existence in that position was laid down.

After continuing his explorations of the Antarctic Continent as far to the westward as longitude 97° east, Captain Wilkes, finding his provisions short and the season far advanced, turned his ship's head to the north and quitted those frozen latitudes.

I regret that it is impossible, within the limits of this address, to do justice to the contents of the five volumes in which Captain Wilkes has described the progress of the expedition; but I trust I have done enough now to show that the exertions of Captain Wilkes, and the results of the expedition intrusted to him, have, in every respect, been such as to entitle him to the highest mark of distinction which it is in the power of this society to bestow.

The following lines from Coleridge's poem, "The Ancient Mariner," describe the albatross searching for food :

> " The ice was here, the ice was there,
>   The ice was all around :
>   It cracked and glowed, and roared and howled,
>   Like noises in a swound.

THE ALBATROSS IN THE HOLLOW OF A WAVE.

> " At length did cross an albatross :
>   Through the fog it came ;
>   As if it had been a Christian soul,
>   We hailed it in God's name.

> " It ate the food it ne'er had eat,
>   And round and round it flew.
>   The ice did split with a thunder-fit;
>   The helmsman steered us through !
>
> " And a good south wind sprung up behind,
>   The albatross did follow,
>   And every day, for food or play,
>   Come to the mariner's hollo !
>
> " In mist or cloud, on mast or shroud,
>   It perched for vespers nine;
>   While all the night, through fog-smoke white,
>   Glimmered the white moonshine."

We left the Vincennes on the 21st of February, standing north. The 22d being Washington's birthday, the old commodore showed his patriotism by having all hands called to splice the mainbrace. We were now short of water and were put on half-allowance.

The happiest man on board our ship was John Sac, a New Zealand chief. His native name was Puatti. He left his home on the island, about ten years previous to our visit there, in an American whaler. During this time he had made two whaling voyages from New Bedford : one to the coast of Japan, the other to the Arctic seas. He had also made one voyage to Cronstadt, one to Havre, and two to Liverpool. John was every inch a man, an excellent sailor, and a jolly good fellow. His form was manly and robust, and his face, like many of the natives, was elaborately tattooed. In the estimation of his countrymen he presented quite a noble appearance. He was very fond of his home, and enthusiastic in praise of his country and people, and longed to return to his wigwam. "New Zealand, New Zealand, no place like New Zealand !"

At night we had another very grand display of the *aurora australis.* It first appeared in the southern heavens, and was more brilliant than any we had ever witnessed. Its beautifully-tinted orange-colored waves would flash across one another in quick succession, and anon seem to fold, one within another, like a fan.

February 23. A strong gale blowing from the south-west, with much sleet, hail, and snow.

INCLINED ICEBERG.

February 24, 25, 26. The gale still continued. It was very severe. We passed many icebergs, and had many narrow escapes from disaster. We left the last iceberg 53° south ; at noon, by observation, 50° south. In taking a cast of the lead, we lost it with eight hundred fathoms of wire line. The sea was of such a clear, deep blue that a white object could be seen at the depth of fifteen fathoms.

March 1. Made a sail two points on the weather bow, the first we had seen for sixty days, which made us think we were in an inhabited quarter of the globe.

March 2. Thick, misty weather.

March 5. The wind prevented our continuing our course for New Zealand. We gave the ship all the sail she could possibly carry, and headed for Sydney. Our convict shipmates seemed very sad, and had grown thin and pale. They had the sympathy of all the crew.

March 11. At noon we passed the head of Port Jackson and took a pilot. Shortly after, dropped anchor in Farm Cove, abreast Fort McQuire, after an absence of three months. All hands well and hearty, including those frozen aloft on the 21st of January. We found the country looking quite green and beautiful, and the air deliciously sweet.

The authorities were notified of the three stowaways we had on board. When the sergeant of the 56th regiment, and others in authority, came on board and looked over the crew, the sergeant claimed the youngest one, who had been a drummer-boy in his regiment. He was court-martialed, and sentenced to receive one hundred and five lashes. It was stated that he received ninety-three ; five of them applied after the breath had left his body. As the lad was a young London prig, he was nicknamed Oliver Twist. He was slenderly built, very intelligent looking, seemingly of good morals, and was becoming a favorite with all on board. He used to tell me about the old Jew Fagins in London, and about his mother and sister, and what he was going to do when he got back home. We all regretted his sad fate. May he rest in peace.

The *Peacock* arrived here on the 22d of February in a sinking condition, her cut-water, as well as her rudder and part of her bulwarks, having been carried away.

H. B. M. transport ship *Buffalo* arrived the same day with the Canadian convicts on board. The Sydney people seemed much delighted at our return. While here we heard of the arrival at Hobart Town of the two ships belonging to the French expedition under command of Commodore d' Urville. He afterwards published in the papers a report of his discoveries while in the Antarctic seas. He had been quite unfortunate in losing four of his officers and twenty-seven of his crew. In overhauling our ship, we found our fore and maintop masts both sprung, a part of our cut-water carried away, and our ship's hull considerably bruised. When viewing her from the shore she looked more like an old Dutch galiot whaler than a trim Yankee sloop-of-war. Having refitted, provisioned, and watered ship, and bidden our English friends a final adieu, on the 16th of March we weighed anchor and stood out to sea.

On the 23d spoke the French ship *Ville de Bordeaux*, which we supplied with provisions. She had been out three years, and had on board four thousand barrels of oil. The crew were on a short allowance of bread and water. We rendered them medical assistance by sending our surgeons on board, and supplied them with a barrel of beef, one of pork, one of flour, some small stores, and some preserved soup for their sick, after which we parted company.

I still practice my writing lessons, and Mr. Stuart and Mr. Green both tell me I can write " mother " first-rate ; yes, and I can just write the words, " home," " sisters," " brothers," " Roxbury," " Boston," " Big Dick," " Torrent 6," and " Hurrah for Jackson, all nations ! "

March 25.   A light wind from the nor'east.

March 26.   Fair, with a light breeze from the north.

March 27.   Wind hauled to the sou'-sou'east, and blew a stiff breeze.

March 28.   Weather fair, wind from the south.

March 29.   Made North Cape of New Zealand.

On the 30th came to anchor in Kawa Kawa River, Bay of Islands.   Here we found, quietly lying at anchor, the " Daughter of the Squadron," the *Flying Fish*, also the brig *Porpoise* and a number of English and American whale-ships.   All the officers were made happy by receiving letters from home.   Billy Roberts and others of the crew were sadly disappointed at not receiving any.   We had parted with our tender, the *Flying Fish*, in a terrific gale in the Antarctic seas, and all sorts of yarns had been spun about the distress she was in when last seen.   All hands were not slow in assigning to her the same fate that befell her unfortunate mate, the *Sea Gull*, off Cape Horn.   Sailors are superstitious, and prone to anticipate evil ; and on this occasion they were full of all kinds of surmises imaginable.   So it cheered our hearts to have her once more in our company.

The following is by J. C. Palmer, surgeon on board the *Flying Fish :*

THE ANTARCTIC MARINER'S SONG.

Sweetly, from the land of roses,
  Sighing, comes the northern breeze;
And the smile of dawn reposes,
  All in blushes, on the seas.
Now, within the sleeping sail,
Murmurs soft the gentle gale.

Ease the sheet, and keep away:
Glory guides us south to-day.

Yonder, see! the icy portal
　　Opens for us to the Pole;
And where never entered mortal,
　　Thither speed we to the goal.
Hopes before, and doubts behind,
On we fly before the wind.
Steady,— so — now let it blow!
Glory guides, and south we go.

Vainly do these gloomy borders
　　All their frightful forms oppose;
Vainly frown these frozen warders,
　　Mailed in sleet, and helmed in snows.
Though, beneath the ghastly skies,
Curdled, all the ocean lies,
Lash we up its foam anew —
Dash we all its terrors through!

Circled by these columns hoary,
　　All the field of fame is ours:
Here to carve a name in story,
　　Or a tomb beneath these towers.
Southward still our way we trace,
Winding through an icy maze.
Luff her to — there she goes through!
Glory leads, and we pursue.

Undaunted, though, despite their mirth,
　　Still by a certain awe subdued,
They reach the last retreat on earth
　　Where Nature hoped for solitude.

Between two icebergs gaunt and pale,
　　Like giant sentinels on post,
Without a welcome or a hail,
　　Intrude they on the realm of Frost.

Cold, cold as death ! the sky so bleak
  That even daylight seems to shiver;
And, starting back from icy peak,
  The blinking sunbeams quail and quiver.

They smile, those lonely, patient men,
  Though gladness mocks that scene so drear;
They speak — yet words are spent in vain
  Which seem to freeze upon the ear.

Mountains on hoary mountains high,
  O'ertop the sea-bird's loftiest flight;
All bleak the air — all bleached the sky —
  The pent-up, stiffened sea, all white.

Amid the fearful stillness round,
  Scarce broken by the wind's faint breezing,
Hist ! heard ye not that crackling sound?
  That death-watch click—the sea is freezing.

They breathe not — speak not — murmur not;
  But in each other's face they gaze,
While memory, fancy, tender thought,
  Turn sadly back to other days.

Long years roll by in that wild dream —
  Long years of mingled joy and pain;
But like a meteor's erring gleam,
  'T is gone — there stands the ice again.

The ice, the piles of ice, arrayed
  In forms of awful grandeur still;
But all their terrors, how they fade
  Before proud man's sublimer will !

With straining oars and bending spars,
  They dash their icy chains asunder;
Force frozen doors — burst crystal bars —
  And drive the sparkling fragments under.

On, little bark! On, yet awhile!
  Across the frozen desert flee;
For yonder, with its welcome smile,
  Now sparkles bright thine own blue sea.

The baffled monsters fall behind,
  Nor longer urge pursuit so vain;
One moment more, and rest we find —
  'T is past; she 's safe, she 's safe again!

With drooping peak now lying to,
  Where sea-fowl brood she checks her motion,
Like them to plume herself anew
  In the bright mirror of the ocean.

All signs of strife soon wiped away,
  They northward turn — God speed them on!
To climes beneath whose genial ray
  Repose is sweet when toil is done.

We learned that the brig *Porpoise*, after having been deserted by the two French ships, had cruised along the icy barriers to longitude 100° east, latitude 64° south. On March 5th she had made Lord Auckland's Isles. The 27th she anchored in the harbor of Sarah's Bosom, in twelve fathoms of water. These islands were resorted to by whalers and sealers, to overhaul, refit, wood, and water ships.

March 17. They spoke the whale-ships *Mary and Martha*. Captain Coffin informed them that there were at least one hundred whale-ships cruising in these seas, several of them being in sight. This will give some idea of the number of ships employed in the whale and seal fisheries in this quarter of the globe.

CHAPTER IX.

New Zealand was discovered by Tasman, in 1642, and visited by Captain Cook in 1769. It consists of two large and several small islands, the largest being something over three hundred miles broad. They are mountainous, and of a volcanic nature. Mounts Egmont and Looker-on are from 8,000 to 10,000 feet high. The native population was at this time about one hundred and fifty thousand. This group, like all the Pacific islands, is very beautiful, so much so as to tempt the English government to get possession of them, and establish its colonies wherever a foothold could be obtained. An old proverb says, " Brag is a good dog, but Hold Fast is a better one." Some conceited Englishmen have boasted that England girdles the world with a chain of fortifications ; that in the East Indies she is supreme ; in China her power has been felt ; in the Eastern Archipelago she knows no rival ; and from the " Lion's Rump " at Cape Town she looks forth over the broad ocean with the air of a conqueror. The banner of St. George waves in solemn majesty over the rock of St. Helena and is seen far out in the Atlantic. She has planted herself firmly on the coasts of Africa and of North and South America, and the best of the West India Islands are hers, and the sun always shines on some of her dominions ! That is all English, you know.

Her Most Gracious Majesty, Queen Victoria of England, issued her proclamation, and took possession of these islands a few months before our arrival. The English changed the names of the two largest of these islands, which lie between 35° and 40° south latitude, formerly known and laid down on the charts as the North and South Islands. They are now called New Ulster and New Munster. Stewart's Island is now called Leinster, and that beautiful beach, the residence of numerous runaway English convicts from Hobart Town and Sydney, is very appropriately named " Blackguard Beach." It is not the runaway sailors, as has been said, but the escaped English convicts, who have found their way to many of the islands of the Pacific, that has been the greatest drawback to the missionary enterprise.

While lying here all hands had liberty on shore, and we had a jolly time. Twenty of us hired a large canoe and went up the Kawa Kawa River about nine miles with John Sac, to his home. Arriving at the village or pass, as it was called, we found all the natives, men, women, and children, armed with old guns, spears, or war-clubs, awaiting the coming of their young chief. They had heard of his arrival on an American man-of-war. As soon as John stepped on shore, they fired off their guns, brandished their war-clubs and spears, and shouted and yelled like so many demons. Fancy four or five thousand of these natives, many of them tattooed over the whole face, armed to the teeth, half-naked, some with a piece of an old mat thrown over the shoulders, others perfectly nude. Some wore red flannel shirts, or sailors' old blue jackets, buttoned, and nothing else. They were wild with delight at the return of their young chief. Finally, after a tremendous yell, the old chief, John's father, made his appearance. He was a very large man, and was tattooed all over his face. He wore over his shoulders a very fine, large mat, beautifully bordered with many rich feathers. His son, our John, wore nothing but his blue dungaree trousers and tarpaulin hat. As they advanced, they eyed each other, and purred like two cats. Finally, when they met, they touched the ends of their noses together, then, placing their hands on each other's shoulders, they would purr and rub noses again and again. All this time we were standing beside John, while the natives were moaning, wailing, and making all kinds of hideous noises. In fact, they all seemed to be crazy. At a signal given by the old chief, they suddenly departed to their huts. We followed John, his father, and others of the royal family to the palace, or White House. It was a very large building, low studded, and contained but one room. On the dark, dirty walls were hanging old flint-lock guns, war-clubs, spears, mats, calabashes, sailors' sou'westers, old pea-jackets, junk bottles, skulls, and human heads dry as those of mummies. Presently we were served with peaches, boiled fish, fresh pork, and sweet potatoes. After this we were treated to some of their dances.

The war-dance, in which John took part, was confined to the young men, and was very interesting. The peace-dance was quite affecting, as were several of the others. To give them a rest, we danced several fore-and-afters, and all-fours; but the "Sailor's Hornpipe" "took the cake." They were fairly overjoyed with it. The love-dance brought this New Zealand ball to a close. Of course we chose partners and joined in this dance. All the while John and his father were in close consultation. Occasionally John would sing out, "Sail in, shipmates, and rake her down." We did enjoy skipping the "light fantastic toe" with those fairy-like natives, immensely.

Just before sunrise, after the dance had been brought to a close, John called all hands to "splice the main-brace." After this we breakfasted on a New Zealand "hishie-hashie" of fresh fish and sweet potatoes boiled into a scouse, and seasoned with something that gave it the flavor of a charlotte russe. It was very palatable, and we stowed away a good share of it in our lockers. Shortly after our usual smoke one after another complained of a strangely disagreeable sensation in the stomach, bearing a strong resemblance to sea-sickness, and soon all of those twenty healthy, manly-looking sailors had become as helpless as "babes in the woods." The only relief was to lie down flat with our faces to the ground. After a sound sleep under a pile of native mats, we awoke quite refreshed, finding ourselves guarded by our fair partners in the dance, who were sitting beside us. It was not long before we had our sea-legs on, all but John Sac, who was a very sick chief. The time of our liberty having expired, we heeded John's advice, and after the native fashion of embracing and rubbing noses, left for the ship.

After we had arrived on board, the larboard watch went ashore to enjoy their liberty. They had a good

frolic and returned the next day on time. Shortly afterward John Sac came on board with his father and several
other chiefs. We hardly knew John, as he was dressed
like all the rest in native attire,— a mat, made of native
flax, large as a blanket, very fine, ingeniously made, and
beautifully embroidered. These mat-cloaks were tied
around their necks, and hung gracefully about their persons. The entire company, forty in number, were beautifully tattooed all over their faces, which gave them a
very fierce aspect. All wore ear-rings of jade or shark's
teeth ; a green stone, held sacred by them, was tied
about their necks, and small, bright-colored feathers
were stuck in their hair. They were of nearly uniform
size, about six feet in height, and were a manly-looking set
of men. John, his father, and several of the others
pleaded earnestly with the commodore to purchase the
territory of Muckatoo, a part of New Zealand which had
once belonged to the old chief's tribe, but had been
seized by the English. The commodore told them that
he could not interfere in a feud. We made them some
very nice presents, and they left the ship.

While here we collected many curiosities, among them
several rare specimens of tattooed heads. These New
Zealanders, like nearly all other islanders, are great beggars. A big chief, whose hut was near the landing, was
a continual bore to the commodore. At length he gave
him an old uniform coat and a cocked hat. With these
as his entire costume he promenaded the beach all day
long, feeling very grand.

April 6. While we were heaving short this morning
John Sac came on board dressed in his trousers and

tarpaulin. He told the commodore that as he had been robbed of his home and country he must seek another island home. We all felt sorry that the anticipations which John had cherished, only a few weeks before, of

NEW ZEALAND CHIEF.

serenely spending the evening of his life at home in his own native country, had been forever blasted. After breakfast we weighed and catted our anchor and stood for those islands so famous in the song of " Hokey, Pokey, Winke, Wanke," " I am king of the Tonga Islands."

There are six principal islands in the Tonga group, several small, uninhabited ones, and many coral reefs and shoals.   They were discovered by Abel Janssen Tasman, the eminent Dutch navigator, in 1642.   They were visited by Captain Cook in 1773, and are often called the " Friendly Islands of Captain Cook."

During our passage of sixteen days we were favored with light, balmy breezes.   We passed Sunday and several other islands.   Witnessed several very remarkable halos around the sun, in circles, half-circles, and segments of circles.

On the 22d we made the island of Tongataboo right ahead, rounded its eastern end, and stood down Astrolabe Channel.   While in the middle of the channel the ship ran upon a coral reef.   We hit it in the center and split this huge coral mushroom in halves.   As the two halves fell over, the ship settled to her water-line unhurt, and in a short time we came to anchor off Nukualofa, the residence of King Josias, or Pubou.   While lying here we found our tender, the *Flying Fish*, and the British brig *Currency Lass* at anchor.   We surveyed the channel and found no shoal in the place where the ship had struck, and we had the satisfaction of knowing that we had rid the channel of one great danger without injury to our ship.

Mr. Tucker and Mr. Rabone, two Wesleyan missionaries, lived at Nukualofa.   Mrs. Tucker took great pride in teaching the native children to read and write.   The island was extremely fruitful, and was covered with rich foliage.   At that time it contained ten thousand inhabitants.   The highest part of Tongataboo is sixty feet above the level of the sea.   The inhabitants were warlike ; and war councils, speech-making, and drinking ava constituted the chief business of their lives.

While we were here two parties, called the Christians and the " Devils," were at war.   Our commodore strove earnestly to restore the blessings of peace.   The head chiefs of each party, with fifty of their followers, were invited on board to a peace council.   They came the next day in two large canoes and several small ones, the Christians taking the starboard side, and the " Devils" the larboard side.   All had their faces profusely adorned with war paint.   Some were painted white ; some black, with vermilion circles around their eyes, and their noses of the same bright hue ; some with jet-black faces, vermilion around their eyes, and with white or yellow noses ; others with yellow, red, black and white stripes crossing their faces in all directions ; some half red, black, or white ; and others completely covered with small dots of red, white, yellow, and black. Besides the small piece of *tapa* worn around the waist, they had orange and straw-colored ribbons, made of the pandanus leaves, tied around their legs and arms, above and below their knees and elbows.   Some wore them around their necks, and others over the left or right shoulder, or both.   The bands were three inches wide and very pliable.   The Christians wore turbans, called *sala*, adorned with beautiful flowers.   The " Devils" had their hair tied in a large knot on one side of the head. They were armed *cap-a-pie* with spears and war-clubs. Only the big chiefs—there were over a hundred of them—were allowed on board.

The scene was novel and picturesque in the extreme. There they squatted in a body on the quarter-deck, all eager for the fight, and all eagerly listening to the great pow-wow. The Christians were represented by the missionary, Mr. Tucker; the "Devils," by a runaway English convict from Sydney. At the close of the great pow-wow we understood that peace was declared between them. Then the commodore made them presents of a lot of beads, several yards of bright-colored calico, some harmonicas and jews'-harps, and a number of large, bright-red, cotton umbrellas, with which all were highly delighted, and soon left the ship. Before they reached the shore, however, hostilities recommenced. The fight lasted all night. Next morning we learned that both parties were victorious; so they called it a drawn battle. When we went on shore the missionaries told us they had gained a great victory over the "Devils," and were now in possession of their yam grounds which the latter had taken from them several months before.

How the missionaries and their wives could live among those savages, in danger of their lives night and day, was more than we could comprehend.

On May 4th we bade our Christian friends adieu, and after taking a final leave of the "Devils," we got under way at daylight and left the harbor of Nukualofa. I doubt if any of our crew ever forgot this place, if for no other reason than because of the mosquitoes. They were so thick that when we went below on the gun or berth decks, it sounded as if there were several hundred music-boxes playing together. Like Job's "comforters" they smote us from the crowns of our heads to the soles of our feet. To escape from our tormentors we sought shelter in the tops and cross-trees. Here they were not so numerous, but they were just as ravenous, and their bite equally venomous.

At noon we passed the islands of Honga Tonga and Honga Hapai. On the 5th we made Turtle and several other small islands. After leaving Tonga all hands were more or less afflicted with ulcers, caused by those terrible mosquito bites. The sores were inflammatory, and difficult to cure. During the night we had a strong wind from the sou'east. The ship was hove to, to wait for daylight. Just at dawn we discovered several small islands close aboard on our lee bows, also a large reef right ahead. Our close vicinity to them was caused by a strong current setting to the northward. Had darkness continued a little longer, no doubt our ship would have been wrecked, and the crew massacred by the natives.

May 6. Weather hazy, with heavy gale blowing from the south. Ship under close-reefed top-sails. It is not very pleasant to cruise in bad weather where there are so many sunken reefs and shoals as are found in these seas.

May 7. Weather fair, with a light wind from the south, and a heavy, chop sea. At daylight we found ourselves surrounded with several beautiful islands, girt about by coral reefs. It was a grand sight to view them from aloft, and see the deep-blue waters of the ocean curling into white foam, and dashing its silvery spray over them. When the rising sun shone upon them the scene was gorgeous, the surf having the appearance of beautiful rainbows resting on the bosom of the ocean.

We shuddered, however, as we gazed upon this fair group of islands, and remembered that they were the homes of a ferocious race of cannibals, or man-eaters, and that we had so narrowly escaped being wrecked upon their shores.

CHAPTER X.

The Fiji Islands were discovered by Tasman in 1643. There are about one hundred and fifty islands in the group, sixty of which were then inhabited by one hundred and fifty thousand cannibals.

During the forenoon of May 8th we came to anchor in the harbor of Levuka, island of Ovolau. Thousands of natives lined the beach, watching our manœuvres with their usual curiosity. When all hands, dressed in their white frocks and trousers, mounted the rigging, ran up aloft, and lay out on the yards to furl the sails, the wondering natives screeched like so many hyenas, and performed such antics that we could hardly believe they belonged to the human race.

We soon had a visit from Tanoa, the king of these cannibal islands, with several of his chiefs, and an American sailor by the name of David Whippy, who had run away from his ship on account of ill treatment, and had lived on this island eighteen years, acting as interpreter for the king. They were nearly naked, after the native fashion. The king wore a scanty *maro* about his loins, with the long ends hanging down in front and behind. He had a large turban of white *tapa* cloth upon his head, and a mother-of-pearl shell as large as a dinner-plate, beautifully " crimshonned " or carved, hung from his neck upon his breast. Above the elbows he wore armlets made from tortoise-shell. His hair was so bushy that it would have been impossible to cover it with a

A FIJI BEAUTY, ONE OF TANOA'S DAUGHTERS.

bushel basket. His face and long beard were bedaubed with rancid cocoanut oil and ivory-black, which gave him a very hideous appearance. His body, like those of all his people, was very hairy. He was about six feet in height, slenderly built, with small, piercing, black eyes. He looked very cunning, and every inch a savage. As he and his suite came over the gangway and stood on deck, the ship's pet, Sydney, a beautiful, large Newfoundland dog which had been presented to the commodore by the governor of Australia, got sight of him. The chief's appearance did not make a very favorable impression on Sydney, for the dog kept in front of him, growling and looking savagely at him. When within a few feet of the dog the king took the front end of his *maro* and shook it at him. The dog grabbed it and tore it entirely from his body. The king was so frightened that he fell on the deck. One of the quartermasters seized the dog by the collar, and, by order of the commodore, put him in the brig.

I believe Sydney was the first dog that the king had ever seen. He soon recovered from his fright, and, with his suite and Mr. Whippy, was shown over the ship. He took a great fancy to the ship's wheel, and wanted the captain to make him a present of it. He was very much astonished when told that we steered the ship with it. When he saw the battery he wanted to know if the guns were not black dogs. Two of the guns were fired off, double shotted. Seeing the balls skip over the surface of the water and throw up its spray into the air, he was greatly surprised, and requested that no more guns be fired. They were much pleased with the ship and everything they saw. Lunch was served for them in the wardroom, of which they partook most heartily, evidently enjoying it much, especially the nuts and raisins and some old Dutch cheese. The military exercises of our marines, their marching, counter-marching, halting, and forward marching, to the music of fife and drum, and the commands to shoulder, carry, present, and ground arms, highly delighted them. After remaining on board several hours they were given presents of whale's teeth, axes, accordions, boxes of Windsor soap, plane-irons, jews'-harps, red paint, and large, bright, brass buttons. They then departed for the shore, greatly pleased with their visit and presents.

The next day, as usual on our arrival at any prominent place, we erected our observatory. We chose a hill about a quarter of a mile from the beach. The observatory consisted of several portable houses, built in New York. The pendulum house was about twenty feet square, and eighteen feet in height. The transit and telescope buildings were somewhat smaller. These, with six tents, made quite a village, and greatly astonished the natives.

May 9. Two small trading sloops arrived to-day, the *Who'd Have Thought It* and the *Nonesuch*. They were tenders to the ship *Leonidas*, Captain Eggleston, which was at another island. The *Leonidas* was a South Sea trader, for tortoise-shell and *beche de mer*. Among the runaway English convicts here was a short, red-headed, wrinkled old Irishman, by the name of Paddy Connell. He had a long gray beard, which hung down to his waist. He had lived on these islands forty years, and in dress and looks strongly resembled these Fiji cannibals. He said it seemed to him sometimes as though he was living out of the world ; but that he was very happy, for he had five wives and forty-eight children.

Here, as at all the islands we visited, our boats, the
Greyhound, Lion, Fox, Turtle, Nightingale, Lizard,

ONE OF PADDY CONNELL'S FIVE WIVES.

Leopard, Elephant, White Handkerchief, and *Bear,*
and the two cutters were fitted out and provisioned with
eight or ten days' rations in order to survey the different
islands, reefs, and bays.

No doubt it would sound odd to a countryman to hear the boatswain and his mates blow through their silver calls (whistles), which are about four inches long, and sing out, one after the other, "Away, there, you Leopards, away!" "You Foxes, away!" · "You Lions, away!" "Come, hurry into your boats!" "Away, there, you Elephants!" "You Turtles, and White Handkerchiefs, away!" It might be that some of the boats' crews were down on the berth deck, and then it was, "Hurry up, there, you Penguins, you Nightingales, you Albatrosses, and man your boats!" There were two officers and five men attached to each boat while we were surveying.

The following were the orders given by the commodore to the officers of the boats :

1. You will avoid landing anywhere on the mainland or islands, unless the latter should be uninhabited.

2. Every precaution must be observed in trading with these natives; and no native must be suffered to come alongside, or near our boats, without our boarding-nettings being up. All trading must be carried on over the stern of the boat, and your arms and howitzers ready to repel attack.

3. You will avoid any disputes with them, and never be off your guard, or free from suspicion. They are in no case to be trusted.

4. Your two boats must never be separated at night, but be anchored as close together as possible.

These and other instructions were often given while standing in the bow of the boat, heaving the lead, or resting on our oars while the officers were measuring base by sound.

When looking down into the water upon the coral

reefs, we could see coral shrubs of pink, yellow, white, green, orange,— in fact, of all colors, forms, and sizes. There were also many shell-fish ; and everywhere beautiful fishes were swimming among the coral branches. It was amusing to watch the shell-fish as they crawled from their shells, and then dragged them behind. Beautiful orange-colored cowries, harp-shells, pearl oysters, conchs, and many other odd-shaped shells and fishes were plainly visible. There seemed to be continual war among these finny tribes and *testacea* in the midst of their fairy-like regions. Sometimes a small fish would swim along over a shell-fish, when the latter would seize it and draw it into his shell. When a lamprey eel or a shovel-nosed shark made his appearance, which was very often, every living thing disappeared in an instant. The shell-fish suddenly crawled back into their shells ; all the other fishes quietly hid away among the coral bushes ; and the turtles drew their heads and feet well into their shells. We often saw small, ravenous, cowardly sharks gulp down many small fishes, more beautiful than butterflies or humming-birds. Frequently a lamprey eel would attack a large conch, tear the fish from its shell and devour it.

One morning our second officer, Midshipman Thompson, espied a beautiful Venus shell lying at the bottom, on the weather side of the boat. He partially undressed, and was in the attitude of diving into the water for the shell, when a white, deep-sea shark, fourteen feet long, swam from under the boat. The sudden appearance of the shark so completely paralyzed Mr. Thompson with fear that he fell down in the boat unconscious, and it was some time before consciousness could be restored.

The white shark is worshiped by the natives as one of their gods. They are considered sacred and are never harmed by them.

On the morning of the 18th of June David Bateman, of the brig *Porpoise*, breathed his last and his spirit took its flight to God who gave it. He was buried in our

CANNIBAL CHIEF, VENDOVI.

small garden on the hill, close by the observatory, with martial honors. The impressive burial service of the Episcopal Church was read by our chaplain ; three volleys were fired over the grave by the marines ; the earth thrown in, and the grave filled up ; thus the melancholy scene was closed.

While the *Peacock* was at Rewa surveying the island,

Captain Hudson captured the celebrated chief, Vendovi, who in 1834 massacred eleven of the crew of the American brig *Charles Dagget* of Salem, Captain Batcheller commander. The *Dagget's* boat went ashore early one morning, and the crew had proceeded half-way up to the *beche de mer* house when they were suddenly surprised by a party of these cannibals who had been lying in ambush. They were seized and firmly held, while the chief, Vendovi, knocked them on the head with his handy billy, a small war-club made of iron-wood. This horrible crime was committed in order to get possession of the trading or Jew box, containing cheap trinkets, and some hatchets, plane-irons, etc. The *Dagget* was a South Sea trader, for sandal-wood, tortoise-shell, and *beche de mer*, which were taken to China and traded for teas and silks. Nearly all the Pacific and Chinese trade carried on in this country eighty years ago was confined to Salem. The sandal-wood referred to is a deliciously fragrant, scented wood. The Chinese burn it in their temples as incense to their gods. The *beche de mer*, or sea-slug, is a sort of round jelly-fish, from six to twelve inches long, and two in diameter, and of a reddish-brown color. They are found in great abundance on the coral reefs. The natives fish for them at night by the light of the moon, and with torches. These fish hide themselves during the day in the crevices of the coral reefs. They sally forth at night and creep out upon the reefs like caterpillars. After they are gathered they are thoroughly dried, or cured, and then resemble a well-fried sausage. The Chinese make an excellent soup of them ; the natives eat them raw.

This town, or *koros*, as it was called, contained about fifty houses. They were built of the same material as those at the other islands, but were differently constructed : the roofs being very steep, and the ridge-pole projecting at each end, often ornamented with shells.

FIJI CHIEF, TUI LEVUKA.

This *koros* was situated in a grove of mangrove bushes, surrounded by many bread-fruit, cocoanut, and banana trees. The interior of their houses was kept quite clean. The house of the chief, Tui Levuka, was a large, barn-like structure, nearly two hundred feet square. The roof was very high and peaked, and there were two narrow openings, or doorways, one at each end. Several of us entered it one day, and found it to contain but one large room. The floor was partially covered with mats and *tapa*. In the center, at one end of the room, was a large pit, lined with stones, where they built their fires and did their cooking. It was inclosed by seven posts, about six feet high. The roof was covered with the leaves of the pandanus. Earthen jars, holding from one to eight gallons, oval at the bottom, and with a small opening at the top, together with a lot of junk-bottles and drinking-vessels were hanging from the posts and the roof. These utensils were made at the pottery by the women. Nearly all the labor, both indoors and out, was performed by the women. They were kept in subjection and in a state of great degradation, and were often tied up and flogged. They were the abject slaves of their lords and masters, who, if not at war with some neighboring tribe, might be found in their huts or in some shady nook asleep or telling stories. Of the latter amusement they were very fond, especially if the stories were false. It might be truly said that the one who could tell the biggest lie was held in the highest esteem by them.

Nearly all their food was cooked in the jars of which we have previously spoken. A very little water is put in the jar with the food to be cooked; the mouth is then stuffed with green plantain leaves, and the jar placed on the fire. Some of these jars were held sacred, and nothing but human flesh was cooked in them. These were kept in the *mabure*, or spirit houses. These cannibals considered the fleshy parts of the arms and legs the most palatable portions of the human body.

Another method of cooking human bodies was this:

By means of pointed sticks a large trench was dug in
the earth. This trench was then lined with stones, and
had a fire built in it. After the stones had become sufficiently heated, the bottom was covered with many layers
of banana and plantain leaves. Three human bodies were
then brought from the *mabure* house and laid in the
trench upon the thick bed of leaves, together with some
hogs, and a large quantity of yams and taro. The whole
was then covered with large quantities of leaves, and a
fire built on top. It is a great cause for gratitude that the
light of Christianity has penetrated to these dark regions,
and that such horribly barbarous customs have ceased
to exist.

A favorite pudding among these natives was called
okalolos, of which they made several kinds. The following
is the recipe : Half a calabash was first lined with a few
plantain leaves. A layer of the golden banana. cut in
slices was placed on the bottom, and on this was laid
another layer of a different flavor, and so on. The meat
of the cocoanut, which is, when ripe and freshly gathered,
as soft as jelly, was placed between the alternate layers,
which were continued until the dish was filled. The milk
of the cocoanuts was then poured over the whole, and
then the ends of the plantain leaves, with which the dish
was lined and which had projected above the top of the
dish, were gathered up and tied around with a string
taken from the bark of a tree, after which the jar was
placed in the trench, under the leaves, to steam. It
takes about four hours to cook a dinner in this manner,
but these Fiji *okalolos* were steamed in about thirty
minutes, and I can testify that they far excelled all the

cakes, pies, and puddings which I ever ate elsewhere.
I have eaten suet and minute puddings, English plum
duffs, Jennie's kisses, "my Mary Ann's cookies," angel
cakes, Satan's best cakes, charlotte russes, pies of all
kinds, and many other dishes with euphonious names,
but the Fiji *okalolos*, or fruit puddings, leave all of
them far "astern."

While here, we visited the chief Tui Levuka. One
day, while at his house, I walked on my hands, turned
several hand-springs and two or three somersets, that I
learned while attached to the circus. The old chief
and Tanoa the king, who was a guest of the chief, were
greatly surprised, and always afterwards pointed to me
as a spirit.

One afternoon we were invited to the *mabure*, or
priest's house. These houses were about twelve to fifteen feet square, with the roof about thirty feet. They
are built on a mound or a pile of stones. It is here
they hold their councils and entertain strangers.

On our arrival we were assigned seats in front of the
mabure, on some stones. Presently a big, muscular
native made his appearance from behind a high rock,
with something under his arm which resembled a short
hog-trough, which he dropped on the ground. A group
of one hundred young Fiji women, whose heads were
profusely adorned with orange blossoms, were seated
upon the ground. When the native arrived in front
of the group he commenced beating on the trough,
or Fiji drum, with a small war-club. It produced a
loud, hollow sound, anything but musical. Then the
orchestra, consisting of a group of maidens, commenced

to play ; some on two joints of small bamboo, with two holes at one end, two in the middle, and one at the other end. To this latter the left nostril was applied. Others had four or five joints of large bamboo, opened at each end, which they beat upon with a small stick. Some beat two sticks together, and some clapped their hands to make a sharp sound, while others gave a sort of grunt down in their throats, which produced a sound similar to that of a weak-toned bass drum. Occasionally the musicians would sing a monotonous song on one note, the bass alternating with the melody. The whole produced discordant sounds, which could hardly be called music, and I fear would fail to be appreciated by a Boston audience. They kept excellent time, however.

While the musicians were playing, the major drummer made his appearance from behind the huge rock. He was completely covered with green and dried leaves. Vines and creepers were bound about him in every way. On his head he wore a mask resembling a boar's head, painted red on one side and black on the other. His baton was a huge war-club. He would turn around at times and " present arms " with it ; then toss it up in the air end over end, and catch it as it came down. His movements were quite similar to those of our major drummers. He was greatly applauded by the spectators.

He was followed by a procession of natives, all dressed in gala attire, wearing white *salas* and new *masi*. The chiefs had wreaths of natural flowers and vines twined around their turbans, which gave a pretty effect. Their faces were painted in various styles, some wholly vermilion, some half vermilion, the other half black, with

white or orange-colored noses; others with white or
black faces, and red or yellow noses. As they entered
the area, their progress became slower. They walked
six abreast, taking three measured steps, then halted.

FIJI MAJOR DRUMMER.

The first three divisions then bent forward, and when
they straightened up the eighteen in the rear would bend
down, and so on, till all had gone through the bending
process. At the close of each strain of music they placed
their war-clubs in a variety of positions, as our soldiers
do their guns when training; such as "shoulder,"
"carry," and "present arms." When all had entered

the square, they bowed very gracefully to us, and then suddenly became quite violent in their actions, jumping up and down, treading the ground furiously, brandishing their war-clubs, and all of a sudden gave some of the most unearthly yells imaginable. We were all well armed, kept a bright lookout, and feared no danger. Finally they gave a tremendous " wha-hoo," then fell to the ground and kissed it. This ended the Fiji club dance.

John Sac, or Tuatti, our New Zealand shipmate, then danced his country's dance, which was one of great energy and violence, and greatly astonished the Fiji natives. After this there was a " love dance" by the young women musicians, which consisted simply in bowing very prettily to us, bending and twisting the body backward and forward, and throwing the arms about, without moving the feet. The performance closed by a loud clapping of the hands. This ended the matinee.

The natives were very fond of sports and games. The girls played *vimoli*, which was performed by tossing up and keeping five or six oranges circling around the head. Another game, called *libigilla*, was wrapping a girl up in a mat, and carrying her to another to guess her name. If she guessed wrong, a forfeit of yams and taro must be given for a treat. The boys pitched quoits with a mother-of-pearl shell, and also played at hide-and-seek. Another of their games was called *vitaki*, which consisted in throwing a stick from a length of bamboo. The one who could throw it the highest or farthest was considered the winner.

The Peacocks treated the natives to a regular, old-

fashioned negro entertainment. Juba and Zib Coon
danced and highly delighted them, and the Virginia reel
set them wild. Then followed a novel representation of
a donkey. Two of the *Peacock's* crew stood back to
back, and were tied loosely together about the waist.
Iron belaying-pins were put into their hands, which
served for feet. They then bent forward so they could
strike the deck with the iron pins. A Mackintosh
blanket was thrown over them, a pair of old shoes served
as ears, and a ship's swab for tail. When this
donkey, with his comical looking rider, Jim Crow Rice,
on his back, made his appearance from between two of
the guns which had been screened off with a tarpaulin,
they were frightened, but the sound of the animal's feet
on deck and the braying of the beast fairly terrified
them. When the blanket was removed and they saw
only two men, they expressed the greatest astonishment,
and even laid their hands on them to satisfy themselves
that they were not two mules.

In the afternoon the officers heard that an attack
would be made on the observatory during the night by
a party of warriors from the chief Vendovi's district, as
they had learned that the chief was a prisoner in irons
on board our ship. Their object was to secure Captain
Wilkes, and by that means compel an exchange of prisoners. The commodore immediately came on board
ship. The observatory was re-inforced by the first part
of the starboard watch, armed and equipped for any
emergency. The ship was laid broadside to the shore,
with springs on her cables, so as to bring the guns to
bear on each side of the observatory.

Just before sunset six large war-canoes came to anchor behind a point about a mile ahead of the ship. Our guns were loaded with canister and a stand of grape and the tompions were left out. The battle-lanterns were lighted and placed between the guns. During the night many natives were seen skulking about the observatory. The night passed, however, without any disturbance, except a false alarm caused by the accidental discharge of a musket in the hands of one of the sentinels, John Van Cleck, a big Dutchman, who swore that " the gun was not loaded," and that " it went off itself." In the morning we commenced breaking up the observatory, and carried all the instruments on board ship.

CHAPTER XI.

WHILE here, besides the vessels, seventeen boats had been actively engaged in surveying the different islands, reefs, and bays. We were sometimes absent from the ship fifteen or eighteen days at a time, without ever being out of the boats, and were continually in danger from the treachery of the natives, who were ever watching for an opportunity to entrap us.

The ship's launch, Lieutenant Oliver H. Perry, grandson of Commodore Perry of Lake Erie fame, and the first cutter, Lieutenant Samuel R. Knox, grandson of General Knox, one of the old Revolutionary heroes, while surveying one of the Windward Islands experienced a very heavy gale from the south. We sought shelter in Sualib Bay. Here we lay five days waiting for the gale to abate. During this time we saw but few natives. Our store of provisions was exhausted, and we subsisted upon the few fish we could catch, and those we were obliged to eat raw. Occasionally we would secure a few cocoanuts which were drifting by the boats. The third night the rain came down in torrents, and we filled our ten-gallon breaker. This precious supply we used sparingly. On the fourth day a native swam out to the cutter with five bananas, which were equally divided between the

two boats' crews, numbering fourteen men. Our boats
had left the ship with ten days' provisions, and this
was the twenty-first day we had been absent. At noon
the weather was a little more moderate, and we prepared to leave the bay.

When we got under way to beat out, standing close in
shore, in going about we missed stays and the cutter was
thrown upon the reef. After several ineffectual efforts,
we found it quite impossible to get the boat off. When
Lieutenant Perry saw our condition he dropped anchor
a quarter of a mile away, in order to assist us if necessary.
At the time of the accident not a native was in sight, but
soon after they were seen flocking down to the beach in
scores, armed with war-clubs and spears. All our arms
and ammunition were soaked with salt water. We were
trying to save something in the cutter when Lieutenant
Knox sang out, "They are coming! the 'devils' are
coming! Make for the launch, my men!" It was
fortunate that all could swim, and that, too, on our backs,
for the splashing of the water with our hands and feet
frightened away those horrible shovel-nosed sharks that
are so numerous about the coral reefs.

Even in our perilous position we could not help feeling
amused to see the "devils" trampling one another under-
foot in their eagerness to secure whatever plunder there
was to be found in the cutter. In their greed they even
allowed us to escape, only throwing a few spears, and
ulas, or short clubs, at us, which we managed to dodge.
After stripping the cutter of everything, they dragged
her over the reef, up into a grove of mangrove bushes.

As soon as all were safe in the launch we got under

way and stood out ; but, making no headway against the wind and sea, we anchored a good gunshot from the shore. Late in the evening the "devils" built fourteen separate fires on the beach opposite our boat. Any ship or boat, or even one of their own canoes, when driven on shore, was by them considered an offering to the gods. The crews of these fated crafts, even though they numbered among them the fathers, mothers, brothers, and sisters of those on shore, were also accounted as offerings to the gods, and, accordingly, were clubbed, roasted, and eaten. This, of course, would have been our fate had we been taken.

The savages had quite a number of muskets, and, after building their fires, they waded out on the reef to windward and fired at us, but we were too far away to receive injury from their volleys, though several of the spent balls fell in our boat. During the night many of the natives swam out and, diving, tried to lift our anchor or cut our cable, and thus cause us to drift ashore. We shot quite a number of them and captured two. Of the latter, one proved to be a great chief, the other an inferior one. They had swum towards us to spy out our weakness. We bound them hand and foot and placed them in the bottom of the boat. As soon as those on shore missed their chief they danced and wailed around their fires like so many fiends.

Sunday morning was ushered in with clear weather and scarcely a breath of wind. At sunrise we got under way and stood out. When going over the bar a big roller came head on, which filled our boat half full of water, and came very near swamping us. The two chiefs in the bottom of the boat floundered about like two big lamprey eels on dry land. We soon bailed the boat out and proceeded in quest of our ships.

At six bells, eleven o'clock, we made Mbua Bay. In doubling the point we saw our ships lying quietly at anchor. How our hearts bounded with joy at the sight, and how we cheered the dear old flags floating from the mizzen peaks! It was the hour of Divine service on board, but this was soon brought to a close. The rigging was soon manned, and we were hailed with cheers, for all hands had given us up for lost. After " splicing the mainbrace " and eating a hearty dinner of plum duff, we were given our hammocks, and, turning in, very soon visited " Beulah Land" (home) in our dreams.

A little past midnight the schooner and eight boats, well manned and armed, set out for Sualib Bay, arriving early in the morning. After an early breakfast on board the *Flying Fish*, all hands went ashore, except the boats' keepers and a dog-watch on board the schooner. Soon after landing we met a small party of the natives, and among them the chief of Sualib. Through the interpreter, Mr. Whippy, Captain Wilkes demanded of the chief the cutter and everything that was stolen with her. The chief replied that it was a tradition of theirs, handed down from their fathers, that when a ship, boat, or one of their own canoes was cast away on their islands they had a right to take possession of both boat and crew in the name of the Great Spirit to whom they belonged, and offer up the crew as a sacrifice to him.

Captain Wilkes with great patience explained to him how he should act in such cases. To this parley the

chief paid very little attention, but wanted to rub noses
with the commodore and be friends. The commodore,
finding the chief deaf to all reason and all demands,
piped all hands to quarters. Then it was, " Boarders,
away ! " and two hundred jolly tars armed with cutlasses,
bowie-knives, and pistols, were soon running up a hill,
inland from the beach about a half a mile, through a
beautiful grove of palms, to a town of about sixty houses.
As we advanced towards the town the natives retreated
into a grove of banana bushes a few hundred yards in
the rear. Occasionally they would run out from their
hiding-places among the bushes and jungles, and bran-
dish their war-clubs at us in a defiant manner. Finding
their women and children had fled, we set fire to the
village, and it was soon laid in ashes.

The natives fired a few random shots at us from the
bushes, but their powder was poor, and no damage was
done ; but when they showed their dusky forms they
felt the deadly power of our carbine rifles. Many sky-
rockets were also thrown into the bushes among them,
which nearly frightened them to death. We could see
them leap up into the air, and hear them yell out, "*Curlew, curlew, curlew,*" meaning " spirits, spirits, spirits."

After seeing the town of Sualib reduced to ashes,
we followed our file leader and returned to our boats.
On our way we burned the town of Tye, containing about
a hundred dwelling-houses, and many yam houses built
of bamboo. We also came across our cutter, covered
with many leaves and bushes.

All hands returned to the beach without receiving
even a scratch. We felt very jolly because we had, as

we thought, taught the savages a lesson which they would not be likely soon to forget.   Arriving on board the schooner we " spliced the mainbrace " and partook of a lunch strongly resembling gun-flints and mahogany. Our ship's bread was extraordinarily hard, and in small pieces about the size of a flint, and our salt junk was as hard and dry as a piece of old mahogany.   Jack before the mast can, at a glance, determine to a certainty whether the so-called " beef" set before him is really bovine or horse flesh.   Old Jack Weaver, after taking an observation of the sun with the thigh-bone of a horse, soliloquized as follows :

> " Old horse, old horse, what brought you here,
>   From Saccarappa to Portland pier,
>   Where you've carted stones for many a year?
>   They treated you with much abuse,
>   Then salted you down for sailors' use.
>   They curse your eyes when they've picked your bones;
>   Then give you a toss to Davy Jones."

We returned to Mbua Bay, arriving at midnight. The next morning the chief came on board our ship and demanded the two chiefs whom we had captured at Sour Laib, saying that they were their prisoners, and that they wanted to roast and eat them as a sacrifice to the gods. The request was not granted.   A few days afterward the commodore learned that they belonged to another town, and that they swam off to assist us.   We gave them some presents and sent them home.   In the afternoon we got under way and proceeded farther up the bay, coming to anchor in twenty-eight fathoms of water off Waimea, or the boiling springs.

July 4. The commodore allowed us to celebrate the Glorious Fourth by visiting the springs. There were quite a number of them, eleven on the beach above high-water mark, some below, and some on the hillside, from which flowed a streamlet, three feet wide, of delicious cold water. This streamlet flowed in such close proximity to the springs that a person could place one hand in the cold water and the other in the hot at the same time.

The latter experiment one would scarcely care to try, as the water was so hot that the yams and taro which we boiled in one of them were cooked through in twenty minutes ; and the natives do all their cooking in them. They vary somewhat in size, but are about three feet in diameter. The largest was held sacred by the natives, and was used only for cooking human flesh. In the neighborhood we saw piles of the bleached bones of their victims.

The coral beach was so hot that we could not walk on it with our bare feet. While we were at the springs many people came to do their cooking. They were all young people. On inquiring for their old people we were told that they were all buried. These natives appeared very friendly, though the young men were wild and savage-looking fellows. The women were much more prepossessing in appearance than those at the other islands.

While here we mastered much of their language and had many social chats with them. They favored us with the K. K. U. dance, which was very pleasing.

After the dance was over they chanted the following,

their manner reminding us of Jews chanting in their synagogues :

> " Antiko maina tambu tang-ane
> To-ahula katan gita kare andratha
> Ha-ti-ke kaung-ai tang-i kow-m lau tu na
> Se-ni-kun-dra-vi sa-lu ni vu-thu ma ke va ke."

The chief of this bay had twenty wives. He lived at the foot of a hill, in a house surrounded by those of his wives, each of whom had a separate house. He spent the most of his time lounging in these, one after another. Mrs. Tandi Muthuata, the head wife, was over six feet in height and very stout. She fully understood her posision, and kept all the others in subjection, ruling them as with a rod of iron. His seventeenth wife was called Henrietta. She was a young Tahitian with whom the chief had become smitten. In order to secure her he had killed and eaten her husband, and then compelled her to become one of his wives. She was of fair complexion, and very good looking. Her hair was naturally black and straight, but, by twitching, twisting, frizzing, and coloring, it had become very bushy.

Having finished our surveys here we weighed anchor and stood for Waialaithake, or Waia Island, Bay of Waialailai, or Porpoise Bay. This island was the most hilly, broken, and romantic of any in the group. On landing we saw no natives, and thought the island uninhabited, but while ascending a hill we fell in with several who were skulking in the groves, and keeping close upon us. The constant fear of being surprised by these savages was very far from pleasant. The more knowledge we obtained of them, the less disposed were we to trust them.

As soon as we had reached the top of the hill, we fired off several sky-rockets and discharged our muskets, the reports of which seemed to frighten the natives. It was amusing to see them jump from their hiding-places in the groves and call on their gods, " *Curlew, curlew, curlew.*"

The observations taken while up here proved quite satisfactory. The height from the level of the ocean was fifteen hundred feet, and the view of the ocean and the numerous islands and reefs, with the sea dashing over them, was truly grand.

The Waia-no were independent of all authority except that of their own chiefs. All endeavors to subjugate them proved unavailing ; and they kept themselves close in their own fastnesses, shunning all communication with all other natives, except making occasional incursions, with a strong force, on the defenseless towns of some other islands. Owing to their cruel conduct and treachery, they were called by their cannibal neighbors savages !

Nearly all the chiefs kept a turtle pen. When they had a chance to dispose of the shell, they removed it from the living turtle by holding a burning brand close to the outer shell until the edge curled up ; then a wooden wedge was inserted, by which the whole head of shell was removed from the back of the living turtle. This was, in every sense of the word, cruelty to turtles. Each turtle is covered with thirteen pieces, which together are termed a head. Tortoise-shell was the chief article of trade in these islands, and its export was the principal business of the whites who lived on this group, and endeavored to monopolize the trade.

The traders in tortoise-shell came here in small vessels, and at great risk, as the natives resorted to every expedient to capture them. The crews were compelled to be on the lookout night and day. Sometimes, when the winds blew fresh towards the shore, the natives would swim off by the hundreds, dive down and endeavor to lift her anchor, part or cut her cable, or tie a rope to it, by which means the vessel would be dragged to the shore, when she was considered and treated as a prize sent by their gods. Another way was to board her by climbing up over her side. Unless the crew were surprised, an attack was often repelled by the use of the vessel's boarding-pikes and cutlasses.

CHAPTER XII.

On the 22d of July, while our first cutter, Lieutenant Alden and Midshipman Henry, and the *Leopard*, Lieutenant Underwood, were surveying the island of Malolo, they ran short of provisions. Lieutenant Underwood and Midshipman Henry, with several of the boat's crew, landed upon this island and attempted to purchase food from the natives. While engaged in trading, the hostage in the cutter under Lieutenant Alden, jumped overboard and swam for the shore. Lieutenant Alden immediately leveled his rifle and shot at him, but he dodged the ball. The natives, seeing that the hostage had escaped, raised the war-cry, and then a bloody work commenced. Our officers and crew retreated to the water backwards, at the same time firing and warding off with their bowie-knife pistols the arrows and spears which were flying thick about their heads. Our little band fought bravely, and many of those savages were made to kiss the coral reefs. Midshipman Henry was knocked down by a blow from a club on the back of the head. He quickly arose, however, and seizing his assailant, plunged his bowie-knife deep into the savage's breast. The two then fell together, never to rise again.

Lieutenant Underwood, struck on the side of his head

by a club in the hand of a gigantic savage, fell face
downward into the water. This seemed to revive him,
for he regained his footing and dealt the savage a terrible
blow on his head with his bowie-knife pistol, which split
his head nearly in two. He then turned towards the
boats, when he was struck on the back of his head with
a *ula*, or handy billy, which was thrown with tremendous
force by a native a short distance off, and fell senseless
into the water.

In the meantime Lieutenant Emmons in the *Greyhound* had joined Lieutenant Alden in the cutter, and
then made for the shore to recover the bodies of their
brother officers. They found them stripped of their
clothing. Lieutenant Underwood was just alive, and as
they lifted him he faintly breathed the words, " Tell — her
— that — ." These were his last. He had been married
but a few weeks before we sailed from Norfolk. Beside
him lay Joseph G. Clark, and not far from him Jerome
Davis and Robert Furman. Close by the body of Henry
were William Leicester and John Sac. They were all
stunned. Clark's upper lip was partly torn away, and
was hanging down to his chin. The natives were kept
at a distance by the *Greyhound's* crew, while others were
bearing the bodies of their shipmates to the cutter. We
soon got under way and pulled for the ship. Arriving
on board, every attention that affection could suggest
was paid to the wounded. Clark's lip was a horrible
sight. It was sewed up by our surgeon, Dr. Gilchrist.
None of the others were wounded, but were quite
severely stunned.

The next morning the *Flying Fish*, on board of which

MASSACRE OF LIEUTENANT UNDERWOOD AND MIDSHIPMAN WILKES HENRY.

the bodies of the slain had been transferred, got under way and proceeded towards the island chosen for the place of burial.

The sun never rose more clearly, and nothing could have looked more beautiful and peaceful than did the little group of islands as we passed them in succession on our melancholy errand. Arriving at the last one, which was about ten miles from Malolo and uninhabited, we came to anchor. Two of the officers and three of the crew went on shore to select a place and dig a grave for both the victims. At one bell all hands were called to bury the dead. The two bodies were placed in the commodore's gig, side by side, wrapped in their country's flag, and rowed to the lonely little island, followed by other boats with the commodore, several of the officers, and twenty of the sailors (all dressed in white), who landed to pay this last tribute of respect to those who had gone through so many hardships and shared so many dangers with them.

The quiet of the scene, the solemnity of the occasion, and the smallness of the numbers were calculated to produce a deep impression. The bodies were borne to the grave, which was in the center of the little island, amid a small grove of ficus trees. It was a lovely spot that had been chosen. The grave was dug wide and deep, in the pure white coral sand. The funeral services were conducted so calmly, and yet with such feeling, that none who were present will ever forget that sad half-hour. After the bodies had been lowered, and the grave filled, three volleys were fired over it.

This pretty cluster of islands was named Underwood's

Group, the little island, Henry's Island. We wandered
about the beach a short time, then reshipped and
returned to Malolo. Preparations were at once made
to punish the actors in this foul deed. The rest of the
day and during the night, the ship's small arms were prepared, and parties duly organized for the fight. Several
boats, well manned and armed, were stationed around
the island, so that none of the natives could escape. At
nine o'clock we landed well armed, and provided with
port-fires and rockets (fiery spirits), which we had found
so efficient on a former occasion. Orders were given to
spare all women and children.

The first town we arrived at was entirely deserted.
The natives had even taken all their household goods
with them. We reduced it quickly to ashes, destroyed
their yam and taro patches, and made the next town.
When the natives first got sight of us, they sent up a
shout of defiance. They exhibited no signs of fear, but
rather defied us. While awaiting the arrival of Captain
Ringold's and Lieutenant Johnson's parties, we descended the hill, and advanced towards the ditch of the
town. The natives boldly came to meet us, with a discharge of arrows, and exhibited the utmost confidence.
They in truth believed their town to be impregnable,
for it had hitherto withstood every attack made by the
Fiji warriors. Its defenses showed no little engineer-
ing skill. A ditch twelve feet wide, and full of mud and
water, surrounded the whole. Next came a stong palisade, built of cocoanut trunks, placed four or five feet
apart, among which was here and there a living tree.
This palisade also included a fence of wicker-work, about

ten feet high, so strong and dense as to defy all attempts to penetrate or even see through it. Inside of this was a second ditch. In this ditch the natives sought shelter and defended themselves, only exposing their heads when they rose to shoot through the loop-holes left in the palisade.

As soon as we neared the fortification, we spread out so as to outflank the skirmishers, and by a few rockets and a shower of balls showed them that they had different enemies from Fiji men to deal with. This compelled them to abandon all the outer works to destruction, and to retire within, where they all united in giving a loud shout of "*Lako-mai*," "Come on," at the same time flourishing their war-clubs and spears.

Having arrived within about seventy feet, we fired on the fortification. Now was seen what many of those present had not before believed ; the expertness with which these savages dodge a ball at the flash of a gun. Those who were the most incredulous before, were now satisfied that they could do this effectually. A stubborn resistance was kept up with musketry, arrows, and war-clubs, which lasted about twenty minutes. In this the women and children were as actively engaged as the men. They believed that it required a larger load to kill a large man than it did to kill a small man. The bows and arrows were for the most part used by the women.

The defense soon slackened, and many natives could be seen escaping from the rear with their dead and wounded on their backs. A rocket, of which several had already been tried without any visible effect, now struck one of the thatched roofs. Several natives sprang up to tear it off, but that moment was their last, as the roof immediately burst into flames. As soon as the flames were found to be spreading, a scene of confusion ensued that baffles description. The deafening shouts of " *Curlew, curlew, curlew*," by the savages, with the cries and shrieks of the women and children, the roaring of the fire, the bursting of the bamboos, and an occasional volley from our rifles, will always be impressed on our memories. In about half an hour this whole town or stronghold of theirs was reduced to ashes. It was evident that large quantities of water, provisions, pigs, etc., had been stored up in the anticipation of a long siege. In the ditch we picked up a number of war-clubs, spears, bows and arrows, several old muskets, fish-nets, *tapa*, etc., and the cap of Lieutenant Underwood. Many of the dead were lying in the ditch.

Our party sustained but little injury. Only one man was struck by a ball, which did no other harm than to leave a scar on his right arm. Several were wounded by arrows, but only one, Samuel Stretch, dangerously. In crossing the island to another town, we found the scenery extremely beautiful. In the valleys below us and on the declivities of the hills were to be seen yam and taro patches kept in the neatest order, with the small yam houses, or *lololo*, in the midst, surrounded by groves of tall cocoanut trees and plantations of bananas. All looked quiet and peaceful, in strong contrast to the exciting contest in which we had been engaged, and the character of the ruthless and murderous race who had been the occupants of the smiling valley.

Soon after descending the hill we came upon another stronghold. We soon set fire to this town by throwing in rockets. It became too hot for the savages, and as they attempted to escape in fives and tens, they were riddled with bullets. Here we were re-inforced by Lieutenant Murray's and Lieutenant Emerson's forces, who had destroyed several towns. The natives made a stubborn resistance and even stood a charge of bayonets.

While these transactions were taking place on the island, the water also became the scene of many conflicts. Every canoe that attempted to escape from the island was overtaken by our boats, destroyed, and its occupants became food for hungry sharks.

We destroyed all the towns, and by five o'clock all hands had returned on board ship. The boats on guard around the island were relieved every four hours. The night passed as quietly as in a country churchyard, save for the singing of some tropical bird, or the splashing of the water, occasioned by some monster of the deep.

Early the next morning several natives were seen on the beach, waving pieces of white *tapa*, the emblem of peace with them. The commodore, with the interpreter in his gig, pulled for the shore. As they neared the edge of the reef, which was bare now, it being low water, all the men retired, leaving a young native woman standing with the different articles of Lieutenant Underwood and Midshipman Henry near her. She held a white cockerell in her arms, which she wanted the commodore to accept. He declined to do so, but took the articles of clothing. The commodore knew it to be the custom

of the natives, when defeated and at the mercy of their
enemies, to beg pardon and sue for mercy before the
whole of the attacking party, in order that all might be
witnesses ; and he also knew that they never acknowledged themselves conquered unless this was done.

Many messages were delivered to the commodore by
this young woman from the chiefs, saying that they were
sorry for clubbing and killing our little chiefs. This,
however, amounted to nothing. The commodore sent
word to the chiefs and people that they must come and
beg pardon and sue for mercy before all our warriors,
on a hill that he pointed out, on the south end of the
island, saying that he should land there in a little while
and receive them. In a few hours our whole force went
ashore and took our station on the hill.

The day was perfectly serene, but the island, which a
few days before had been one of the loveliest spots on
earth, was now entirely desolate, showing the place of
the massacre, ruined towns, and devastated plantations.

The eye wandered over the dreary waste, to the beautiful expanse of waters beyond and around, with the long
lines of white, sparkling reefs, until it rested, far in the
distance, on the small green island where we had performed the last rites to our murdered shipmates. A
gentle breeze stirred the lofty palm trees and produced
a moaning sound as in the forests of our own country.
A feeling of depression, inseparable from the occasion,
rested upon us and brought vividly to our thoughts the
grief which these melancholy deaths would bring upon
those who were far away.

After watching several hours with much patience, we

heard the sound of distant wailings, which gradually drew nearer. Presently the natives could be seen coming over the hills towards us, making a scene which will be long remembered. They at length reached the foot of the hill, when about forty of them advanced, crouching on their hands and knees, pausing occasionally to utter piteous moans and wails.

When within about thirty feet of us, they stopped, and an old chief, their leader, in the most piteous manner begged pardon, supplicating forgiveness and pledging that they would never do the like again to a *papalangi*, or white man. He said that they acknowledged themselves conquered, and that the island belonged to our big chief (the commodore), and that they were his slaves and would do whatever he desired. He said that their head chiefs and most of their wives had been killed.

He offered several of the slain chiefs' daughters, as a present to the commodore.

During the whole time that the old chief was speaking the other natives remained bowed, with their faces to the ground.

A few words of advice were given them by the commodore, and they were then dismissed. They were not long in leaving ; the chiefs' daughters with them. The young women were all very pretty.

Orders were now given to man the boats, and we reached the vessels at sundown.

Midshipman Wilkes Henry was the only son of his mother, and she a widow, the sister of Commodore Wilkes. His death was a deep affliction to his mother, who could be sustained under it only by Divine grace.

The following lines were written by Joseph G. Clark, one of the crew, who fought so bravely and had his upper lip nearly cut off in the fight :

WILKES HENRY.

He went to his home, where his kind mother dwelt,
    To tell her the squadron was ready to sail,
And merry the heart of the young sailor felt,
    For bright was the morning and fair was the gale.

In vain were his efforts her tears to restrain,
    By reciting the hopes that inspired him with joy,
For she secretly felt, — oh, how keen was the pain ! —
    That this was the last she would see of her boy.

The hand of his mother he grasped in his own,
    And bade her farewell as he rose to depart;
She could breathe no response, for to her 'twas the tone
    Of the death-knell of all that was dear to her heart.

He hastened on board and the anchors were " home,"
    The wide canvas spread, his ship started from shore;
But ah ! who can tell of the evil to come, —
    He had left her indeed, to behold her no more !

To the Isle of Malolo, the lonely abode
    Of a cannibal king and his murderous train,
The youth in the path of his duty trod,
    Was attacked by the natives and treacherously slain.

I saw from his eye flash the heroic fire
    Of a brave and true heart that was born to command;
He could not advance, and he would not retire,
    But he stood, fought and fell with his knife in his hand.

To a desolate island his body we bore,
    And laid his remains with his comrade to rest.

That island ne'er held such a treasure before,
  As the jewels we buried so deep in its breast.

Dear youth! he has gone to his rest with the brave,
  To the source whence true glory, true happiness springs;
The tears of his countrymen sprinkled his grave,
  And the blue, rolling ocean his requiem sings.

CHAPTER XIII.

AFTER surveying several small islands and reefs we arrived at Muthewater. The next day King Tuembooa came on board with many hogs and yams as a present to "the big white chief," the commodore. They were accepted.

August 10. Sunday morning at four bells all hands were called to Divine service. The flags of the squadron were at half-mast, and a deathlike silence pervaded the ship. All hands, officers and men, listened to the solemn discourse of our chaplain, from the texts, "Boast not thyself of to-morrow, for thou knowest not what a day may bring forth;" and "It is even as a vapor, that appeareth for a little time, and then vanisheth away."

In the afternoon signal was made to get under way and proceed to Mali, an island about thirty miles north. Here we found all towns deserted, and all canoes hauled up and hid away among the bushes. These natives were getting very shy of us since the news of the destruction of Sualib and Malolo had spread among them.

After having completed our surveys here we weighed anchor and revisited Ovolau. We found the place nearly deserted. Our garden that we had planted on Observatory Hill was looking finely, but many of the vegetables

had gone to seed, and it needed weeding.   A white man
by the name of George said he would attend to it.

The chief of this district, Tui Levuka, was overjoyed
to see us back again.   One afternoon when our observatory was established here, Tui Levuka and King Tanoa
were shown the instruments.   Looking at the great pendulum swinging to the right and left, they both tried to
keep time with it by swaying their bodies the same way
at the same time, and singing out, "*Tui i tuku, tui i tuku,
tui i tuku,*" meaning "Here she goes and there she goes,
here she goes and there she goes."   After repeated
efforts to keep pace with the pendulum their patience
became exhausted, and they gave it up.

They were also shown the transit, the dipping-needle,
and horizontal horizon.   A small quantity of quicksilver
was poured into the hand of one of them.   They tried
to pick it up with their fingers; but, finding they could
not do so, and that it did not even wet their fingers, they
would look at each other, grinning and laughing most
heartily.   But when they were permitted to look through
our large telescope and take a view of the planet Saturn,
with her two rings and seven moons, they were completely nonplussed.

After this a large globe was shown them, and our own
and other countries pointed out, and finally their own
little, insignificant islands; but we could not make them
understand.   They had not the slightest conception of
the magnitude of the earth, having no knowledge of any
lands excepting their own islands, the Tongas, and a few
others.

It was a common belief among the natives upon the

islands of the Pacific that the little *papalangis* (white people) were little spirits, and that their homes were in the skies; that they were subject to one great spirit, and that the ships ascended to and descended from the skies when out of sight of their islands.

One afternoon I was ordered into the *dinky*, a small shell of a boat, with lead line and compass. I was to pull to a point about a mile ahead of the ship, run off thirty fathoms with the lead line in a nor'easterly direction from a large tree at the back of a small hill, stick the boat-hook into the ground, fasten a cornet, or signal, to the upper end, and return in an hour.

Obeying orders, I doubled the point and took a short cruise up the beach, out of sight of the ships. While strolling along I suddenly fell in with Tanoa, the king of the island, and a part of his crew. His large war-canoe was at the edge of the reef. He came toward me, took my right hand and rubbed it across his nose — this being his mode of salutation. Then he rolled up the sleeve of my frock to the shoulder; took hold of me by the wrist and shoulder, opened his big mouth, grated his beautiful white teeth, smacked his lips, and said, " *Mite kuai,*" "What a sweet morsel." Then, in a few minutes, he commenced to spit terribly, pressed his hands on his stomach, as though he felt sick, and then made up an awful face and cried out, " *Oui miti,*" "No good, bad." He then in very broken English, with many signs and gestures, and in a joking kind of way — though I think he meant it — pointed to the mountains, the horizon, and the sky, signifying that I should go to the mountains and remain there until the ships had returned home, when

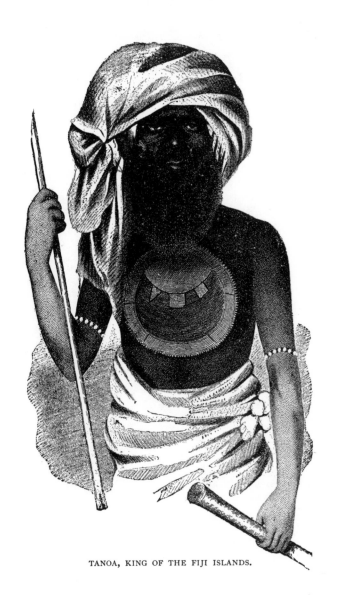

TANOA, KING OF THE FIJI ISLANDS.

he would send for me, make me a chief over some district, and give me three of his daughters for wives.

I did not feel that I could accept the old king's offer and become his son-in-law, and so fulfilled my commission and returned to the ship. This kind of talk was very common among the Fiji chiefs, for deceit was a part of their national character. They were very quick in discerning what would please those whom they wished

to conciliate and readily acceded to their views. That this was the case with these people there can be no doubt.

King Tanoa's canoe was a very rapid sailer. It was a single canoe, over a hundred feet long, with a very large out-rigger. About midship was built a hurricane deck, the place of honor, the king's quarter-deck. Her crew, numbering about sixty, were nearly all Tonga men. She

FIJI DRUMMER.

was ornamented with over two thousand very beautiful *cypræa*, Ovula shells.   When this canoe was launched, eighty of his victims were clubbed that she might be launched over their bodies.   He used to take great pride and pleasure in running down smaller canoes and drowning their occupants.   It was said that King Tanoa was the greatest cannibal that ever lived.   He was, in every sense of the word, " King of the Cannibal Islands."

The habits and customs of these Fijians were in the highest degree interesting.

On board the *Flying Fish*, or *Kai Nite*, Midshipman Sinclair outrageously abused one of the crew, William Smith, for some neglect of duty.   He first denounced him in the most abusive and aggravating terms, and then administered several severe blows with a rope's-end. This was more than Jack before the mast could stand. Smith sprang at him, seized him in his arms, and jumped overboard.   Smith was unarmed, and was drowned ; Sinclair was armed with a dirk, and escaped by swimming to the fore-channels and climbing on board.

We found old red-headed Paddy Connell in rather ill health, but happy in having had, during our absence, an addition to his family, another " young brat of a boy." This was the forty-ninth child, and now his prayer was that he might live to see the fiftieth.

The old chief of the town, Tui Levuka, spent the most of his time at home with his wives, muskets, and junk-bottles.   The natives here seemed to have a sort of mania for collections of bottles.   A few weeks before we arrived, the *Currency Lass*, a trading schooner, had visited this port and disposed of several hampers of bottles.

The old chief had increased his stock, and now had them suspended from every available place both within and without his house.

Fiji mothers used to anoint the bodies of their children all over, early every morning, with rancid cocoanut oil. This was liberally applied and vigorously rubbed in until the skin fairly glistened. This was supposed to prevent the pickaninnies from catching cold, and from contracting various diseases.

Many of the natives wore necklaces composed of rare shells, and those who could get them wore several whale's teeth, strung on a string, hanging down on their breasts. A whale's tooth was the price of a human life at these islands. The men here did not tattoo, but many of the women had the corners of their mouths tattooed in circles of a blue-black color.

Both men and women spend a great deal of time at their toilets. The prevailing style among the men was to wear the hair around the forehead, not parted in the middle, but from ear to ear. The front part was dyed brown or red, and the back part white or yellow. The hair was so thick that no comb could possibly penetrate it. On measuring the head of one of the men we found it to be sixty-two inches in circumference. The larger and more bushy the head the more pride was taken in it, and the more it was admired by the women. Their heads were literally alive with vermin, and it was a common sight to see them eagerly searching one another's heads for the insects, and sharing the spoil. One-third of the vermin secured belonged to the searcher, and no greater insult could be offered a native than to appropriate more

than the allotted share. It was considered a crime to
search the head of a child, as that was considered to be
the particular province of the parents.

The women wore their hair in long locks, few or many
in number according to their fancy. These locks were in
cork-screw form, and were called *tombi*. The head was
dipped in lye made from the ashes of the leaves of the
bread-fruit tree. When the head was raised the lye ran
down in little zigzag rivulets over face, neck, and body,
showing, when dry, in distinct lines, which were considered very ornamental, and were called *ulu-lase*.

The dress of the women was very scanty. It consisted
of a kind of band about eight inches in width, and bordered with a fringe dyed in various colors. Some of
these garments were quite pretty. They were made
from the bark of the hibiscus and were very elastic.
This dress was called the *liku*, and it was worn around
the waist. The Fiji dressmaker used neither needles,
thread, thimble, nor wax, but simply moistened the bark,
tore it into long, thin strips, then tied one end to the
great toe of her right foot and braided the strips together
toward her.

In upper Fiji society, in asking a woman in marriage
the consent of the father, mother, and brother had to be
obtained. The refusal of the brother was sufficient to
prevent the marriage. If the suit was accepted, rolls of
tapa, whale's teeth, provisions, etc., were presented to
the parents. Marriages among the "blue blood" Fijians
were sanctioned by religious ceremonies. After parties
had become engaged they might often be seen strolling
about arm-in-arm. Several times we saw the bride, after

the ceremony was over, go down to the reef, into the
water, and disfigure her face and body with the sharp

QUEEN EMMA, ONE OF TANOA'S WIVES.

edge of a small shell, causing the blood to flow. After
such a performance she looked as if she had been dragged
through a thicket of brambles.

Among the common people, marriage was a mere matter of bargain. The usual price of a wife was a whale's tooth, an old musket, or a hatchet and some tobacco. A man could have as many wives as he could afford to buy and support. Once paid for he had an entire right to them and might club, roast, and eat them if he so desired. Elopements were rare, but did sometimes occur, for there were several runaway matches while we were at these islands.

One day the funeral of a chief occurred. Before the burial took place the mother of the deceased chief declared that she was old and had lived long enough, and requested that she might be strangled and buried, in order that she might go to the spirit-land with her son. One of the wives of the dead chief expressed the same desire ; so they were both partially strangled by their friends and placed in the grave, one on either side of the chief, each with the right hand placed upon his breast. Several of the mourners also cut off their little toes or the first joint of their little fingers and placed them in the grave as tokens of grief. A few strips of *tapa* and a mat were thrown over the bodies, then some sticks were laid across, and the grave filled with earth. We could hear the faint moans of the two poor women, not yet dead, as the clods fell and were trodden down upon them.

The old and infirm, all who suffered from lingering diseases, and even children, often requested their nearest relatives to either wring their heads off or strangle them. An instance of this kind happened while we were lying here. A boy, while hunting on the reef for *beche de mer*, had one of his legs bitten off by a shark. His parents at once strangled him, giving as the reason that if he lived he would be a disgrace to the family in consequence of having but one leg.

The usual sign of mourning was to have the hair and beard cut short. Women in mourning burned themselves with hot irons, raising large blisters, the scars of which might be seen long afterward upon neck, shoulders, breast, and arms. It was called *loloe mate.*

The eating of human flesh was not for the love of it, nor to appease hunger, but was one of their religious rites or was due to habit or revenge. One morning a big canoe came alongside our ship with two chiefs and nine roasted human bodies. The chiefs were bound for one of the leeward islands to have a feast with their brother, the head chief of the island. Three of the victims were chiefs, and were tallied as such, their faces being painted black. None but chiefs were allowed to partake of the flesh of a chief. The brains were equally divided among the participants. They believed that if they ate the brains of a chief they would inherit his warlike qualities.

Our prisoner, Vendovi, the chief who had been captured by us through the treachery of one of his nephews, declared after he had been on board a few weeks that if ever he had a chance he would club, roast, and eat the treacherous fellow, dry and grind his bones, and drink them in his *ava*. Six months afterward the old chief had become so much civilized that the irons were taken off him. He appeared to be a very thoughtful, genial, and pleasant sort of a man. After he had been with us eighteen months, seeing and learning our manners and customs and listening to the many long yarns spun to him by our signal quartermaster, old Tom Piner, a converted sailor, such a wonderful change was wrought in him that the sailors used to call him "The old Christian, cannibal, man-eater." He died soon afterward.

The situation of the missionaries and their families here was a most trying one. They lived in constant fear of their lives. Their worst enemies, however, were not the heathen Fijians, but the civilized English runaway convicts from Australia. While cruising among these cannibal islands and during our intercourse with these savages, we witnessed many scenes and incidents so unnatural and shocking that the mere mention of them would offend the moral sensibilities of my readers, therefore I refrain from speaking of them.

"It has been said that the Fijian is not deficient in intelligence; that he is shrewd, apt to learn, skilful, and cunning. But his soul is uninformed by that moral beauty which might conceal the dark and repulsive features of his character. In this respect how great is the contrast between him and the matchless scenery by which he is surrounded, whose purity he has desecrated, and whose beauty sullied by crimes the most odious and customs the most abhorrent. In the midst of all that can please the taste, charm the fancy, or gratify the imagination; where everything is fair, and bright, and beautiful; where the dreamy haze of a tropical clime rests lovingly on hilltop and valley; where the sun smiles in gladness upon landscapes as picturesque and charming as the sweetest spots, buried in foliage and flowers, that nestle in the bosom of the Italian Alps ; where brooks and fountains send forth unrestrained their unceasing melody ; where the breezes are soft and balmy, and the perfumed breath of an unending summer fills the air with its intoxicating odor,— man alone is debased. Nature displays her brightest charms and revels in her gayest attire ; but God's own image is loathsome and deformed. Here is indeed a field for the missionary ; and laborers are not wanting in fulfilment of the Divine command, 'Go ye into all the world and preach the gospel.' The humble, self-denying followers of Wesley have found their way to this group."

Looking backward fifty years to these islands, one of the loveliest spots on this huge globe, and visiting them in my imagination to-day, and listening to the cries and sighs of the natives, perhaps I may be pardoned for thinking it would have been better if the islands had never been discovered by Europeans ; not that Christianity is a failure, but that our civilization is. Nations are like individuals — selfish, selfish, selfish. The more they get, the more they want.

The Fiji Islands to-day are an English colony, and the Fiji cannibals are British subjects to Her Most Gracious Britannic Majesty, Victoria, Queen of England, Ireland, Scotland, and Wales, that kingdom whose unity, it is claimed, has never been broken. Yes, it is " rule, Britannia." She rules in the north, in the south, in the east, and in the west. How did she come into possession of these lovely islands ? In the same way, no doubt, that she acquired New Zealand — through the treachery of the American consul, who was an Englishman.

The condition of these islanders is, in many respects, very much changed. We do not read in the papers of to-day of ships being cast away and their crews clubbed, roasted, and eaten by the South Sea cannibals. In contrast we read in the English papers of the wonderful progress of the Christian religion among them, and how the Salvation Army is turning many of them into "blood and fire" soldiers.

A few months since I found myself in the Salvation Army barracks at Camberwell, George Street, London, and had the pleasure of listening to Colonel Barker, who had just returned from New Zealand. He stated that many of the natives had been converted and had joined the army, and that Adjutant Holdaway had a Salvation band, composed of Maoris, who could play and sing many of the army tunes and hymns equal to any army corps to which he ever listened; and that the uniform just suited them, and was becoming very common among them. The red *ganges*, with the word "Salvation" in large, white letters across the breast, was very fashionable with them.

I make a few quotations from "Cries from Fiji, and Sighings from the South Seas," by Dr. T. P. Lucas of Melbourne:

The labor traffic has for some time occupied the attention of the British nation. It is nothing more or less than a veritable British slave-trade. What means the old song, "Britons Never shall be Slaves"?

Where is all the glory of the British liberty, battled for and obtained by Wilberforce, Buxton, and a host of others? Where is the brightness and grandeur of the British flag, which the Queen of the Seas displayed before all nations and peoples? Destruction to slavery and to the slave-trade forever! Who are those who stand in the plaçes of the heroes of the past, and fear to speak out the national watchword, " England and Liberty"? Is there no national honor left? Is England to be cowed by any and every opposing nation, while she herself descends to imbue her hands in the shed blood of the accursed slave traffic? Rise up, ye spirits of the departed, and weep for your sons! Lament, ye sages, for England is once more a slave-holding nation!

The reasons which have led to this are the desire of aspiring subjects to possess large estates, and the difficulty of making those estates pay, except by working them by labor at a price low enough to allow competition with similar estates and industries in other countries.

A company wants two hundred men. It opens relations with the chief and government, and the two hundred men, as slaves, have to go, leaving wives and homes, whether they will it or no.

Slaves? Yes; the people are slaves. Lest the white man should put upon them they are not allowed to work of their own free will.

Who are these savages, and of what use in the world, lazy dogs, and cumberers of the ground?

> Dogs, they are dogs, and nothing more;
> No soul to love, no spirit to adore,
> But fit for slaves, as slaves they were at first,
> No mind to ken, though kicked and cuffed and cursed.
>   Depravity! Well may the angels weep:
> While He, who counts the sparrows as they fall,
> In vengeance waits to hear each feeble call.

I will only add that it is sad to think that in so lovely a part of God's creation, in this enlightened nineteenth century, there should exist anything so vile, putting it in its true light, as a South Sea English slave-trade, a traffic which is more infamous than any African slave-trade. And this traffic, this " trade in human beings," is carried on by civilized Englishmen! May God save the queen!

The survey completed, we took leave of the Fiji group on August 11th. Our hearts were sad as we thought of the fate of Lieutenant Underwood and Midshipman

Wilkes Henry, for these two officers had been great favorites with the crew. We felt very thankful, however, that no more of our number had met the same fate.

On clearing the reefs, we shaped our course for the Sandwich Islands. On the 13th we passed from east to west longitude, and consequently changed our reckoning by a day.

August 28. On board the *Peacock*, another island was discovered, and named Bowditch Island, for the author of "The American Navigator." The people found on this island had no knowledge of fire, which is, I believe, the only instance of the kind on record. They appeared to be wild with fright when they saw the sparks fly from the flint and steel; and when we lighted our pipes, and they saw the smoke issuing from our mouths, they cried out, "*Debolos, debolos,*" "Devils, devils." When we made a fire on the reef they looked on with the greatest curiosity.

Yet these strange people had their gods to worship. I think there has never been a race of people discovered who did not acknowledge some power superior to their own. Near the center of the island was their *tui-tokelau,* or house of their gods. It was oblong in shape, about sixty by eighty feet, and twenty feet in height. It was built of cocoanut wood, and thatched with pandanus leaves. It was open at the eaves, from which hung many beautiful cowry and mother-of-pearl shells. Their gods, or idols, were placed on the outside of the building. These idols were mostly made from blocks of coral, and were covered with many mats. The largest was fourteen feet high and was named *Tagaloa-ilaya-i-te-layi-Tagaloa*

(Above, in the heavens). The smallest idol was made of stones and was about four feet high. These natives thought that we came down from the skies. Cocoanut Island would have been a very appropriate name for this one, as it was nearly covered with groves of these trees.

After visiting Oatafer, Utiroa, and several other islands in the Ellis, Gilbert, and Kingsmill groups, we steered a

KINGSMILL IDOL.

direct course for Oahu. For several days the weather was changeable — short calms, sudden squalls, with fresh breezes, both fair and foul — and the wind dead ahead most of the time. Quite a number of flying fish were picked up on deck, some of them measuring fifteen inches in length. We also caught several porpoises.

August 20, 21, and 22. Light breezes and fair weather. Early on the morning of the 23d land was reported from the mast-head, two points on the weather bow. For several days the weather continued fine. We came across several islands not laid down on any chart. One was named McKean's Island, for the man who first saw it. Another was named Hull's Island, for Commodore Isaac Hull. The last named lies in 4° 29´ south latitude, and is about thirteen miles in circumference. It was a coral island with a lagoon in the center, which was dry, and nearly filled with coral slabs about the size and thickness of tombstones. These were scattered about, and piled up in a variety of ways. There were many large turtles on this island, and some rats, or a kind of animal whose tail resembled that of the rat. These little creatures would sit up on their hind legs like squirrels, and stare at us. There were also many birds of beautiful plumage, which were very tame, and did not flinch when we pulled the bright feathers from their tails. There were no natives upon this island.

August 25, 26, 27, and 28. We had frequent thunder showers.

September 4. Crossed the line in longitude 169°. Many birds, including the tropical bird, booby, tern, and plover, hovered about the ships. At noon the sun was directly overhead, and there was not a shadow to be seen.

It is a singular fact that the natives living near the equator are of a lighter complexion than those in higher latitudes.

On the evening of the 5th we took a light, southerly breeze, which we held until the 8th, when it left us, and then for one long week we experienced a dead calm, during which time we drifted about, backing and filling, in the doldrums, hearing not so much as a whisper of the wind nor the flapping of a sail. But for the long, huge, heaving swell of old ocean's mighty bosom, I might say that we were in the ocean's graveyard.

There is a dreary monotony in a dead calm at sea which vividly calls to mind Byron's striking pen-picture :

> "The rivers, lakes, and ocean, all stood still,
> And nothing stirred within their depths;
> Ships, sailorless, lay rotting on the sea,
> And their masts fell piecemeal as they dropped.
> They slept on the abyss without a surge;
> The waves were dead; the tides were in their grave;
> The moon, their mistress, had expired before
> The winds were withered in the stagnant air
> And the clouds perished."

CHAPTER XIV.

At daylight on the morning of the 23d of September we made Oahu, one of the Sandwich Islands, and about eight o'clock entered the harbor of Honolulu. A couple of small hawsers were run out from the starboard bow, and these were seized by several hundred natives, men, women, and children, who were on the reef, up to their necks in water, and very soon the ship was warped over the bar and into port, amid such shouting and singing that it seemed as though bedlam had broken loose. All Honolulu, including its land-sharks, was at the waterside and joined in the shouting and cheering. It was not the novelty that created the excitement, for the arrival of a man-of-war, in their port, was no uncommon thing; but they looked upon the event as a sort of golden shower which was to fill their pockets. They had been expecting our arrival for six months.

By eleven o'clock we had the ship safely moored close to the consul's wharf. After dinner all hands were called to muster on the quarter-deck, when Commodore Wilkes informed us that he wished to re-enter us for eighteen months longer, saying at the time that it was impossible to sooner complete the work which he had undertaken. He told us that those who re-entered should have three months' pay and two weeks' liberty, and that their wages would be raised one-fourth.

Nearly all our ships' crews had entered for three years, and, as their time had expired, all hands had an idea that when we left Honolulu it would be to up anchor for " home, sweet, sweet home."

Like all the young men and boys in the squadron, I felt heartily sick of the navy. We learned nothing but to pull and haul, handle the light sails, holy-stone decks, clean bright work, do boat duty, etc. None but able seamen were allowed to go to the wheel, heave the lead, or work on the rigging. As young as I was, before I entered the navy I had learned to box the compass, heave the lead, knot a rope-yarn, haul out an earing, work a Matthew Walker, and Turk's head, strap a block, knot, hand, reef, and steer. I learned more seamanship on board the merchantman *Rainbow*, during an eight months' voyage from New York to Canton, China, than in my seven years in the navy.

Quite a number of the men who had families and had not seen their dear ones for years, left, and went on board three whale-ships which were homeward bound. After listening to many long yarns spun upon deck, I consulted my own mind, and came to the conclusion that I would not leave the ship short-handed in a foreign port.

The next morning the purser, Mr. Waldron, told me that the four dollars a month to my mother was for only three years, and had now expired. I asked him if there was any way for me to send some money to my mother, and he told me that one of the whale-ships would sail in about a week for New Bedford, and that the money could be sent by her. I had now fully made up my mind to re-enter, and so, with others, wrote my name in full, and felt as big and grand as though I were an officer.

The next day the purser gave me a paper on which was written the following :

U. S. Ship Vincennes, Honolulu, May 7th, 1841.

I have charged to Charlie Erskine, ord'y seaman, One Hundred Dollars, to be sent per order to F. D. Quincy, Esq., of Boston, for his mother, which sum is to be repaid to C. Erskine in case it should not be received, by R. R. Waldron, purser.

My First Letter.

"the Sandwich Islands year 1841.

on board of ship Vincens

Mother, Mother, Dear Mother,

while fair away a cruseing amoung the islands of the sea, I never, Oh no Dear mother, I never, never will forget to think of the. by going to Mr. F. D. Quincy 25 Commercial Street You will get one hundred dollars from

Your absent son Charlie."

When I re-entered, and signed the ship's articles, I was paid three months' wages and twelve dollars grog money. During the day all the foreign consuls, missionaries, and many of the residents visited the ship. A young English naturalist wanted to match a beautiful orange-colored cowry shell. I had its mate, and he gave me ten dollars for it, and twenty dollars for a head of tortoise-shell.

There were nine whale-ships lying here, besides our squadron. Five of them were American. The next morning between five and six hundred American sailors, all dressed in white frocks and trousers, black tarpaulin hats and neckerchiefs, and their pockets well filled with Spanish dollars, went on shore. Passing the American consul's house, half-way up Main Street, we hove to, and saluted the Star Spangled Banner, which was proudly waving from his house. The consul, Mr. Brinsmade, and his wife, bowed very gracefully to us from the veranda.

It astonished the natives greatly to see so many sailors let loose at once. The principal street of the town was Main Street. The first settlers lived on this street, in frame houses. Some of these were painted white, with green blinds, and were inclosed with neat picket-fences. The next street was about half a mile back, and ran crosswise. The buildings on this street had thatched roofs and sides, with glass windows and frame doors. Here were located the grog-shops, dancing-halls, billiard-rooms, cock-pits, sailors' boarding-houses, and gambling-saloons. Some of these houses were inclosed by walls of brick, dried in the sun, and were whitewashed. These were occupied by the middle classes. European garments were worn by this class of people. On the next street the houses were rudely fashioned. They were built of sticks, vines, and half-formed sun-dried bricks, and plastered with mud. The residents on this street were not quite half-dressed. Some of the men wore hat and shirt, and some wore trousers and no shirt. The dress of the ladies was made very much like a bag with a hole in the bottom, for the head to be slipped through, and arm-holes in the sides. It reached to the ankles, and appeared to be of the same width throughout its entire length.

In the outskirts, mud huts were found, which once formed the only habitations of the Sandwich Islanders.

THE SEAMAN'S BETHEL, HONOLULU.

The natives occupying these were dressed in the garb of the heathen, a narrow strip of *tapa* tied around the loins, or a blanket of the same material thrown corner-wise over the left shoulder and tied in a large knot on the breast.

The greatest curiosity I saw while here was the Seaman's Bethel. This was built in Boston by the Boston

Seaman's Friends' Society, taken down and shipped to this port in 1826 or 1828. It was in this bethel that Father Damon preached so many years.

The third day we were on shore anybody would have known to be Sunday, because it was so quiet. It was impossible to get a native to play a game, neither could any of them be hired to do anything. In the forenoon, about a hundred of us went to the Seaman's Bethel to hear the pastor, Rev. Mr. Diell, preach. In the afternoon we listened to a missionary by the name of Bingham, who preached to the natives in their own language.

We passed our time on shore very pleasantly, in the sailors' boarding-houses kept by "Yankee Jim" and "Old Smith," and in visiting the distant villages, Diamond Hill, the Punch Bowl, the Plains of Waikiki, and the Valley of Nuuanu. It was rare sport for us to frolic in the surf with the natives, join with them in their dances, slide down hill with them on the *holna* (a kind of sled), sing songs, play cards, and games, such as hide-and-seek, tag, and see-saw, and last, but not least, paying forfeits. We had a jolly time together.

Our holidays came to a close at last, and all hands returned to our respective ships, minus dollars and somewhat under the weather from our frolic. To give Jack before the mast his due, I will add that not one of us was put in the fort or even complained of during our two weeks' liberty on shore.

After we returned on board ship a court-martial was held for the trial of two marines for refusing duty (they asserting that their time was up), and an Englishman, by the name of Peter Sweeney, who shipped at New Zealand. Sweeney was very conceited and disagreeable. At all times, whether drunk or sober, he would curse everything American, using such expressions as "the bloody ship," "the bloody grub," "the bloody Yankee tars," "the bloody Stars and Stripes," "the bloody Yankee commodore," and so on. He was no sailor, and was as useless as a spare pump on board, and the ship's crew requested the commodore to discharge him from the ship and the expedition.

The court-martial sentenced the men to receive a certain number of lashes on their bare backs, with the cat-o'-nine-tails. The ship's launch was rigged with a half-deck and gallows. A number of marines, with the boatswain and his three mates, were appointed to guard the prisoners and inflict the punishment. The launch was towed by another boat alongside the *Peacock*, *Porpoise*, and *Vincennes*, when the rigging was manned and the men flogged, one after another.

The culprits were lashed to the shrouds by their wrists, with a piece of spun-yarn, and by their ankles to a grating, with a shot-box between their feet. When the order was given, "Boatswain's mate, do your duty," one of the quarter-gunners, with his thumb and finger, removed the shirt which had been placed on the man's back, with the sleeves over his shoulders. The boatswain's mate then drew the lines of the cat through his fingers, raised them above his head, and let them fall upon the man's back.

Riley received sixteen lashes, Sweeney eight, and Ward a baker's dozen, thirteen. The eagle buttons were then cut from Sweeney's clothes, and he, with his bag and hammock, was placed in the *dinky*, which was towed to the shore, stern foremost, by another boat, while the ship's fifer and drummer played the " Rogue's March."

During the exhibition, the decks and rigging of the nine whale-ships, many boats and canoes in the harbor, and on shore the fort, housetops, and beach, were covered with a mass of human beings, all eager to witness this barbarous spectacle.

I quote from the commodore's own language : " Understanding from our consul that the sailors of the whaling fleet, as is most generally the case, were disposed to be disorderly ; and my interference being several times asked for, I thought it a good opportunity to show the crews of all these vessels that authority to punish offenders existed. I therefore ordered the sentence of the court to be put in execution publicly, after the usual manner in such cases : ' Flogging through the fleet ' ! "

This example was set before a half-civilized people, who were just emerging from heathen darkness into Christian light ! Well might it have been asked, " Where is our Christianity ? Where is our civilization ? "

There were in Honolulu at this time many beer-drinking Germans, pipe-loving Dutchmen, French dandies, conceited Englishmen, Yankees, Hoosiers, California Indians, and almond-eyed, sallow-faced Chinamen. Of the latter class were Sam and Mou, who run a bakery. The sign over their door read as follows :

> " Good people all, come near and buy
> Of Sam and Mou good cake and pie;
> Bread, hard or soft, for land or sea,
> Celestial made,— come, buy of we."

Note the last line, " Celestial made "— from dogs and cats raised for the purpose.

There were two weekly newspapers printed here, called *The Polynesian*. One was in English, the other in the Hawaiian language. Eleven thousand copies of the Bible had also been printed in the native language, and distributed among the islands.

Some sixty or seventy Kanakas, or natives, were shipped to take the place of the crew who had left. The two whale-ships sailed for the United States. How I longed to be with them. The ships of the squadron had been thoroughly overhauled, smoked, and repainted. The ships had been overrun with rats and cockroaches. Some of the latter were three inches long. On the berth deck at night swarms of them might be seen flying about. They were so ravenous that they even ate the horn buttons off our clothes, and attacked our toe-nails while we were asleep in our hammocks.

Early in the morning, on the 3d of December, we weighed anchor and put to sea, with the American consul, Mr. Brinsmade, and a missionary by the name of Judd.

The Sandwich Islands were discovered by Captain Cook in 1778. They are eleven in number, situated in the tropics between 19° and 23° north latitude. We headed for the island of Hawaii, formerly called Owhyhee. It is nearly ninety miles long and seventy broad, being the largest of the group. It blew pretty fresh, the sea was somewhat rough, and our Kanaka shipmates were quite indisposed. They lay about on deck like so many landlubbers, as willing to die as to live.

Our supply of provisions, which we took on board at Honolulu, had been stored in the consul's house a number of years, and our hard-tack was very moldy, and alive with grub-worms. We used to soak the bread in our tea, when the animals would float on top, and we would skim them off. We did not exactly relish this at first, but soon got used to it, however.

CHAPTER XV.

On the 9th we made Hilo Bay, and took a pilot, who proved to be John Ely, who had been a shipmate of the commodore when he was a midshipman in the *Guerriere* frigate in 1820. Meanwhile both had grown into manhood and forgotten each other. Ely said that he had been living among these ignorant savages ever since.

At five o'clock we dropped anchor in six fathoms of water with muddy bottom. The two great mountains on this island offer a grand sight. They can be seen out at sea at a distance of sixty miles. Their summits were covered with snow, and a belt of dark, heavy clouds hung below. Father Coan lived in this village, in a little red house with white sills and a double row of small windows. Nearly all hands went to his church on Sunday. It was a very large building, seating nearly seven thousand people. Many of the native houses were surrounded by bread-fruit and cocoanut trees, clusters of pine-apples and rows of sugar-cane.

On arrival, our observatory was established at Point Waiakea. An expedition to the mountains was fitted out, consisting of the commodore, ten officers, Mr. Brinsmade, Dr. Judd, a number of seamen, and two

MISSIONARY PREACHING TO NATIVES.

hundred natives to carry the portable houses, instruments, tents, and provisions. The natives were separated into parties, numbered, and loaded. It was three o'clock when we started, with our two hundred bearers of burdens, forty hogs, a bullock, and a bullock-hunter, fifty bearers of poe, twenty-five with calabashes, large and small, others with iron pots, kettles, frying-pans, etc. Some were lightly and others heavily loaded, their burden being lashed to their backs, or carried on each end of sticks balanced across their shoulders, which is their usual mode of carrying burdens.

We encamped for supper about six o'clock at a village called Olaa, having traveled about eight miles. Here we waited until the moon arose, which was at midnight, when we again got under way, making Kapuanhi, or Flea village, about ten P. M. Here they had some of the largest, as well as some of the smallest, and spryest fleas I have ever seen. I have been in a number of fleay regions, but never found them so numerous nor knew them to bite so spitefully as here. Here we made quite a stop for breakfast and for rest, but the fleas gave us no rest. Besides these tormentors there were mosquitoes of enormous size, scorpions, and centipedes. But the fleas "took the cake." The natives told us that the mosquitoes and fleas were brought to their island by the first ships years and years before, and that they had been " biting, flying, and hooping about " ever since.

On leaving Kapuanhi we found the road very hard to travel. The next village was Kappaohee. Here we refreshed ourselves, took a siesta, and then got under way again, heading for the summit of Mauna Loa.   In about a couple of days we arrived at a plain on the side of the mountain, where is situated the volcanic crater called Kilauea, eight thousand feet above the sea-level. We pitched our camp in full view of one of the largest volcanoes in the known world.   The crater of Kilauea is seven times as large as Boston Common.   Imagine yourself, kind reader, standing at its edge, looking down into this huge pit one thousand feet deep, and beholding at its bottom lakes of liquid fire, boiling over into each other, dashing their fiery waves against the dark sides, and throwing up fiery jets sixty to eighty feet into the air.   The view at night is sublime in the extreme. While a dog-watch of us were seated on its edge, with our feet hanging over, another pool burst forth, with a hissing, rushing roar.   As it boiled over, the cherry-red liquid lava ran in streams to another pool.   In less than an hour it formed a lake a mile in circumference, as large as Boston Common.   It kept on hissing, roaring, boiling, and sending up its fiery red liquid lava jets sixty to eighty feet.   A vast cloud of silvery brightness hung overhead, more glorious than anything we had ever beheld.   This scene was well worth a voyage around the world.

While sitting here, Bill Richmond, one of our boatswain's mates, began to spin a yarn about the kind of a purchase he could rig in order to hoist one of the big icebergs we had seen in the Antarctic seas so as to drop it into this volcano.   What a sizzling it would make !

Just then the commodore, with other officers, hove in sight a short distance off.   He called us "a pack of

foolish virgins," and said, " I don't believe you could
find half a dozen landlubbers so silly as to perch themselves there," and ordered us to go and turn in. The
camp was about two hundred yards off, and when we
made it it was two bells, one o'clock.

At daylight the mortar was fired, when all hands
turned out, raising a great hubbub. All were grumbling
and complaining about their burdens. Shaking their
heads, they pointed to their loads, and growled out,
"*Oury miti*," and, to cap the climax, they even struck
for higher wages. The commodore acceded to their
demand, and seeing that they were all tired out, and the
shoulders of many were sore, sent down for fifty more
natives without their " fraus," and concluded to lay to
until the next day in order to give the natives a rest.

There were a large number of hangers-on, in the shape
of wives and relatives. Some had two wives, and some
had their sisters-in-law. These young ladies greeted
the rising of the sun with their native dance. When
they had become somewhat excited in it, the bullock,
which was half wild, got loose, and such a rush in all
directions to get beyond the reach of his horns. It was
really a very amusing scene. The bullock was soon
secured by the hunter, and driven on in advance of the
party. During the day the burdens were more equally
divided among the natives.

While here, a party of us descended to the bottom of
the crater, and poked sticks into a small pool of lava.
The sticks immediately took fire. There are many
caves on this mountain. We ventured into several of
them. Some of them are of unknown extent. In one

that we entered we found it so carved and finished as to resemble a work of art. A projection, some three feet high, ran along on either side far down into the passage, very elegantly molded, and making splendid seats. The floor was smooth. Overhead were hanging lava " icicles," two to three feet long, from which was slowly dripping very sweet but extremely cold water. We penetrated this cave for more than half a mile. Once there flowed through it a stream of boiling lava which has so completely inundated the whole island.

In another cave we found the remains of birds and the skeleton of a human being. On the plain were many chasms and crevices, from which steam issued. In these we scalded our hogs and cooked our food.

The next morning we resumed our journey up the mountain. The hangers-on, in the shape of wives and sweethearts, were so much in our way, and such consumers of our food, that all of them were forbidden following us, and so they went back to their wigwams.

As we advanced the air grew cooler, and the way rougher. In two days, after much hard traveling, we had left all shrubbery behind us, and had ascended above the clouds and could look down upon them. After leaving here we had no path to follow, the whole surface being a mass of lava.

The next day was Sunday, and a day of rest to our weary limbs. In the afternoon of Monday, finding it impossible to drive the bullock any farther, he was killed. Water had become very scarce, and the natives were hawking it about the camp at half a dollar a quart. They did not sell much.

One of our shipmates, William Longley, was missing for several days. When last seen he complained of being sick. Many of us had the mountain fever,— that is, a shortness of breath, sore eyes, with much headache, and a dryness of the skin.

The next morning after we had got fairly under way, we were overtaken and enveloped in a snow-cloud. The natives became much frightened, and shouted out, " *Oury miti*," " No good," and nearly all of them left and ran down the mountain. They had nothing on but a narrow strip of *tapa* tied around the loins, and a scanty blanket over the shoulders, leaving the body, arms, and legs exposed to the weather. The thermometer was at thirty degrees, and they had been accustomed from childhood to a temperature of seventy to eighty degrees. Fortunately the commodore had previously sent down to the ship for a hundred or more men.

It cleared away in the afternoon, leaving the snow a foot deep. We could not make much progress through the snow, with our heavy loads, so we sought shelter in one of the caves, where we passed rather an uncomfortable night. In this cave we found a small pond of water frozen over. The ice was about eight inches thick. At sunrise we came forth from the lava cave to behold a sublime scene. The lofty dome of Mauna Loa was covered with a mantle of snow. The effect of the rising sun upon it gave it the appearance of a fairy dome. It would quickly change from a blush-rose color to a bright scarlet, then light purple. Finally, it assumed its pure white mantle.

Looking down on the valleys and the plains below us

we could see the waving of the lofty palms in the morning breeze. Looking farther down into the bay we could see old ocean's waves rolling in and throwing the silvery spray high in the air over the coral reefs. We could but admire the wonderful contrast. By ten o'clock nearly all the snow had disappeared.

About eleven, fifty of our ship's company arrived, bringing the glad tidings that our lost shipmate, Longley, had been found near one of the caves, though in a very feeble condition. He said he had seen people pass and repass, but had not had the strength to attract their attention. He had been exposed to the cold and rain three days and nights. The best of care was taken of him and he soon recovered. The day proved fine, and we got everything in readiness for an early start in the morning, and after a hearty supper of hard-tack, boiled fresh beef, and boiled tea without sugar, we made for the cave, rolled ourselves up in our blankets, turned in on our lava beds, and tried to go to sleep. At daylight the next morning we turned out and breakfasted on a most delicious scouse and Scotch coffee, after which we made a move for the summit, arriving there the next day noon with weary limbs and sore feet. The ascent for the last five or six miles was very rough. The whole surface was covered with lava clinkers, much resembling those from a blacksmith's forge. We were provided with green raw-hide sandals to travel over this steep, rough road, and it was no boy's play to travel it for five or six miles, carrying heavy boxes of instruments, pieces of the portable house, and provisions. But Jack before the mast carried the whole lot to the summit, singing, laughing, and joking, as if on a picnic party. Place the sailor in any situation you will, you cannot deprive him of his mirth and gayety.

The commodore having selected a suitable place, we pitched our camp, satisfied the inner man the best we could, spun several yarns, then turned in.

The next morning the sun rose clear and bright, and everything was tranquil. After an early breakfast we erected the portable houses, and the instruments were put up and the pendulum set in motion. We then commenced to build a wall as high as we could reach, with the lava clinkers, around the whole camp, to protect the houses from the force of the wind, the commodore and officers working with us, and as hard as the best of us.

A number of stations had been established on the route down to the ship, so we heard from her every few days.

The summit of this mountain is nearly fifteen thousand feet above the level of the sea. Old Tom Piner used to tell us that we were then as near to heaven as we ever would be unless we mended our ways. My prospects of a berth in that port are much brighter to-day than they were then.

There are four craters on the summit of Mauna Loa, but they are nearly or quite inactive. We descended into one of them and traveled over it for a distance of two miles. As we had looked into it from the brim the bottom had appeared smooth and even, but after having descended we found it filled with heaps of clinkers and massive blocks of lava. Little patches of beautiful snow, which had drifted into the crevices, formed a striking contrast to the dark lava. One crevasse sent forth hot dust or ashes. From others hot steam rushed, sometimes with a loud and hissing sound, like that of a locomotive. After collecting many specimens, we about ship and stood for the camp. The east side of the mountain was one vast plain of unbroken lava, which had at some time flowed from one of the craters. It was dazzling to the eyes to behold it, resembling, as it were, a limitless sheet of bronze, radiating all the colors of the rainbow from its burnished surface. The vast dome, which is the summit of Mauna Loa, is about twenty miles broad.

We made the camp at two bells, five o'clock ; at six o'clock had our usual supper of hard-tack and boiled tea, our dessert consisting of bananas. The dog-watch was spent in smoking, mending our saddles, singing, and spinning yarns.

Standing on the summit of this mountain, and viewing the scene before me, I was reminded of the expression of an old lady when carried for the first time to the top of a mountain. Looking all around, and seeing hill and valley, village and river beneath her, the good old lady raised her hands and exclaimed, " Good Lord a massy, wall I declare to gracious what a big world it is, after all ! "

During our stay of three weeks above the clouds we were exposed to many hardships, the weather being as changeable as off Cape Horn. At times the winds were cold and boisterous, and the thermometer often dropped to eighteen below. The pelting rain, the driving snowstorms, and the furious blasts, laden with hail and sleet, would come howling and whistling over the frightful chasms and craggy peaks so suddenly and with such force that it reminded us of our sojourn in the frozen regions of the Antarctic. Jack before the mast did not expect to fall in with such weather within the tropics.

It was interesting to watch the various movements of the clouds floating below us, with the horizon above them. At times they would be seen, as it were, resting on the sides of the mountain, some looking a dark indigo color, others white as the purest snow, others resembling huge bunches of fleecy wool, while the sky above was of the deepest blue. Some, floating by, would graze the base of the mountain and leave traces of snow. The stars looked very near and large. As the sun arose it seemed as if it were rolling over towards us.

This night was like most of the nights we experienced while on the mountain, very stormy and cold, the temperature being down to sixteen below. I will not say that I never saw it blow so hard, but I never saw it blow any harder. For fear of some damage to the instruments we were ordered to turn out and take them down. We had no sooner got them stowed away snug in their cases than our camp was struck by a terrific hurricane which raised the roof of the pendulum house high into the air and scattered its fragments on the sides of the mountain. The other house was demolished and several valuable instruments badly injured. Pieces of canvas from our tents, spread out as big as table-cloths, might be seen floating in the air. The wind was so violent that it was impossible to keep our footing, so we laid down and clung closely to the side of the mountain. Amidst all this Jack had his jokes, you may be sure. You might hear one sing out, " I say, old gruffy, my lad, did you ever fall in with anything like this off Cape Cod?" " No, my hearty, it even beats Cape Horn." Another would shout, " I've seen it blowing like blue blazes, but this is a regular old blow-hard, hard enough to blow Yankee Doodle on a frying-pan."

" Silence fore and aft ! " sings out old Tom Piner, " you never knew anything about its blowing above the mast-heads. Just heave to until all hands are called up higher ; then you will find that you cannot weather the gale even by lying down to it."

At two o'clock the gale abated ; at daylight everything was as serene as a morning in the tropics.

At sunrise we were astonished to behold the Star Spangled Banner still proudly waving far above this scene of desolation, on the brim of one of the craters.

I feel proud to know that my country's flag, the broad stripes and bright stars, has been borne by brave men, north, south, east, and west, and waved to the breeze in as high an altitude as the flag of any other nation.

The words, " Pendulum Peak, January, 1841, U. S. Ex. Ex.," having been cut in the lava within our village, we picked up the remnants of the camp, and were all glad to bid adieu to the bleak and dreary summit of Mauna Loa.

On our return we made the first station about eleven o'clock, when we " spliced the mainbrace " for the first time since we had left the ship. At noon we dined on a good hot soup, and after a short rest went on our way rejoicing, fetching up at Sunday Station, at six o'clock, with aching limbs, scarcely able to drag one foot after the other. After a slight repast we made for one of the caves and turned in. After breakfast the next morning we resumed our journey.

We were so stiff as scarcely to be able to move, but felt better as we proceeded. We arrived at the volcanic

CAMP ON PENDULUM PEAK.

crater Kilauea about four o'clock, and there found summer weather.

Cheered by the natives and their hangers-on, all of us went through the process of the *loomi loomi,* a kneading operation somewhat like shampooing, which is performed by the natives. It relaxes the muscles and joints, and after undergoing the operation I think that I felt as young as I used to be.

After an excellent supper we soon rolled ourselves up in our blankets, lay on the dried grass, and fell asleep.

The next morning it seemed as if all nature were alive ; the waving of the green foliage, the singing of the birds, the cheerful voices of the natives, gave everything the air of summer.   Here we made a stop of four days, during which time a complete survey of the crater and surrounding country was made.

The sea of fire at the bottom of the crater appeared to be larger and in greater agitation than at our former visit.   While a party of us were viewing it one night, it boiled up, and the red, molten lava ran in streams over the dark bottom of the crater in all directions.

The big cloud that hangs over this volcano is, at night, a cloud of fire, which can be seen by mariners at a distance of seventy or eighty miles out to sea.   In the daytime it is of a silvery hue, with burnished edges.   Under some of the lava clinkers we found sulphur and beautiful white magnesite.   We also found what is called Pele's hair in the crevices of the lava.   This is a glossy material, resembling loose tufts of tow.   The ground on the leeside of the crater seemed, in places, to be covered with it, as with patches of golden cobwebs.

Bidding the fiery crater of Kilauea and Madame Pele a final adieu, we steered for the ship.   It being fair weather and easy traveling, we were soon aboard ship, glad to stand once more on the decks of our own swift-gliding craft.

We had been absent from the ship just forty-two days.   We found all our shipmates well, and very glad to see us back again.   The next day the pendulum was put up on shore, but it would not work.   It would stop every few minutes.   The cause was found to be the jarring of the island by the heavy rolling of the surf upon the beach.

About one-third of the distance from the shore to the ship we discovered a spring. We pulled out to it and found that the water was fresh and boiling hot.

While here at this island we visited Kealakeakua Bay, the place where Captain Cook was massacred. His monument was the stump of a cocoanut tree, on which was a sheet of copper with the following inscription :

NEAR THIS SPOT FELL

CAPTAIN JAMES COOK, R. N.

THE RENOWNED CIRCUMNAVIGATOR,

WHO DISCOVERED THESE ISLANDS, A. D. 1778.

———

HIS MAJESTY'S SHIP IMOGENE,

OCTOBER 17TH, 1837.

This sheet of copper and cap put on by Sparrowhawk,
September 13th, 1839,
In order to preserve this monument to the memory of Cook.
Give this a coat of tar.

Formerly the natives were very superstitious, and they sacrificed a great deal to the gods. They would visit the crater of Kilauea and throw in rolls of *tapa*, hogs, both cooked and alive, bunches of bananas, and cocoanuts, as offerings to the goddess Pele.

The evening before we left the volcano, one of the natives was caught in the act of throwing a calabash of poe into the volcano as an offering to the dread goddess. He was ever after called by his Christian countrymen a " backslider."

Kapiolani lived in this village. She was the woman who ate berries which were sacred to Pele, and even stood on the brink of the crater, before her people, and threw stones in at the goddess. Addressing her people she said :

"Jehovah is my God ; he kindled these fires. I fear not Pele. Should I perish by her anger, then you may

HAWAIIAN TEMPLES AND GODS.

fear her power ; but if Jehovah saves me when breaking her *tabus*, then must you fear and serve Jehovah. The gods of Hawaii are vain. Great is the goodness of Jehovah in sending missionaries to turn us from these vanities to the living God."

The people, seeing that the power of Pele was broken, and that the *tabus* of the goddess were vain, returned to the village with their leader. Kapiolani was truly a genuine heroine.

CHAPTER XVI.

AFTER completing the researches and observations of this island, we got under way and stood to sea, bound to Lahaina, island of Maui, the residence of the king, who was a natural son of Kamehameha I. The wind, during the day, was light, and we made slow progress; but as evening advanced, we took a light sea-breeze from the southwest, which soon wafted us to an anchorage in Lahaina Road, abreast the king's palace.

The next day we had a visit from the royal family. There was a great display of epaulettes, gold lace, swords, and cocked hats. The king was a portly young man, between twenty and thirty years of age, and of a commanding figure. He was very richly dressed, being nearly covered with gold lace. He was received on board by the yard being manned, our marine corps parading on the quarter-deck, presenting arms, and our ship's band, consisting of drum and fife, playing "Hail to the Chief." He was soon conducted to different parts of the ship, accompanied by Captain Wilkes and other officers. The berth deck was lighted fore and aft, all the pots and pans, and the tinware of the messes, as well as the hoops on the kids, were burnished, and displayed in front of the mess chests, and the rooms of the forward officers were brilliantly illuminated. The whole display was, no doubt, very interesting to the native king and his family.

After a sumptuous dinner, which was specially prepared for the occasion, and served in the cabin, the king and his suite left the ship. As they took their departure the yards were manned, the marines presented arms, and three cheers were given the king by all hands. He acknowledged the compliment by waving his cocked hat. A few days later they again dined on board our ship, this time in the ward-room. It was said that the king liked wine and spirits, and made free use of them, but on both of these occasions he drank very sparingly. Mrs. Kekauluohi, the king's wife, was a very portly woman, and was said to be the handsomest on that group of islands. She always looked smiling and happy.

While prospecting in the interior of this island, we came across a mound of human bones, a perfect Golgotha. It was one of their burying-places after a battle, for the place where the bones were found was known to be one of their old battle-grounds. Some of the skeletons were in a perfect state of preservation.

Lahaina was the headquarters of the missionaries, and also a great resort for our whalers to wood and water ship. There were no grog-shops in this place, and the captains knew it. For quiet on the Sabbath it would shame many a New England village. No natives were astir until meeting-time, and then they might be seen only as they passed quietly to and from church.

After surveying Maui and several other islands, we got under way and stood for Oahu, where we arrived on the

19th of March.   There we completed our repairs, and
on April 5th set out for the Columbia River, north-
west coast of North America.   By the way, while in
Oahu we heard of the dispute, between Old Mother
England and Brother Jonathan, about the northwest
boundary line.

For several days and nights a very bright lookout was
kept for land, said by whalers to exist in this quarter,
26° north latitude.   We saw nothing, however, that
looked like land, though islands might once have existed
there and sunk.   We saw myriads of birds which are
found only in the vicinity of land ; among them were
many small birds and quantities of villula, which gave
the ocean the appearance of being covered with floating
cinders.

The commodore was a great disciplinarian and always
kept all hands at work when there was nothing to do.
When the weather permitted he would have the quarters'
beat take charge of the quarter-deck, and would sing out
through his speaking-trumpet, " Silence fore and aft, wet
and sand the decks, knock out your ports, take off your
muzzle-bags, withdraw your tompions and cast loose your
guns."   Then the captain of the gun (one of the crew)
would take charge and say, " Chock your luff, stop, vent,
and sponge your guns, cartridge, wad and ram home,
round shot, canister or stand of grape, wad ram home,
man side tackle falls, run out.   Crows and hand-spikes,
elevate your guns for a long shot, two points abaft the
beam to the enemy, cock your locks, blow your match,
watch the weather-roll, stand by, fire."   Sometimes, in
an undertone, Jack would add, " A couple of round

shot, canister, stand of grape, two midshipmen and a
master's mate, wad and ram home the charge."

> " Though far from our homes, yet still in our land
> True Yankee enterprise will ever expand
> And publish to all each side of the main
> We triumphed once and can do it again.
> A problem, a problem, oh ! hear, great and small,
> The true owners of the country are still on the soil,
> While Jonathan and John Bull are growling together
> For land which by right belongs not to either.
> Let philosophers listen, and solve the question
> Which has troubled the statesmen of each nation,
> By what right Big Bull claims sustenance here
> While he has plenty of pasturage elsewhere."
>
> — *By one of the crew.*

Early in the morning of the 28th we heard the cheerful cry of " Land-ho ! " It proved to be Cape Disappointment, Columbia River, our own native land.   At
about nine o'clock we entered a strong tide-rip and
soon after came within sight of the Columbia River.   It
was blowing pretty fresh, with a considerable sea on, and
heavy breakers extended from Cape Disappointment to
Point Adams, in one unbroken line.   Nothing could
exceed the grandeur of this scene when viewed from
aloft.   The Columbia is a thousand miles long, and has
its source eight hundred feet above the level of the sea.

To view its powerful floods of light, milky water
rushing down and contending with the tides of the blue
water of old ocean and see the marked line of separation
between the sea and the river water, and a line of breakers nearly seven miles long dashing its silvery spray high
in the air, is a wild sight.   All who have seen it have

spoken of the incessant roar of the waters, representing it as one of the most awful sights that can possibly meet the eye of the sailor.

On heaving the lead we found only five, eight, and nine fathoms of water, where on the chart it was laid down twenty-eight fathoms. The two quarter boats were lowered to sound for the channel, at six bells, three o'clock ; but the wind beginning to freshen and the weather to thicken, they were recalled, and we hauled off with the tide, which was running with great rapidity and soon carried us back into the blue waters of the ocean.

During the night the weather was very boisterous. The following morning it was quite foggy. We bore away for the Straits of Juan de Fuca, and at eleven o'clock the man at the mast-head cried out, " Breakers on the lee bow ! " The ship was at once brought by the wind, the studding-sails taken in, and a cast of the lead taken, when we found ourselves in five fathoms of water. The fog soon lifted and we saw, not half a mile off, a high point of rocks. Had we continued on our course fifteen minutes longer the ship must have been dashed to pieces and all hands sent to Davy Jones' locker.

This place proved to be Point Grenville, off Vancouver and Destruction Isle. This is one of the hair-breadth escapes from wreck incident to this cruise.

A canoe soon came alongside with two old Indians, who kept singing out, "*Squik quak manash, squik quak manash. Nusk quall, nusk quall. Miso Wilszon Misoly, Miso Wilszon Misoly, Bosson, Bosson.*" Then they would turn one hand over the other with great rapidity. Some time after we found the meaning of the first three words to be, "Give us some tobacco"; the next was "Nisqually"; the other words meant a Mr. Wilson, a missionary from Boston. The motion of the hands was to describe a small stern-wheel boat at Nisqually, belonging to the Hudson Bay Company. After giving the Indians some tobacco we put to sea.

The morning of the 30th was still foggy. We saw a great abundance of wild geese and ducks flying in almost every direction and appearing very tame, probably having never heard the report of a gun. We captured many of them with little trouble.

During the night, which was very dark and rainy, the ship was hove to, a cast of the lead being taken every fifteen minutes. The morning of the first of May proved to be fair and beautiful. With a light sea-breeze we doubled Cape Flattery and entered the Straits of Juan de Fuca. While beating up the straits we were boarded by many canoes. At nine o'clock on the 2d we made Port Discovery. We came to anchor close in shore, in twenty fathoms of water. While surveying this place we came in contact with many of the Indians, who, in their broken language, would ask if we were Boston or King George ships. There was a great difference between the islanders of the Pacific and these Indians, both in language and appearance. They seemed to have scarcely any idea of decency or cleanliness, and seemed to be almost as low in the scale of humanity as the Terra del Fuegians.

It was indeed amusing to observe the contempt that

our prisoner, the Fiji chief Vendovi, entertained for these Indians. He would hardly deign to look at them. While here we were plentifully supplied with venison, ducks, geese, pork, salmon, cod, flounders, herring, clams, quahaugs, mussels, long oysters, and small crabs.

Our general orders at this time were as follows :

The undersigned informs the officers and crews under his command that the duties on which they are about to enter will necessarily bring them in contact at times with the savage and treacherous inhabitants of this coast, and he therefore feels it his duty to enjoin upon them the necessity of unceasing caution and a restrictive and mild system in all their intercourse with them.

In my general order of July 13, 1839, my views are expressed fully respecting our intercourse with savages, and I expect that the injunctions therein contained will be strictly regarded.

No officer or man will be allowed to visit the shore without arms, and boat's crews when surveying or on other duty will be furnished with such as are necessary for their protection.

CHARLES WILKES,
Commanding U. S. Ex. Ex.

At daylight on the morning of the 6th we got under way and proceeded to Puget Sound. After having finished our work here, we commenced beating up the bay for Nisqually Bay. We arrived on the 11th, at eight P. M., dropping anchor close in shore in seven fathoms of water. The *Flying Fish* and *Porpoise* were also here, safely moored, and with the boats hoisted out. We were now on our native soil, and, though more than three thousand miles away from the place of our birth, could not resist the sensations kindled by the remembrance of " home, sweet, sweet home."

On May 15th surveying parties were sent out from the

various ships. The *Porpoise* was to survey Hood's Canal; the boats of the *Vincennes* were to survey the rivers and bays in the vicinity; a land party was sent to

FLAT-HEADED SQUAW AND CHILD.

explore the interior, and another was assigned to the Cascade Mountains.

Your humble servant was left, with others, to establish the observatory. This was done near a brook, abreast of the ship, and within hail of it. We built a log-cabin for a pendulum house, to take the place of the old one which was scattered to the four winds of heaven from the summit of Mauna Loa. It was soon finished, the instruments set up, and everything complete.

The Indians at this place belonged to the flat-headed tribes. When infants their heads are compressed by a sort of clamp, which gives them a wedge-shape. The females, commonly called squaws, were very scantily attired, and were very fond of ornaments. A small, dirty bone, two or three inches long, was stuck through the cartilage of the nose. All the unmarried squaws wore small brass bells suspended around the rims of the ears. Most of the women were bow-legged. The men were rather short and thick-set, with high cheek-bones, fine eyes, set wide apart, and black hair, which was worn long and flowing. The countenances of both sexes wore an expression of wildness.

On the banks of the river is dug a kind of ochre, both yellow and red, with which these Indians paint their faces. Their language was the strangest we had yet heard. Such words as *klick, kluck, tsk, sustiki*, and *squassus*, we did not understand; but *saantylku* and *selamp* both meant hot, gathering brooms, and August; *skelues* meant exhausted salmon, and September; *skaai* meant dry moon, and October; *kinni-etylyutin* meant house-making, and November; and *kumakwala* meant snow-moon, and December.

Independence Day fell on Sunday, so we celebrated on Monday. We commenced at daybreak by firing a national salute of twenty-six guns, one for each State in the Union, two brass howitzers having been brought on shore to the observatory for the purpose. The reports of the guns not only astonished the natives, but waked up the red-coats in the fort, who came running up to the observatory with the Indians, nearly out of breath, to inquire the cause of the racket. We pointed them to our country's flag, which was so proudly waving in the breeze over our observatory. They looked thunder-struck, and wanted to know what we meant. We told them that it was Brother Jonathan's birthday. They then called us a crew of crazy Americans.

At two bells, nine o'clock, all hands, including the officers, with the exception of Mr. Vanderford, our master's mate, who remained as ship-keeper, went on shore. At the observatory the commodore formed us into a procession. The starboard watch took the lead, then came the *Vincennes'* band, fife and drum, then the master-at-arms with Chief Vendovi dressed in the Fiji fashion, and leading our ship's pet, the dog Sydney, by two fathoms of marling; then the larboard watch, and finally the marines. We were all dressed in span-clean white frocks and trousers. The commodore led the procession, followed by the other officers, and we all marched off, with colors flying and music playing. In passing Fort Nisqually we gave three tremendous cheers, which were returned very faintly from the ramparts by several red-coats.

We soon arrived at a clearing near the edge of the prairie, a spot which the commodore had chosen for the Fourth of July exhibition. Here we found an ox which had been slaughtered and dressed on the preceding Saturday. We ran a pole through the ox from end to end, and then placed the ends of this pole upon two forked tree-trunks which had been securely planted in the earth. A trench was dug under him in which a fire was built, and a windlass arranged with which to turn him at inter-

CELEBRATION OF THE FOURTH OF JULY.

vals, while a committee detailed from the crew dredged him with flour and basted him every hour.

At ten o'clock all hands were called to "splice the mainbrace." Not a man being sick, all indulged. After this the commodore ordered the starboard watch on the right and the larboard on the left, and then he produced a foot-ball, gave it a tremendous kick which sent it high into the air, and sang out, " Sail in, my shipmates !" We did sail in. With others I got my shins barked from my ankles to my knees, but never got so much as a kick at the ball.

At eight bells, noon, the grog was rolled and all hands piped to dinner. When we repaired to the barbecue the Indians had gathered in large numbers, looking silently but wistfully at the novel sight before them. The ox proved to be as tender as a lamb.

In firing the salute at midday, Daniel Whitehorn, one of our quarter-gunners, ramming home a charge, had his arm dreadfully lacerated by the unexpected discharge of the gun. This accident put a momentary stop to our hilarity. His messmates took him in charge and soothed his wounds. Jack before the mast is familiar with such scenes as this. A shipmate falling from aloft, thrown from a yard, getting washed overboard in a gale, getting tied up to the rigging or his back lacerated with the cats, getting knocked down with a hand-spike by the captain or one of his mates,— witnessing such scenes it becomes his nature to weep with them that weep and to rejoice with them that rejoice.

After dinner the amusements proceeded, but not with the mirth of the morning, for the accident threw a gloom over all hands. Some ball and card playing, chatting with the Indians, and taking a cruise into the woods wound up the day. At night all hands returned on board excepting two, who had become lost in the woods. They were found three days afterward by the Indians, more dead than alive. They were nicknamed the " Babes in the Wood."

The next day the surveying parties were sent to survey Puget Sound. The scenery from the observatory was grand. In the distance, far beyond the prairie, might be seen the snow-capped summits of Mount Hood, Mount St. Helen's, and Mount Ranier. They are beautiful to view at sunrise and at sunset. The woods were very thick, the trees large and close. Wolves were very numerous, and also foxes. Deer and bears were common, but not so much so as the treacherous wolves. Birds of all kinds were plenty, especially wild ducks and geese, which appeared very tame. While here we saw many of the Crows, Shoshones, Apaches, and Blackfeet Indians.

The survey of Puget Sound having been completed, the observatory was broken up, the instruments taken down, packed, and sent aboard ship.

On the morning of the 17th we weighed anchor and took our departure for Point Dungeness, arriving there on the 22d. The boats were immediately sent away on surveying duty. Here another accident happened. Samuel Williams, gunner's mate, was firing a four-pounder for the purpose of measuring base by sound, when, as he was priming from a well-filled powder-horn, a terrific explosion took place, sending him with much force to the other side of the deck. His hand, arms, and face were much burned, but no bones were broken. On coming to, he wanted to know " if the powder-horn had busted." He was soon taken below and cared for.

We had scarcely dropped our anchor ere we were surrounded by many canoes bringing salmon, codfish, venison, and bear meat for sale.

On the 28th we got under way again and stood down
the straits.   When off Cape Flattery, the wind being
ahead, we put into Neah Harbor.   It is the first in the
straits after rounding the cape, and is sheltered on the
northeast by Neah Island.   While surveying this harbor
the ship was fairly surrounded by canoes.   A vigilant
watch was kept on them, and only a few Indians were
allowed on board at a time.

There were two tribes, the Classet and Patouche.
They brought many fine furs, seal and sea-otter skins, to
trade, and were taken all aback when they found that
we were not eager to make a bargain.   The furs were
cheap enough, but we did not want them.   They offered
us two or three fine fur-seal skins for a pound of tobacco,
a pound of powder, or fifty leaden bullets.   A bottle of
New England rum would fetch half a dozen of the
finest furs.   This showed what sort of trade was carried
on when the Boston ships traded on this coast for furs
and salmon.   They would keep asking, " What for so
big ship?   What for so many mans? and no trade for
furs for a lite rumie ? "

This would be a good field for a missionary, for these
Indians appear to be quite ignorant of any religious
notions.

On the 1st of August we witnessed a beautiful eclipse
of the moon.   We found the Indians very numerous in
the woods, wearing nothing but old dirty blankets.   The
men were very short and had extremely broad faces,
which were besmeared with salmon oil, soot, and red
ochre.   The inside of their wigwams was very filthy.
The squaws of the Classet tribe were much better looking

and more lady-like than those of other tribes. Their hair, which was jet black and very long, hung loosely about their shoulders, and most of them had fair complexions and rosy cheeks.

On the 3d a carrier arrived from Nisqually, bring-

LOSS OF THE PEACOCK.

ing news of the loss of the *Peacock* on the bar of the Columbia.

We soon weighed anchor and put to sea. The weather for several days had been cold and foggy. We ran down the coast in eighty and ninety fathoms of water. At daylight, on the 6th, we made Cape Disappointment, Columbia River, and soon after sunrise came up with the cape and fired several guns. Shortly after, the *Flying Fish* hove in sight, coming down the Columbia. About nine o'clock the *Flying Fish* came alongside, when Captain Hudson came on board and informed Commodore Wilkes of the total wreck of his ship, the *Peacock*, on the bar of the Columbia. After the ship struck, everything that skill and seamanship could devise was resorted to in order to save her, but all to no avail.

In leaving the ship some of the boats were turned end over end, but other boats, being near at hand, rescued their crews. The ship soon went to pieces and everything was lost. But, happily, the crew was saved.

They stated that Captain Hudson was the last man to leave the ship, and that the coolness and calmness displayed by him during the wreck had secured the admiration of all hands.

The commodore, fearing to attempt crossing the bar in his own ship, the *Vincennes*, two days afterward transferred his broad pennant to the brig *Porpoise*, and with the schooner, and boats of the *Peacock*, remained here to survey the Columbia River and its bar, while Captain Ringgold proceeded in the *Vincennes* to San Francisco with a part of the *Peacock's* crew on board.

So we soon squared away and stood to sea. On the 12th we approached the shore and took a look at the land about Cape Blanco. The coast everywhere presented a dreary prospect. On the 14th we made Port San Francisco and ran in. We crossed the bar in five fathoms of water, and having a fair wind proceeded up the bay and anchored off Yerba Buena, a small Spanish settlement. Several vessels were lying at anchor here, among them were two American ships and a brig. We were soon boarded by Captain Phelps of the ship *Alert* of Boston, who informed us of the death of the President of the United States, Wm. H. Harrison.

On the 17th we up anchor again and stood over to Sansalito, or Whaler's Bay, not far from Captain Suter's fort. Here, as at other places, land and boat expeditions were fitted out for survey and research. While surveying the Sacramento, Feather, and other rivers, it was a beautiful sight to see the elks and deer coming down from the mountains to the river to drink. The kiotes, or dog-wolves, were also very numerous. We used to build fires around the camps to keep them away ; but they would come, and that in droves, and stand howling, yelling, and barking at us. It was enough to frighten a tribe of Indians. A few shots, however, from our guns and they skedaddled into the woods.

Grizzly bears were also very plenty. The little cubs were very cunning and playful as kittens. One must be careful not to hurt them, if he does he may expect a tight hug from the mother.

We penetrated up the Sacramento as far as we could in the launch. The peak of Shasta is magnificent to view from here, rising as it does to a lofty height, its steep sides emerging from the mist which envelops its base and seems to throw it off to a great distance. It is at times an active volcano.

One day we witnessed the funeral of one of the Shasta Indians. Some wood was gathered, a fire built, and the dead body laid thereon. Then the Indians, dressed in blankets, with their faces painted, and their long, jet-black hair streaming in the air, danced, sang, wailed, and made all kinds of hideous noises, and waved their blankets in the air, in order to drive away all evil spirits. They believe that when the body is entirely burned up, and the heart consumed, that the spirit has flown to the far-off hunting ground, there to enjoy everlasting peace.

Our botanist, Dr. Pickering, while digging up a rare plant, felt something brush against him behind. Turning around he saw, sitting on his hind legs watching him, a large grizzly bear ; feeling a peculiar sensation coming over him, he pretended not to notice his bearship, who still sat there watching his every movement. Finally, the bear's patience gave out, and he walked leisurely off, to the great relief of the doctor.

Having finished our work up here, we returned to the ship, where we found the brig *Porpoise*, schooner *Flying Fish*, and the brig *Oregon*, late the *Thomas Perkins*. She was purchased by Commodore Wilkes, at Columbia River, for the purpose of carrying home the officers and crew of the *Peacock*. While here, we lived on bear meat, wild game, fresh fish, and a thin cake made of coarse Indian meal, baked on a piece of sheet iron. Vegetables were scarce, the Spaniards being as lazy as the Indians, and neither troubled themselves about raising any.

Some of these Spanish families were very large, fifteen to twenty odd. Did it ever enter your mind how nice it would be to have twenty sisters, or ten sisters and ten brothers? They learn to ride as early as the Sandwich Islanders learn to swim. Large numbers· die from falls from the horses. They are generally robust, and left to take care of themselves, and run about naked and dirty.

Both sexes were equally fond of gambling, horse-racing, cock-fighting, bull and bear baiting, and dancing, which almost always ended in a row, especially at their weddings.

Before we left here, we had a circus on board. By invitation of the ward-room officer, a large number of Spanish ladies visited the ship. The quarter-deck was decorated with the flags of almost all nations. There were many dances danced, among which were the Spanish fandango, the love, courtship, marriage, and bull-bait dances, all of which were most gracefully executed. Both ladies and gentlemen seemed to enjoy the dances ; also the wine, which was flowing about pretty freely. The music from the guitars was so inspiring that we on the forecastle put in several fore-and-afters, all-fours, break-downs, and sailors' hornpipes. Late at night, both men and women retired to the shore, with a good freight of wine on board.

All the surveying parties having returned, the observatory was taken down, and all the instruments carried on board ship, the boats were hoisted in, and everything was stowed snugly away.

On the 1st of November signals were made to get under way, when we weighed anchor and stood out of the harbor, with the two brigs and the schooner. At sundown, the wind dying away and a strong tide setting against us, and the weather becoming foggy, we came to anchor in seven fathoms of water. Signal was made to the other vessels, which were a mile ahead of us, to anchor. It was calm at the time, and the bay was as smooth as a mill-pond, while not a breath of air was stirring. At four bells, ten o'clock, all hands turned in except the first part of the starboard watch. About eleven o'clock, the sea swell suddenly set in, and all hands were called on deck. By midnight the swell had so increased as to cause apprehensions of great danger. By three o'clock the old ship might be said to be riding in breakers of gigantic size. The estimated height of these breakers was over thirty odd feet. At eight bells, four o'clock, one of these huge breakers struck the ship broad on the larboard bow with such force as to sweep

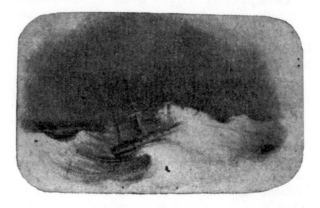

THE VINCENNES ON THE BAR.

the spar deck fore and aft. The boats and booms were broken adrift, the boats stove in, and the spars and every other movable thing were washed from one side of the deck to the other.

One of the marines, Joseph Allshouse, was struck by a spar, and died in a few hours. By eight o'clock the swell abated and the rollers ceased to break. A light breeze sprung up, when we got under way and stood for the Bay of Monterey. At two o'clock all hands were called to bury the dead. The body was carried to the

lee gangway, wrapped in an American flag, while the bier
was a rough plank.   The funeral services were conducted
by Captain Hudson.   A deathlike stillness pervaded the
ship.   At the words, "We commit his body to the
deep," a plunge was heard, and a momentary melancholy seemed to impress the minds of all hands.   Three
volleys were fired over the lonely ocean grave, and the
boatswain's call announced that all was over.   The yards
were braced, and we kept on our course.

EATING POE.

Early the next morning we made Monterey Bay.   The
Porpoise was sent in with the letter-bag and we then
directed our course for the Sandwich Islands.   On the
18th we came to anchor in the harbor of Honolulu.
While here, we had one day's liberty on shore.   The
natives were highly delighted at our return.   While on
shore the boys, Kinney, Roberts, and myself, took a
cruise out to the "Punch Bowl," where we dined with
one of the chiefs and his family.   The dinner consisted
of half-cooked fish and poe.   The latter was made from

the taro, a vegetable root, ground into a sort of paste. They ate it by thrusting their fingers into the calabash containing it and carrying quite a quantity to the mouth. When the paste was as thick as baker's sugar molasses they used but one finger. Then it was *miti rud* (very good). When thin they used four fingers. Then it was *oura miti* (very bad).

Baked dogs, rats, and mice were once considered dainty dishes by the natives, but of late years they have not been regarded as luxuries.

Yankee Jim, Johnny Smith, and other sailors' boarding-house keepers, and land-sharks and land-lubbers were fairly overjoyed at our return, and received us with open arms. We had not forgotten their tokens of kindness on a previous visit, when we were their guests for two weeks, and nearly every man before the mast with a hundred dollars in his locker. A week had not elapsed before our pretended friends, the land-sharks, had stripped us of nearly every dollar, and all that we had received in return was some scanty meals and oceans of grog.

They were just like sailors' boarding-house keepers all over the world. They appeared to be very kind-hearted and generous. They told us not to mind about the pay, but just give them a little bit of an order on the old commodore and it would be all right. "Come, my shipmates, what are you going to have?" sung out Johnny Smith, the old land-shark. "Let us sing the flowing bowl, drink, dance, sing, and be merry." Then Yankee Jim, the old land-pirate, broke in and sang lustily :

> " Come ye, all my jolly sailors bold,
>   We'll never have it said
>   That the Yankee tars exploring go
>   Were ever yet afraid."

Well, we just did drink, dance, and sing. After a dance it was " All hands splice the mainbrace." Maybe eighteen or twenty would drink, when two hundred drinks would be charged to us.

The commodore had his weather eye open, and had foreseen all this, and had caused notices to be issued forbidding any one to trust any of the crews, as he should not pay any debts of their contracting on any account whatever.

After having a jolly time, if you can call it a jolly time, and our liberty being up, we returned on board our respective ships, every — man — sober. Soon these soul-less landlords and rumsellers presented their bills to the commodore, amounting to nearly two thousand dollars. He asked them if they had not seen the notices. They acknowledged that they had, but made complaints against the measure, and demanded the payment of these bills. The commodore listened to their arguments very attentively, and they inferred that they had softened him somewhat in his resolution, in which, however, they were mistaken, for he told them that he pitied them, and was very sorry, and that his sorrow was still greater that the bills did not amount to fifty thousand dollars instead of two thousand, for in any case he would not allow one cent of it to be paid ; so the bills were squared by the foretop-sails, as Jack before the mast has it.

Having completed our surveys and researches in this

group of islands, on the afternoon of the 27th of November we bade farewell to our kind friends in Honolulu, and, the squadron in company, took our final leave of the Hawaiian Islands, and set sail for the East Indies.

The *Vincennes*  was a rapid sailor, and we had a good, stiff breeze right abeam, and she was given all the sail that she could possibly carry, and our gallant ship reeled off thirteen knots an hour, and we were reminded that at the end of each hour we were thirteen knots nearer our homes. Bright lookout was kept for land, as islands had been reported as having been seen in this locality, but we saw none.

HAWAIIAN IDOL.

On the 7th of December we dropped a day, having passed into east longitude ; the day beautifully clear.   In some parts of the ocean we have sailed in, the sea has been of a dark, or light green, blue, or olive color, and in some places as clear as the raindrops.   Here it was so transparent that our pot, which was a large, old-fashioned, three-legged, iron one, painted white, when lowered into the water, bottom upwards, was seen at thirty-two fathoms (one hundred and ninety feet) deep.

On the 19th we made Wakes Island, which is of coral formation, eight feet above the sea, with a large lagoon, which was well filled with fish.   Here we found the short-tailed albatross.   After surveying this, Gugan, and Assumption Islands, we stood on our course.

On the 8th of January we made the islands of Sabtang and Batan. The wind being ahead we beat through the Balintang Straits. We had now left the North Pacific and entered the Sooloo Sea.

At daylight on the 13th we dropped anchor in the Bay of Manilla, island of Luzon, one of the Philippine Islands. These islands are of a volcanic nature, and no portion of the globe is so much the seat of internal fires ; though none were in action while we were there, some of them were smoking. They were discovered by Magellan in 1521, and are subject to the Spanish government. The city is fortified with walls and ditches, as in all Spanish ports. The streets were narrow and dirty. The houses were two stories high, built of stone, and were either yellow or whitewashed. Outside of the city they were built of bamboo, and elevated on posts to prevent the entrance of the numerous reptiles, centipedes, and lizards.

While taking a cruise up one of the main streets we saw the cooks in movable kitchens, frying cakes, making bird's-nest puddings, stewing, etc. It amused us to see them at work in the streets. Chinese tinkers, blacksmiths, bakers, cabinet-makers, shoe and slipper makers, tailors, hawkers of opium and cakes of coagulated blood and betel nut, were numerous. The betel nut was chewed with the pepper-leaf by the natives of the East Indies. It stained their teeth to a cherry red.

The majority of the population was Chinese. There were also many Malays, and a few Spaniards, Europeans, and negroes. All wore loose dresses and slippers. Those who could afford it carried Chinese umbrellas, very gorgeously painted, to screen themselves from the burning sun. The women were very fond of bathing; likewise of shopping — a favorite amusement, I find, with the fair sex the world over.

While on an expedition with the botanists into the country we met many buffaloes. The natives yoked them together, as our farmers do oxen. They were the beasts of burden. The ladies also rode horseback upon them, with saddles cut out of solid wood. We saw buffaloes near the edge of the lakes, floundering about in the mire, with only their eyes and noses out of water. Their flesh is as tough as sole leather, and as tasteless.

In and about the lakes and ponds we saw many birds feeding; herons, gulls, pelicans with their huge bills, the diver with its long, arched neck, snow-white cranes, flocks of ducks, eagles, and many other beautifully feathered and rare birds.

As for monkeys, I might say some of the woods were full of them. It was indeed amusing to see them, not in a cage in a menagerie, but in their homes in the woods, cutting up all kinds of monkey-shines. They go in troops of from sixty to eighty, chasing each other, and sometimes leaping a distance of fifteen to twenty feet, from the limb of one tree to another, and such a snarling, squealing set we never fell in with before. Some of them had very broad noses, long tails, and were as black and glossy as could be. To see them swing from the limb of a tree, by the end of their tails, was truly laughable. We also started many flocks of beautiful green parrots and paroquets, and came across many hot springs.

Rice is the principal food of the inhabitants of these islands. There are several different varieties,— the bontot-cabayo, birnambang, dumali, quinanda, bolohan, and malagequil—the latter is very much prized. All their dainty and fancy dishes were made from it. A brilliant whitewash, very durable, and capable of standing the weather, was also made from it.

All the tropical fruits grow here,— pine-apples, the best I have seen in any part of the world. The Brazilian, Porto Rico, and Bahama pine-apples were not to be compared to the Philippines. They grow very large, some of them weighing twenty pounds or more. They are the fruit of fruits, and the most delicious in the world. The meaning of pine-apple is, "You are perfect."

The largest building — that is, the longest — that we saw while there, was the Royal Cigar Manufactory, in which fifteen thousand persons were employed, eleven thousand of whom were women. A boat's crew of us were passing by the factory one noon when the employees were coming out for dinner. We had never seen so many women together at once ; many of them were short and stout. Their average height was about five feet. They were clothed in loose jackets and petticoats made from gaudy colored grass cloth. They wore no stockings, and their feet were covered by slippers often very pretty in shape and color. Many of them had beautiful large teeth, stained red by chewing the betel nut. All had glossy black hair. We did not see a red-headed girl among them. Many were extremely pretty, if not handsome. The majority of them, however, were very homely.

Among the shipping which we saw lying in the roads were two American vessels, loading with hemp.

On the morning of the 21st of January we got under way and made sail for the Straits of Mindoro.

On the 6th of February we made and surveyed the Pangootaaraang group, consisting of five small islands.

Early in the morning of the 8th we made the Mangsee Islands. Here, as on many of the islands of the Sooloo Seas, lived crews of freebooters and blood-thirsty Malay pirates, more ready and willing to cut our throats and pick our pockets than to trade. Though not cannibals, they delighted in shedding blood, and were fully as barbarous and treacherous as the Fiji cannibals. Our Sooloo pilot advised us when we landed not to penetrate into the woods.

Here, as on all the islands, we saw many beautiful birds. We found one kind we had not seen on any other island. It was about half as large as a peacock, but clothed in richer colored feathers.

Monkeys could be seen in great numbers. Here we found what was called the "sad-faced" monkey. It was very quiet and slow-motioned, and had a very broad and melancholy face.

While pulling along these shores, we looked over the gunwales of our boats into some of the most beautiful coral flower gardens that are to be found in the world.

The food of the natives was hogs, ground-rats, snails, monkeys, snakes, etc.

While surveying in the boats we fired muskets, in order to measure base. The Malays mistook us for some shipwrecked crew, and thought our guns were signals of distress. They came down upon us in several of their prows at full speed, and armed with their cuirasses and spears. Our boats at once closed together. The pirates came alongside of us, but, having no fire-arms, and seeing that we were numerous and well armed, they sneakingly hauled off again, and had the impudence to hoist a white flag in token of peace. Their retreat was hastened by a shot from our ship, which had just rounded a point a mile to windward, and thus signaled for our return. I never have seen such a bloodthirsty set of thieves and pirates as were these Malays.

On the 18th, at midnight, we made Pulo Aor and Pulo Pedaang. We came to until daylight, when we found ourselves close alongside a large Chinese junk. After breakfast we weighed anchor, but, the wind being light, we did not reach Singapore Roads until the next day, when, in the afternoon, we came to anchor opposite the town. Here we found the flags of all nations fluttering in the breeze, from the mizzen peak of the stately Indiaman, and the bamboo yards of the huge Chinese junk. Many of these flags some of us now beheld for the first time.

Among the shipping found here, we saw American, English, French, Russian, Spanish, Turkish, Greek, and Siamese vessels, Dutch galiots, built out of teak, Baltimore clippers, long, low, rakish brigs and schooners, opium smugglers, Chinese junks with a large eye on each bow so that they might see the Malay prows, prahus, bumboats, and numerous odd-looking boats, called sampans.

Our ship was soon surrounded by a fleet of bumboats

and sampans. On these were washerwomen, many of whom were young and pretty, and venders of all conceivable goods ; soft-tack, fresh eggs of different sizes, a reddish-colored milk, chickens, cockerells, and ducks, both cooked and alive, various kinds of pies, cakes, and puddings, carved fowl, and fish, fruits and vegetables, mats, shells, birds of paradise, pigeons, various parrots, cockatoos, monkeys, singing and talking birds, beautiful specimens of corals, and many other curiosities too numerous to mention. All the venders pleaded piteously for us to buy, declaring that everything was very cheap.

We were homeward bound, so our stay here was short, yet in rowing the officers up to town we had a chance to see the sights of the place. On either side of the river we saw the floating homes of the Chinese, called sampans. They were covered with women and children. The children were all naked, frolicking in the water, and apparently happy as ducks. But what took the wind out of our sails was to see guards of swarthy, brown sepoys, dressed up as English soldiers, in close-bodied, red coats, while the thermometer stood at nearly one hundred. Besides Europeans, we saw many Hindus, Dutch, Chinese, Jews, Malays, Parsees, Armenians, and Buddhists. There was a jargon of languages, but all seemed to understand one another.

Most of the trades were carried on in the streets. Here we found umbrellas and fans for sale, coffin-makers, and money changers whose smaller coins were pieces of melted silver, several copper coins tied on a string, a peculiar kind of fish scales, and small cowry shells.

There were also Chinese barbers who pulled teeth, bled, cupped, and leeched most unmercifully.

Our scientific gentlemen were advised not to visit the woods in search of specimens, as they would be liable to be attacked by tigers.

The pine-apples here were delicious. They were not in the least acid, and did not turn the knife black when cut.

On the morning of the 26th, everything being in readiness, we took advantage of the land breeze and got under way. We passed our Daughter of the Squadron (the *Flying Fish*), which had been sold, the commodore fearing to trust her around the stormy Cape of Good Hope. She had been our companion in many toils and dangers. As we passed her with a strange commander and crew on board, and a foreign flag at her mast-head floating to the balmy breeze, every bosom was filled with sadness.

The *Sea Gull* had foundered off the coast of Terra del Fuego, the *Relief* had been sent home from New Holland, the *Peacock* had been wrecked at the mouth of the Columbia River, so the *Vincennes* and *Porpoise* were all that remained of the squadron which were to return to the United States.

The wind being fair, we sailed through the Straits of Banca, into the Java Seas, and through the Straits of Sunda, into the Indian Ocean. Our ships' supply of stores, which we took on board at Singapore, had been awaiting our arrival for several years, and consequently was rather stale and musty, particularly our hard-tack, which was both moldy and wormy.

> " But who cares? who cares?
> We are homeward bound, we are homeward bound,
> And only fifteen thousand miles away!
> But who cares? who cares?
> We are homeward bound, we are homeward bound."

All was life and gayety on board, and bright visions of home were before us. The weather was fine, the wind fair, and our gallant ship had all the sail on her that she could possibly carry. She made thirteen and a half knots per hour for five days in succession. We did not raise, tack, or sheet, or take a pull at the brace, only the " mainbrace," and that we " spliced."

March 2. This morning our old shipmate, George Porter, the man who came very near being hung while we were off the Carney Islands, breathed his last. He belonged in Bangor, Maine, and how eagerly he looked forward to going home and seeing all the loved ones there ! Poor George ! He was a jolly good fellow, an excellent sailor, and a worthy shipmate. It made us feel very sad to commit his body to the depths of the hungry, restless ocean, there to lie until the sea is summoned to give up its dead.

The weather continued fine and the breezes light until the 20th, when we encountered bad weather, with a very rough, chopped sea, which caused the ship to pitch deeply.

On the 23d Benjamin Vanderford, our trading master and South Sea pilot, died. He had formerly commanded several South Sea trading vessels from Salem. He could converse in the Fiji language, and was well versed in their manners and customs. A strong attachment had sprung up between him and our Fiji chief, Vendovi, whom he was to take in charge on our arrival in the United States. Nothing could induce poor Vendovi to look at the corpse of his friend. His spirits left him. He had been failing for some time, and sailors' rations did not agree with him. He had lost his best friend, and no doubt felt it keenly. Mr. Vanderford's body was committed to the deep with the usual service and honors.

For several days we had delightful weather and strong trades, enabling us to make two hundred and fifty miles a day nearer our homes.

On the 30th we overtook and spoke the ship *Clarendon* of Boston, from Canton, bound for New York.

On April 14th we came to anchor in Table Bay, Cape of Good Hope. The Cape was discovered by the Portuguese navigator, Bartholomew Diaz, in 1486, and named by him the "Cape of Storms." When, on his return to Portugal, he made known his discovery, King Henry gave it another name.

> "Dread roared the blast, the wave;
> O'er the torn heavens, loud on their awestruck ear,
> Great nature seemed to call, 'Approach not here!'
> At Lisbon's court they told their dread escape,
> And, from her raging tempest, named the cape.
> 'Thou southmost point,' the joyful king exclaimed,
> 'Cape of Good Hope be thou forever named.'"

Cape of Good Hope is always hailed by the homebound sailor with as much delight as Cape Horn is with fear. Here we found much shipping lying quietly at anchor. The view of Cape Town from the ship's deck is indeed novel.   On either side of Table Mountain are seen the crags of Lion's Head and Devil's Peak.   The broad, flat top of Table Mountain is always overhung by a great cloud, and when the cloud spreads out and covers the whole town with its broad shadows, it is then termed by Jack before the mast "the devil's table-cloth."

To the south, on the hill, stands the world-renowned observatory, where Sir John Herschell discovered the planet which once bore his name, but is now called Uranus.

Cape Town is an old Dutch settlement, and everything wore a Dutch look.   Almost all the people we met were Dutch.   Both men and women were short and stout, with full, rosy cheeks.   They all dressed in the old Dutch fashion.

While taking a cruise with the botanists in the outskirts of the town, we fell in with some of the Caffirs, Bushmen, Hottentots, and other tribes of South Africa.

On the 17th we got under way, and took our departure from the Cape of Storms, shaping our course for the island of St. Helena.

On the morning of the 19th Joseph Sylva, a Portuguese boy, who had shipped at Oahu, died.   In the afternoon his body, with two roundshot, was sewed up in his hammock, and committed to the deep.   Brave little Joe is now sleeping beneath the blue waters with others of the ocean's heroes.

After a run of thirteen days, we came to anchor in the roadstead of the Valley of Jamestown, island of St. Helena.   Here we found six American and two English ships, one from Sweden, and a Dutch sloop-of-war, at anchor. The island of St. Helena is nothing but a large, barren rock, uprisen from the sea, and so steep that only a short distance from the shores soundings cannot be obtained with a deep-sea line. The only landing place was Jamestown. The population, at this time, including the garrison, some English gentlemen, negroes, a few Chinese, and many quadroons, numbered about four thousand, and all lived in the Valley of Jamestown. Meats, vegetables, and fruits we found very scarce and extremely dear. Rum, however, was plenty, and quite cheap. It was not made here, but was sent out from New England, America !

St. Helena is celebrated only because of its being the place of Napoleon Bonaparte's confinement and death.

The following verses about Napoleon I learned when before the mast :

> " Come all ye nations, both far and near,
>   And listen to my song and story,
>   For by these few lines you soon shall hear
>   How man's deprived of fame and glory.

> " Ambition will have its flight,
>   Fortune is often backward twirled,
>   Old Boney could not be content
>   Till he was master of the world.

> " Oh ! Wellington, he took the field,
>   And brought those British boys to Buffon,
>   When old Boney he was forced to yield,
>   And go on board the *Bellerophon*."

One afternoon a boat's crew of us ascended Ladder Hill, and visited Longwood, the late residence of Napoleon. A short time previous to our arrival, by the consent of the British Government, the *Bellerophon*, the same ship that had borne Napoleon here as an exile, carried his remains back to his native land. Some cedars and weeping willows were growing around the tomb, which was built of English cement. It had partly caved in, and pieces of it were lying about. I have a piece of it in my possession to-day. In the room in which the emperor died was a Yankee threshing-machine. The ceiling and walls were covered with cobwebs, and the floor strewn with chaff and straw.

Among the many yarns that I have heard spun in the ship's forecastle is one about Napoleon's attempted escape from St. Helena. It is said that a Baltimore clipper was watering ship at the island. Large casks were used for the purpose of holding the water, and these had been taken ashore by the crew, filled, and returned to the landing, ready to be taken on board ship. They were, in fact, being rolled over the drawbridge and past the guard house, when a guard noticed that one of the hogsheads appeared very light. He ordered the hoop at one end to be knocked off and the head taken out, when, lo and behold, there was Napoleon !

On the 2d of June, late in the afternoon, we heard the shrill pipe of the boatswain and his mate calling all hands, " Up anchor for the United States ! " Home, sweet, sweet home ! There is no sweeter word that greets the sailor's ear, let his home be in England, Scotland, Wales, Ireland, France, Russia, or in the land of the Stars and Stripes. Yes, when homeward bound after a long cruise, even the bosom of Jack before the mast heaves with joyous emotion. But some of our shipmates who left home with us four years ago are not with us to-day. Some sleep in old Ocean's sepulcher, among other treasures of the deep, and some in coral graves. The *Sea Gull's* crew, who were bound together in ties of friendship and love, had not been separated in the hour of death, but had sunk together to rise no more until the sea is summoned to give up its dead. May they rest in peace !

There was not a man on the sick-list, and the faces of all hands seemed to wear the glow of some bright vision of happiness. The weather was fine, the wind fair, and, with studding sails set on either side,—below and aloft,—our good ship, like a thing of life, bounded onward, as eager to reach home as were her jolly crew. Everything was lovely, and nothing transpired to mar our happiness as we passed through the tropics.

On the 16th crossed the equator. One very warm and pleasant night, in the mid-watch, seeing three of our quarter growlers (old sailors) taking a siesta on deck, and enjoying our big dog, Sydney, as a pillow, I hunted up a bone and placed it about a foot from the dog's nose. As soon as Sydney got a smell of the bone he suddenly sprang up, and the sleepers' heads came down on deck with a thump. Such a growling ! Why, they were like three old bears with sore heads, and if they had known who the culprit was, I verily believe they would have thrown him overboard.

On the 28th we crossed the Tropic of Cancer and sailed through what might be called a sea of sun-fish, for the surface of the ocean seemed to be covered with them.

On the 29th we passed floating fields of gulf-weed, some of them a mile in length. Our prisoner, the Fiji chief Vendovi, was failing rapidly in health. He had been very despondent since the death of Mr. Vanderford. All hands were busily engaged building "castles in the air," imagining what they would do when they got paid off. As regards your humble servant, he had fully made up his mind not to ship again in the navy. This was my sixth year, and I had had enough of the navy during that time to last me a lifetime. I had seen as good men as ever trod a ship's deck, lashed to the rigging—made spread eagles of—and flogged. Truly, " feeble man, clothed with a little brief authority, plays such fantastic tricks before high heaven as to make the very angels weep."

Fifty years have passed, and how little reform has been made in the treatment of sailors ! It is true Jack's grog has been stopped, and flogging has been legally abolished. Still, in this nineteenth century, the sailor is most tyrannically abused, as can be seen by reading the reports in the daily papers. For instance, a naval officer — one high in authority — is court-martialed, and found guilty of abusing and threatening the lives of some of his men. The officer is sentenced to be put on the retired list for a year. This punishment in reality means a twelve months' picnic on full pay. A merchant captain — a very small specimen of a man — knocks down one of his sailors with a handspike, and lashes another to the rigging and flogs him. When the ship arrives in

Boston, the two victims cause the captain to be arrested. The captain is tried and sentenced by the learned judge to a fine of five hundred dollars—two hundred and fifty for each of the sailors. Would His Honor consent to be struck with a handspike or lashed to the rigging and flogged for two hundred and fifty dollars? I cannot help saying, "My God! is this our civilization?"

On the 2d of June we made the outer edge of the Gulf Stream. Here we experienced a change of weather. It is common for sailors to declare that they never saw it blow so hard, or that it is the worst gale they ever experienced. All hands acknowledged now with truth that they had never seen it blow with greater violence. The rain came down in torrents; the thunder and lightning were terrific. It was a regular old-fashioned Gulf gale, and there was scarcely a moment during the twelve hours it lasted that we did not witness the lightning's red glare in some quarter of the heavens.

On the morning of the 9th, it being foggy, we took a cast of the lead and obtained soundings at eighty fathoms. This showed that we were nearing the coast, and our thoughts turned at once to the dear ones at home. Shortly after discharging a gun, a pilot boat hove in sight; and soon a pilot came on board and took charge of the ship.

On the morning of the 10th we made the Highlands of Nevisink, at the mouth of New York harbor. After lying at quarantine a short time to receive the health officers, we held on our course toward the city of New York. Arriving off the Battery, all hands were called to muster, while the commodore expressed to us his thanks for the manner in which we had conducted ourselves during the cruise, and stated the confident belief that we should receive from the Government such reward as the successful result of the cruise and our long and perilous services entitled us to. A national salute of twenty-six guns was fired, and the broad pennant of Commodore Charles Wilkes was hauled down. The commodore then left the ship and proceeded to Washington. In the absence of the commodore, Captain William L. Hudson took command, and proceeded with the vessel to the Navy Yard at Brooklyn. As soon as our gallant ship—our home for four long years—was safely moored, a steamboat came alongside and took all hands with bags and hammocks on board. We soon landed, and were again free men in the land of freedom ; and a jollier set of tars it would be difficult to conceive of. To be relieved from four years of confinement and from the severe discipline of a man-of-war was bliss indeed.

A Sailor's Ditty.

"Huzza, my boys! The ship *Vincennes*
　Comes proudly o'er the wave;
Bold Captain Wilkes in her command,
　Two hundred seamen brave.
With joyful hearts and hopes all bright,
　These Yankee sailors come,
And glorious, full, meridian light
　Shines on their passage home.

"These are my sons," bright Freedom cries,
　"From the Antarctic seas."
And proudly from our mizzen flies
　The stars of Liberty.

"These are the tars that dared explore
  The new Antarctic world,
And nobly on that frozen shore
  Columbia's flag unfurled.

"The Fiji group they have surveyed
  With well-instructed hearts;
And all those islands, reefs, and bays,
  See pictured on their charts."
She paused; and lo! from Freedom's eye
  There fell a crystal tear.
"Two sons I've lost," the goddess cried;
  "Two sons I loved most dear."

"Nay, Freedom, quiet each mournful sigh;
  Those crystal drops restrain;
The sequel shall relight thine eye
  With pleasure's beam again.
We are the men our chieftain led
  O'er dark Malolo's plain;
Before us hosts of Indians fled,
  And left two hundred slain.

"We are the men that burned their town,
  Well fortified and new;
Destroyed their cattle, fruits cut down,
  Because thy sons they slew.
On hands and knees that murd'rous host
  Did crawl our chief to meet—
They owned 'twas retribution just—
  Begged pardon at his feet.

"To Mauna Loa's fiery top
  These daring tars have scaled;
And there, o'er all the science group,
  Our captain has surveyed.

Let England boast her Cook and Ross,
   And other chiefs of fame;
They all must stand like mounds of dross
   Beside our captain's name.

"On Fame's broad pillar, hand in hand,
   Shall stand in bold relief,
O'er all the rest of all the land,
   Columbus and our chief.
Then speed thee on, our gallant ship,
   And homeward bear thy tars;
While proudly glitters from thy peak
   Columbia's flag of stars."

— By one of the crew.

CHAPTER XVII.

ONCE ashore, we headed directly for the sailors' quarters, — the "Hook" and "Five Points," — where the sailors' boarding-houses were located. We were greeted by the landlords, the landladies, and their daughters with a profusion of smiles; and oh, how glad they were to see us! If we had been their own brothers they could not have been more cordial. They showered upon us endearing expressions, such as, "My dear, long-lost Jack, I am ever so glad to see you home again!" "My shipmates," "My messmates," etc. This, however, was all taffy. They loved us only for the shot in the locker. When a sailor was flush they called him "Jack" and treated him like a king; when his money was gone they called him "John" and turned him out.

The third day on shore we heard of the death of Vendovi, the Fiji chief. We also learned that we should not be paid off for a week. Feeling anxious to get home, and, I must add, thoroughly disgusted with the vile set of land-sharks of both sexes, twenty of us started for Boston. Arriving late in the evening, we came to at "Mother Paine's" and "Jack Wright's" sailors' boarding-houses, situated on Ann Street. Sunday morning, after breakfast, the boy, Isaac Carney, made for his home in East Boston; Bill Roberts, in

Chelsea ; and Charlie Erskine sought his home at the West End. At noon, we all three met at " Mother Paine's," neither of us having been successful in finding our parents. While talking over our morning a lventures with each other in the old wood-shed, we could not help giving vent to our feelings. We did, inceed, feel very sad and discouraged. However, after dinner we started again. I revisited the house where my mother had formerly lived in Bridge Street Court. The woman whom I found residing there had just returned from church, and informed me that my mother had moved about three years before to Commercial Street, and said I had better look in the directory. I had already looked there, but my mother's name was not in the book. I continued my search, however, and finally discovered that my mother resided on Canton Street.

Such a joyful meeting as it was ! I shall not attempt to describe it. Carney also was successful in finding his mother, who was living in Chelsea, and Roberts found his in East Boston.

Tuesday we all returned to New York. It was fourteen days from the time of our arrival to the day we were paid off. Mr. Bennett stated in the *New York Herald* that it was a shame and a disgrace for the Government to keep us out of our pay so long, and that he would help pay the expenses of the two hundred of the *Vincennes'* crew to Washington if they would go on and give each member of Congress what they so richly deserved — a good, sound thrashing. He had no doubt but what we could do it, even if there were five hundred Congressmen. At last the day arrived when we were to

receive our wages. Our sailor landlords and ladies —
the land-sharks — were on hand, willing and eager to
take our earnings as we received them from the purser.
These people were in the habit of acting as our treas-
urers. They would take the sailor's money and deal it
out to him from time to time, being sure, however, to
charge enormously for the service. The sailors were, in
fact, swindled without mercy by these pretended friends.
Some of our crew were paid off with six and eight hundred dollars.

The next day about a hundred of us squared the yards
with our landlords and headed for dear old Boston.
When we reached there, several of the crew continued
to their homes on Cape Cod, while others went to
Maine, New Hampshire, and Vermont. Before we separated, however, the land-sharks on Ann Street had reaped
quite a harvest from us.

All were glad to see me home again. My mother
was overjoyed, and told me that the hundred dollars I
had sent to her had been a real Godsend, and that it
came just in the "nick of time."

Supper hour drawing near, my youngest sister said to
me, " Charlie, what do you want real nice for supper?"

I replied, "Some of mother's hasty pudding and
milk."

They were all much astonished at my simple request,
as they had expected to prepare something more elabo-
rate ; but we had the hasty pudding, and I assure you it
was delicious.

I soon went down town and bought a suit of clothes
at John Earle's; but before I could wear the pants, I

had to cut away the straps, take a reef in the legs, and dispense with the suspenders and vest ; even then I felt as if I was in irons. However, I stood it, and with a black beaver hat on the back of my head, felt that my attire was *comme il faut*, and sailed forth.

In a few days I met one of my young shipmates, called Knowles, who invited me to accompany him to his home in Maine. I was pleased to accept his invitation, and the following afternoon we took the steamboat for Bangor. His home was in the country, thirty miles west of Bangor. We rode two-thirds of the way in an old-fashioned stage-coach, and walked the remainder. At last we arrived at the house. It was a very old looking house, and stood a little back from the road. As we advanced, we saw standing in the large front doorway a tall, venerable man, with long white hair, and whiskers reaching to his waist. He was leaning on a staff, and reminded me of Rip Van Winkle.

"Thank God ! father is alive, and mother too !" exclaimed my young shipmate, sobbing.

Soon a kind, motherly looking old lady made her appearance at the door. When he saw her, Knowles cried, " Why, don't you know me, mother? "

Then his good, loving, old mother threw her arms around his neck, and exclaimed, " My God, my God ! it is my boy, my boy, — my own, dear, lost boy ! "

I assisted the old man to a chair, and then, while tears of joy were streaming down his cheeks, hauled off and took a cruise about the yard, and surveyed the hennery and piggery. The pigs amused me very much. There were a dozen little ones, short and fat, and all of the same size. It was quite laughable to see them stare at me with their small, pink eyes for a second or two and then scamper away. Soon I was called back into the house, and my shipmate introduced me to his venerable father and mother and several brothers and sisters. They were all overjoyed at the return of the long-lost boy. They had not heard anything from him since he had left home, seven years before, and his parents had supposed him dead. I was very kindly treated, and remained with them about two months.

While here, I attended the academy every afternoon, for the trifling expense of one dollar a week. The master was a young lawyer. I also went to singing-school one evening in the week, and to writing-school another. Soon, the master of the academy getting married, a vacation was declared for a month. I had been progressing finely in reading, writing, and singing, so every one said, and regretted the interference of a vacation.

The time soon arrived when I had to take a final leave of my shipmate, his father, mother, brothers, sisters, and schoolmates, and return to Boston. Mother and the rest of the family were as glad to see me back as if I had just returned from a long sea voyage.

Upon investigation, I found only one of the *Vincennes'* crew in Boston — Samuel Williams — a gunner's mate, and one of the original crew. He had been shipped over five years, and, with many others, had received more than eight hundred dollars pay. He told me he had then but three hundred left, and that he did not know what to do with it. Said he had grown tired and lonely being on shore so long, and that the very paving-stones seemed to tell him to go home — to sea again. I never heard of him again.

A few days afterwards I shipped in the bark *General Scott*, bound to New York, and thence to Appalachicola. I made one trip in this bark, and several in the brig *Thomas Jefferson* to Mobile and New Orleans, and also two in an old down-east molasses drogher. Nothing of interest occurred on either of these short voyages, and in about two years I found myself at home again in

> " Boston, O Boston, that fair spot of earth,
> Where heaven gave glorious freedom her birth."

I soon obtained employment at painting, and commenced work. For amusement I occasionally spent an evening at the old National Theater. One evening I was sitting in the pit with a number of boys who were making considerable disturbance. " Old Dexter," the constable, had spoken to us several times, and requested us to be quiet. Finding his mandate unheeded, he leaned over, seized me by the collar, and lifted me out of my seat into the aisle. He was a large and powerful man, while I was small and wiry. We had reached the inside door of the pit, when the officer seeing that a fight was in progress in the entry left me to stop the fight. I improved the opportunity and skedaddled for home. The next day, hearing that officer Dexter was in pursuit of me, I remained in the house. Fortunately, in the evening I heard that a New York packet was short-handed. I shipped on her at once, and received four dollars for the run. We reached New York in three days. As we made fast to the wharf we found ourselves alongside a new clipper ship called the *Rainbow*. I soon went aboard of her, and as I did so a brisk, little, old man stepped up to me and said :

" Do you want to ship ? "

" What in ? "

" Why, in this ship, of course."

" Where bound, sir ? "

" To Canton, my lad."

" Thence, where ? "

" Return to New York."

" What wages, sir ? "

" Can you hand, reef, and steer ? "

" Yes, sir."

"Ten dollars per month."

" 1 will ship, sir."

He then handed me the following :

No Grog allowed in this Ship, and no Man received that is not Sober.

JAMES H. DILL, *Notary Public,*

No. 76 Wall Street.

Ship the bearer, CHARLIE ERSKINE, *as* ordinary seaman *on board of the ship* " RAINBOW," *at* $10 *per Month, and pay him* $20 *advance, with Security and Protection.*

New York, Jan. 29, 1845.

Your obed't Serv't,

CAPT. JOHN LAND.

No. 141.

I, CORNELIUS VAN NESS, Collector of the District of New York, do hereby Certify that CHAS. ERSKINE, *an* American Seaman *aged* 22 *years, or thereabouts, of the height of* 5 *feet* 7 *inches,* Brown *hair,* Dark *complexion, Born in* Boston, *State of* Massachusetts, *has this day produced to me proof, in the manner directed by the Act entitled " An Act for the Relief and Protection of American Seamen"; and pursuant to the said Act, I do hereby certify that the said* ERSKINE *is a Citizen of the United States of America.*

IN WITNESS WHEREOF, *I have hereunto set my Hand and Seal of Office, this* 29th *day of* January, 1845.

                                        I. W. T. TALMAN, *Collector.*

Feb. 1, 1845. Found myself on board of the ship *Rainbow*, Captain John Land, bound to Canton. The ship's decks and the wharf were crowded with spectators to witness the sailing of this new and beautiful craft. As we were being towed down the river, we were saluted with shouts and cheers from the shore. Large flags and banners hung from the spacious new warehouse of Messrs. Howland & Aspinwall, and the windows were filled with ladies. We had a very pleasant though cold sail down the Narrows to Sandy Hook. When we reached the light-house, the company on board, which consisted of about fifty gentlemen, left us and went aboard the steamer *Samson* which came after them. As they left, they gave us three times three cheers, which we returned with interest. The *Rainbow* was one of the first vessels of her kind — 750 tons burden, very long and narrow, very sharp, and an extraordinarily fast sailer, passing every vessel we came across. Before the steamer left us, Rev. Mr. Barker offered an appropriate prayer, and distributed several religious books among the crew.

Having made all sail, we bowled merrily along towards the open sea at the rate of nine knots an hour, the wind from the nor'west, we heading east-sou'east; all hands employed cleaning up decks and stowing the anchors. At five o'clock P. M. all hands were called aft and divided into watches.

Six o'clock, went to supper and the dog-watch set. The ship's company consisted of the captain, first and second mates, carpenter, cook, steward, cabin boy, ten seamen, six ordinary seamen, and six boys, making twenty-nine in all. Twenty-two before the mast, and nineteen of them were Americans. We also had four passengers — Mr. Lovett, Mr. Gardner, Mr. Saltonstall, and Mr. Newbold.

Nothing of importance occurred on the voyage, with the exception of passing several vessels, until the 4th, when we encountered a terrific gale. We took a double reef in the topsails and sent down the to'-gallant yards. The yards had no sooner touched the deck than all three to'-gallant masts went by the board. For three days afterward we ran under close-reefed topsails, with a very heavy sea dashing several feet over the monkey rail, flooding the deck and driving everything before it. Several casks of coal, having broken away from lashings, took a cruise about decks and did much damage. Two water casks full of water got loose and were carried over the rail without touching it. It was in this gale that the ships *United States* and *London*, from New York, foundered.

On the 8th it was beautifully clear. Shook all the reefs out of the topsails, and made all the sail we possibly could. Before ten o'clock our rigging resembled a washerwoman's clothes-line, being strung over with wet clothes of every description.

Sunday morning scrubbed decks and bent a new spanker At eight bells — eight o'clock — as the watch were going below, the weather threatening, the order was given to shorten sail. We furled the mainsail, took bonnet off the jib, close-reefed the topsails, and reefed the spanker. We passed a most miserable Sunday, having plenty of work to do.

February 10 and 11. Lying to under close-reefed foretop-sails and stay-sails.

The morning of the 14th was fine. In the afternoon saw land at a great distance to leeward, which proved to be the Azores, or Western Islands. Several sail in sight. For several days the weather continued fair, the wind light. We finished repairing our to'-gallant masts, sent them up, crossed our to'-gallant, royal, and sky-sail yards, and set the sails, with studding sails on either side. The wind being fair, we made rapid progress. The *Rainbow* kept her crew busy night and day, Sundays included. There is always a great deal of necessary work to be done aboard of a new ship on her first voyage, but on the *Rainbow* there appeared to be a large amount of unnecessary labor demanded.

One night the mid-watch had just gone below to turn in when it was called back on deck to take a pull at the weather braces. This was extra work, and unnecessary, and one of the watch began to growl. The captain ordered him aft. The man said he had no business aft. The captain then threatened to put him in irons. The man remained obstinate, however, and the captain, with the assistance of the steward, seized the sailor, and, after considerable difficulty, executed his threat.

The larboard watch, which had been below, hearing the scuffle, rushed on deck ; but before they arrived the man had been ironed and thrust down the booby hatch. The captain, who was very much excited at seeing all the larboard watch coming aft in a body and inquiring whom he had ironed, called for a cutlass. He then came in amongst us and inquired if any more of us wanted to be put in irons. A man by the name of Peter promptly replied that he did ; upon which he was seized by the collar, thrown upon the deck, and held there by the steward. Peter at once showed fight, whereupon the captain ordered him to be tied up to the rigging and flogged. The moment the order was given, Peter struggled to his feet, bared his breast, and, grasping his sheath knife, said to the captain, " You may run me through, but, by the Eternal, you'll never tie me up to the rigging and flog me alive."

The captain drew his cutlass. Up to this point the crew had remained very quiet, but when they saw the captain's action their blood began to rise. Each man tucked a fresh quid of tobacco into his cheek and was ready for a fight. A bloody mutiny might have occurred had not the passengers at this moment interfered, and by their entreaties induced the captain to let Peter go. So the cat's paw died away.

After Peter had been released, the captain ap- proached us and said, " Men, you know, or ought to know, the consequences of a man before the mast giving back lip. Do what you are ordered to do, and that quickly and cheerfully. There must be no swearing, quarreling, grumbling, or humbugging on board of this ship, and no such word as 'I can't' is to be used. You have shipped to work. Your time belongs to the owners, and therefore you are to find no fault. The work must be done, and if it is not done willingly, the sword must see it done."

Taylor, the man who had been put in irons, was now set at liberty, and the crew ordered forward. The larboard watch went below, and the starboard watch gave a pull at the weather braces, but not with the merry song as usual. In justice to the two mates, I will state that they took no part in the affair.

The 22d, Washington's birthday, we celebrated with plenty of hard work, not enough being thought of the day which gave our glorious and ever-to-be-remembered commander-in-chief birth, to make it a holiday. The only alleviation of the injustice was a dish of fried salt cod-fish for dinner, to which all hands did ample justice.

February 29. Sunday. A fairer morning never dawned. After having scrubbed decks, we scrubbed ourselves. At ten o'clock all hands were called aft to prayers. The passengers and crew gathered around the capstan, when the captain made a few remarks, stating the object of our meeting there on Sunday and how we might obtain salvation, and urged us to read our Bibles and other religious books. A chapter from the Bible was then read, and a hymn sung. Then followed a brief sermon, after which the services closed with prayer. Dinner hour soon arrived, when we had the pleasure of eating a plum duff with molasses, which we relished the more keenly as we remembered we had a watch below in the afternoon to settle it. At four o'clock we were again called aft to prayers, the services being similar to those held in the morning.

March 5. A fine, clear day, but very hot. Crossed the line to-day, but without the customary visit of Father Neptune. The only ceremony in crossing was a thorough baptism of rain, by which we were completely drenched.

March 15. We now doubled the "cape of storms," Cape of Good Hope. All the light yards were sent down, and everything made snug. The Southern Cross was now visible in the heavens, and its two polar stars shone as brightly as ever. For several days the ship was surrounded by albatrosses, cape pigeons, and stormy petrels.

April 3. In the morning made the island of Java and spoke the ship *Monument*, from Canton, bound for Boston. We soon entered the Straits of Sunda. The wind failing us, we came to in the roads and took in a supply of fresh buffalo meat, chickens, vegetables, fruits, garlic, and snaps, or Holland gin. Probably in no part of the world are chickens to be found so plenty and cheap as at this island. We could look into the water and see the bottom, fairly white with the bones which had been thrown overboard by the sailors who had visited the place. During the two days we lay here becalmed, it was chicken for breakfast, chicken for dinner, chicken for supper. It is as natural for an old sailor to growl as it is for him to breathe, and, on this occasion, they indulged in it freely. It was amusing to hear one of them growl out, "Oh, if they would only serve old salt horse for dinner!"

Early on the evening of the 5th, a light wind sprang up from the sou'west and we weighed anchor and made sail for Canton.   Shortly after making Macao, we were boarded by a Chinese pilot, who brought us up to our anchorage at Wampo.   Here we lay eighteen days. This was the sickly time of the year for this region. Consequently, each morning, at daylight, all hands had a *tot* (a wineglass) of garlic bitters (garlic steeped in gin), and at sunrise, a half-pint of strong Java coffee. We were also warned by the captain not to drink any *samshoe*, a native liquor.   The ship was discharged of her assorted freight, and we took on a cargo of teas, mace, and silks, which were stowed away in the hold by a Chinese stevedore and his gang of Chinamen.   While lying here we took the opportunity to cut three feet from our lower masts, to turn in and set up the lower rigging back-stays, and to do other necessary work.   Each watch had thirty-six hours' liberty to go to Canton, which was about sixteen miles from Wampo, up the Canton River. The favorite resort in Canton for sailors was Hog Lane and vicinity.   As soon as we had arrived in the lane the shopkeepers began to banter us for our names, which they wished to use as signs over the doors of their shops. The following are some of the names we saw : George Washington, Johnny Bull, Johnny Crapo, Portuguese Joe, Big Dick, Jim Crow, Jimmy Ducks, and many others too numerous to mention.   In many of the shops were notices of "Boston crackers, both hard and soft."   Another bore the sign of "Simmons' Oak Hall, North Ann Street, Boston, — the cheapest place in the world to buy clothing."   The venders of cat, rat, and dog pies, sugared worms, and coagulated blood, were more numerous than our peanut and apple venders.

If the devil should throw his net into Canton he would surely draw in his own. I verily believe every shop-keeper we met, man or woman, was an expert thief, cheat, and liar. They could change a black dog into a white monkey, to say nothing of a Spanish dollar into a counterfeit. We saw many strange sights. Barbers in the streets, shaving with razors that looked like little hatchets, old Chinese women reading large books, and old Chinamen driving hoops and flying kites. These kites were in the form of birds, and had wings. After purchasing several tea caddies, boxes, fans, and other things for the dear ones at home, we steered for Hog Lane, where we spent the night, having what Jack before the mast calls a jolly good time. In the morning, after taking an eye-opener, we breakfasted on cat or dog stew, — we were unable to determine which, though the meat tasted much like rabbit's meat. Of course the stew was plentifully thickened with rice. We returned on board at noon, when the larboard watch took their liberty.

While we were lying here, the residents back in the country were visited by an earthquake, which demolished over ten thousand houses and killed nearly five thousand people.

In the city of Canton there was a large opera house where an opera troupe had a three months' engagement. The Sunday night before we left, a fire broke out while some five or six thousand persons were assembled to witness the performance. Nearly all perished in the flames.

Labor was very cheap. We had all our clothes and blankets washed and mattresses packed for the small sum of one dollar ; also a jar of ginger presented to us as a "*come-ashore.*" The evening before our departure a grand display of fireworks was given in honor of Captain Land by several of his Chinese friends.

All the rigging having been set up, and the ship "all atanto," the hatches battened down, and everything made snug, on the morning of June 1st we weighed anchor and stood to sea.

While passing Hong Kong we saw "Old Ironsides" (the frigate *Constitution*) standing in. She fired a shot across our bow, as a signal for us to heave to. The captain paying no attention to it, or to the second, a third was sent through the foresail, when we hove to. Presently a boat from the *Constitution* came alongside. An officer climbed over the side, and a letter-bag was put on board. As the officer was walking aft with the captain, he espied me at the wheel.

"Why, Charlie, is that you?" he exclaimed.

On looking up, I was surprised at seeing old Lieutenant "D——n Your Eyes," of the *Vincennes*.

"Don't you know any better than to speak to the man at the wheel, 'D——n Your Eyes'?" I replied.

He soon took his departure, when we filled and stood on our course.

Nothing of importance occurred until we arrived off the coast of Cochin China, when we were overtaken by a sou'west monsoon. The captain, having his weather eye open, saw it coming, and we took in our light sails and sent the yards to the deck. The top-sails lowered, courses and crogic clued up, the squall now struck us, and we had lively work before we got the ship under bare poles. The wind blew furiously, lashing the sea into a perfect foam, from three to four feet deep. It was impossible to tell how rapidly the ship was driven through the water. It must have been from eighteen to twenty knots, or more, an hour. The storm continued about six hours.

After the storm had subsided we had fair wind and pleasant weather and "watch and watch," until we reached the cape, when we again experienced very rough weather. One night, the wind, which had been abaft our quarter, suddenly shifted dead ahead. Our sails were taken all aback, and the ship got such stern-way on her that everybody on board felt certain that she would go down stern foremost. It seemed a miracle how she was ever got before the wind. The sea was running very high, and the wind blowing a terrific gale. The ship was taking in water over the bows, and the deck was flooded fore and aft. All the sails were taken in, except the foretop-sail, which was blown out from the bolt-ropes, scarcely a shred of it remaining. One of our boys, by the name of Ambrose Hazard, was knocked off the main-yard onto the deck by the flapping of the sail which he was furling. He was picked up and carried into the cabin and put into a berth. Just then we shipped a very heavy sea which nearly flooded our forecastle and cabin. Poor Ambrose was washed out from his berth, and found floating in nearly two feet of water, dead. This gale was from the sou'east, and continued about thirty-six hours, carrying us well around the cape.

The first duty now devolving upon us was to bury the dead.   Old sailors are always averse to having dead men on board ship.   All hands and the passengers gathered at the lee gangway, where the impressive Episcopal burial service was performed by the captain.   The sun rose in calm sublimity out of the ocean in the eastern horizon as our shipmate's body was launched into its watery grave.   Just then a school of flying fish was seen to fly over the spot, followed by a school of dolphins, then a huge shark.   This shark followed in the wake of our ship for several days afterward.   In the afternoon Ambrose's chest was brought on deck and an auction sale of its contents commenced.   The captain acted as auctioneer.   He first held up several small bundles, but no one bid for them.   He next offered for sale a pair of trousers and a pea-jacket ; then the bedding.   He pleaded earnestly for some one to bid, but no one responded. Finally he took up several small packages which were tied up very neatly and labeled, and read the addresses.

The first was, "To my dear, loving mother, from her son Ambrose."   The next, "To my little flaxen-haired sister, Fannie."   Another, to "Brother Eddie."   The auctioneer, our captain, then made some very touching remarks which brought tears to the eyes of both the passengers and the crew.

For several days after this sad event we were busy sending up the light yards, mending and bending sails, and rigging studding gear.   I have heard of ships carrying many light sails, such as moonsails, star-gazers, skyscrapers, and heaven disturbers, but the *Rainbow* carried nothing above her sky-sails ; but she did carry a standing

crogic, a jib, an outer jib, a flying jib, and a bonnet on
her jib, fore and main lower, top, and top-gallant studding sails, and stay-sails too numerous to mention. She
had fifteen cloths in her lower studding sails, and five
hundred yards of canvas in her main course.

July 20. We were now rolling along by the island of
St. Helena, with studding sails below and aloft, and our
good ship moving through the water like a thing of life.
We were having " watch and watch," so we had plenty
of time to mend our clothes and spin yarns. The 20th
was the captain's birthday, and he celebrated it by having the ship's pet — a good-sized pig — killed. All
hands consequently had a fresh mess. Old Tom Taylor,
the man who had been put in irons, said, " The old man
reminds me of a Portuguese devil — when he is good he
is too good, and when he is bad he is too d——d bad."

The captain had naturally a very ugly temper, and was
a great bully. He was known as a bully captain out of
Baltimore. Just before this last voyage he had been
converted to religion. Probably he had become a
better man, but his old habits were still on him, and he
would often rip out and curse all hands as he had been
used to. He sometimes, however, would become aware
of his brutality, and would then dive down into his
cabin, and, falling upon his knees, would pray for half an
hour afterward ; any one could hear him, he prayed so
loud. Our two mates understood the old man better
than we did, and succeeded in preventing many a row.
We were now nearing the end of the voyage, and the
captain had been so kind in giving us " watch and
watch," which amounted to half time off, that we had

come to the conclusion that he was not such a bad man, after all.

The forecastle of the *Rainbow* was a damp, dark, and narrow little space in the bow of the ship. There was not room enough between where our chests were lashed for ten men to stand. Here we ate, drank, slept, smoked, took everything as it came along, and derived all the pleasure we possibly could. The crew were a manly, jolly set. I acquired more practical seamanship during the eight months while on board the *Rainbow* than in the whole seven years while in the navy, where a man or boy learns nothing but to pull, haul, splice, pass the balls, handle the sails, make grummets, work a Matthew Walker, a Turk's head, and tie a hard, square, hangman's, or a true lover's knot. None but able seamen are allowed to take a trick at the wheel or work on the rigging.

July 23. Our good ship has been making rapid progress towards home. To-day we crossed the equator, or equinoctial line. The Magellan Clouds and the constellation of the Southern Cross are growing fainter and fainter in the distance, while northward we see many of our old familiar friends that have cheered us in our night watches — Jupiter, the Pleiades, and the Big Dipper.

August 8. This evening in latitude 7° north, just above the northern horizon, we made the North Star. It was shining as brightly as ever.

August 10. Weather fair, with a strong breeze blowing from the sou'east. Our ship was making fourteen knots an hour. We carried this breeze until the 18th, when it commenced to slacken. In the evening caught a porpoise, and the following morning had some porpoise steak for breakfast, instead of our usual mess of lobscouse, which was made of bread, potatoes, onions, and salt beef and pork chopped up — the whole stewed together. This mess, with a pot of coffee sweetened with molasses, was generally the standard dish on board of a merchantman for Jack before the mast.

We were so near home now we were taking what Jack calls sailor's pleasure, that is, overhauling our chests, monk-bags, ditty-boxes, and the little parcels marked for brother, sister, or "the girl I left behind me." The small space where our deceased shipmate's chest had been lashed remained unoccupied, and any one of the crew would as soon have thought of jumping overboard as of sitting or standing there. The old sailors swore that they had seen poor Ambrose standing there, shivering in the wind, and looking as pale as a ghost.

As we neared the Gulf Stream the weather looked squally. The sky-sails and royal yards were sent on deck, and the flying-jib-boom housed. While crossing the stream the lightning was very vivid and the rain poured down in torrents.

At eight bells, four o'clock, on the morning of September 17th, took pilot. At daylight made the Highlands of Nevisink, off New York harbor. Soon after breakfast a steamboat came alongside and towed us up to the wharf, when all hands left the ship with chests and bedding. We had made the voyage to China and return in the extraordinarily short space of seven months and seventeen days, the quickest voyage from port to port in a sailing vessel ever made, I believe, before or since.

We arrived home eight days ahead of the *Monument,* though she had three thousand miles the start of us.

My stay in New York was but a few hours.

SQUARING THE YARDS WITH MY LANDLORD.

NEW YORK, Sept. 19, 1845.

CHARLIE ERSKINE

To "SAILORS' HOME," *Dr.*

	To 1 day's board and lodging	$0.50
	" cash cartage	0.25
	" " paid clothing	7.75
	" bill of old acct.	12.46
Sept. 18.	" cash	2.00
	" balance	20.60
		$43.56

Cr. by amt. rec'd from ship $43.56

Rec'd payment,

EDWARD D. STEVENS.

CHAPTER XVIII.

I LEFT New York the same evening for Boston. All glad to see me home once more. My brothers and sisters were much pleased with their little presents. Soon visited the National Theater and saw the officer, "Old Dexter." He gave me some good advice. A few days afterward, met with Father Taylor, who gave me one of the best lectures I ever listened to. He advised me to sail with a good Christian captain, so I next shipped in the bark *Laura*, Captain Leach, bound to New Orleans, thence to London, then to return to some port in the United States. This trip was put into a sailor's ditty by one of the crew.

> " From old Boston city we did set sail
>   In what appeared to be a fine craft, —
> It was the *Laura*, a bark
>   Which looked neat and handy from forward to aft.

> " Our captain's name is Leach, by the way,
>   A moral man he's thought to be;
> But salt water has his conscience stretched
>   In a manner strange to see,

> " As you'll perceive, if you but hark
>   And listen to what I say;
> For he had all hands trimming his bark
>   The first Sabbath at sea.

" He wished to get her by the head
　　That faster she might run;
And, as our noble captain said,
　　The thing it must be done.

" The wood we passed from aft to fore,
　　With ropes we did it bind;
The water casks lashed o'er and o'er
　　To please our captain's mind.

" He is a man that's hard to please,
　　He likes to keep us on the go;
He never seems to be at ease
　　When other folks are so.

" Our captain, he no seaman is,
　　And that we all can plainly see;
Yet he always likes to give orders,
　　And thinks no one knows more than he.

" And when at times there comes on a squall,
　　Our captain, he will frightened be;
He'll stamp and shout and confuse us all,
　　So that we scarce can hear or see.

" Oft by the time the work is done
　　And sails well taken in,
Why, the wind it is all gone,
　　We must make sail again.

" He likes to show the passengers
　　He is a man both smart and bold,
Has been through perilous dangers
　　In storm, and heat, and cold.

" He often tells about Cape Horn,
　　The Mediterranean, too,
When he two years at sea was gone;
　　Heaven knows if it be true !

" Enough I've said of our captain bold,
　　Still this is no jest,
　For there is much remains untold,
　　But you may guess the rest.

" It's of the mate I next shall tell,
　　As being next in rank.
　He's a man we all like well,
　　He's rude, but yet he's frank.

" The mate, he's an old Dutchman;
　　He'd please you, I am sure;
　At any rate, with such a man
　　I never sailed before.

" He's rough and rude, 'tis very true,—
　　And what old sea-dog's not?
　But surely he will well treat you,
　　If you're one of the right sort.

" Our dikey, Mr. Greggs, we all can see
　　How with him is the case;
　He very well would like to be
　　In Mr. Freeman's place.

" And so, to please bold Captain Leach,
　　He tries to keep us on the go;
　But having tried it with us each,
　　He finds it is no go.

" We are but six before the mast,
　　As good a six as ever met;
　For ne'er before was my lot cast
　　With such a manly, jovial set.

" Our forecastle is dark and wet,
　　But still we don't complain.
　Our captain, he will never meet
　　With the likes of us again.

" We've plenty, such as 'tis, to eat;
   A cook we need to make it good.
We don't wish for half-cooked meat;
   We are good men, we want good food.

" The steward, he's a dirty critter,
   And lazy, too, to boot;
Oft while he's mixing up his fritter
   His hands will be as black as soot.

" All hands are at work about the decks
   All the live-long day;
For 'watch and watch' we can't expect,
   We should hardly earn our pay.

" Come, then, my lads, what say you all?
   Shall we this stand a five months more?
Shall we stick by and weather the squalls,
   Or shall we go ashore?

" She is a bark by rig,
   At Boston she belongs.
I've all the crew for evidence,
   And they'll support my song.

" She now lies alongside the levee,
   And soon will want a crew;
But if she receives her just deserts,
   She surely will find but few."

The day after our arrival in New Orleans we heard
that the captain had taken freight for Cronstadt, Russia.
This was contrary to the original agreement, but we would
have stuck to the ship if we had had decent usage. As
it was, we were tired of the ship and the captain too,
and, to a man, we packed our " duds." He was

taken all aback when he saw that all hands were going ashore with their chests. He coaxed and pleaded with us to remain on board, told us that we were a good set of men and that we should have "watch and watch," and was even foolish enough to say that we should have plum duff twice a week. But we didn't feel inclined to accept his flattering offers, and it was several months before he succeeded in shipping a new crew.

The following morning I shipped as a deck hand on board the big *Sultanea*, a Mississippi steamboat. While on this steamboat, I recollect that on one trip we ran alongside a large emigrant ship from Amsterdam, and took on board between six and seven hundred high and low Dutch emigrants. They were short, stout, and thick-set, with round, full faces and rosy cheeks. They took deck passage to St. Louis. Their baggage consisted of chests, which were very heavy, being built of teak. The only bedding they brought with them was feather beds. They would lie down upon one of these and use the other for a covering. They drank the river water, ate green vegetables and other food which they purchased at the different landings. This unwholesome manner of living caused a great deal of sickness among them. I remained on this steamboat about six months, when I shipped in the brig *Thomas Jefferson*, for Boston, and received twelve dollars in payment for the run. We made the passage in eight days. As usual, my friends gave me a cordial welcome home. Shortly after my return I resumed work at painting, but soon abandoned it and shipped in the ship *Charles Carrol*, receiving eight dollars for the run to New Orleans. We lay in

Boston outer bay for six days, in a nor'east snow-storm, and then weighed anchor and put to sea.

This ship, *Carrol,* was one of the old-timers, being sixty odd years old. She was built for strength, and had great breadth of beam and a bow as broad as the stern of an old Dutch galiot. She was also a very dry ship and "laid to like a duck in a gale of wind." Our captain was a perfect fac-similie of old Father Neptune, and treated Jack before the mast as though he was his own son. The ship *Charles Carrol* was, as all ships should be, a floating sailors' home. Our crew were a good set of sailors, and nearly all Bostonians. We were thirty-two days on our passage from Boston Bay to the Balize, where we took steam and were towed up the river to New Orleans. Soon after the ship had been made fast alongside the levee, the captain told us to make our home aboard while the ship remained in port. While here, we heard the glad news that cotton was king, freights high, and that nearly every ship was taken up, and men very scarce.

The day after our arrival the crew formed themselves into two gangs and obtained employment at screwing cotton by the day. We accepted the captain's offer to make the ship our home, and slept in the forecastle and ate our grub at the French market. As the lighter, freighted with cotton, came alongside the ship in which we were at work, we hoisted it on board and dumped it into the ship's hold, then stowed it in tiers so snugly it would have been impossible to have found space enough left over to hold a copy of *The Boston Herald.* With the aid of a set of jack-screws and a ditty, we would stow away huge bales of cotton, singing all the while. The song enlivened the gang and seemed to make the work much easier. The foreman often sang this ditty, the rest of the gang joining in the chorus:

> " Were you ever in Boston town,
>   Bonnie laddie, Highland laddie?
> Yes, I've been in Boston town,
>   Where the ships sail up and down,
>   My bonnie Highland laddie, ho !
>
> " Were you ever in Mobile Bay,
>   Bonnie laddie, Highland laddie?
> Yes, I've been in Mobile Bay,
>   Screwing cotton by the day,
>   My bonnie Highland laddie, ho !
>
> " Were you ever in Miramichi,
>   Bonnie laddie, Highland laddie?
> Yes, I've been in Miramichi,
>   Where you make fast to a tree,
>   My bonnie Highland laddie, ho !
>
> " Were you ever in Quebec,
>   Bonnie laddie, Highland laddie?
> Yes, I have been in Quebec,
>   Stowing timber on the deck,
>   My bonnie Highland laddie, ho ! "

At another time we would sing :

> " Lift him up and carry him along,
>   Fire, maringo, fire away;
> Put him down where he belongs,
>   Fire, maringo, fire away;
> Ease him down and let him lay,
>   Fire, maringo, fire away;

> Screw him, and there he'll stay,
>   Fire, maringo, fire away;
> Stow him in his hole below,
>   Fire, maringo, fire away;
> Say he must, and then he'll go,
>   Fire, maringo, fire away.
> In New Orleans they say,
>   Fire, maringo, fire away,
> That General Jackson's gained the day,
>   Fire, maringo, fire away!"

I found stowing cotton in a ship's hold to be the most exhausting labor I had ever performed. We wore nothing but trousers, with a bandana handkerchief tied over our heads. The hold was a damp, dark place. The thermometer stood at nearly one hundred, not a breath of air stirred, and our bodies were reeking with perspiration. This was more than my frail body could endure. When I was paid, Saturday evening, with eight silver Spanish dollars for my four days' labor, I came to the conclusion that they were the hardest eight dollars I had ever earned, and that there would be no more screwing cotton by the day for me.

The following Monday I went to work at painting ships and steamboats for an old Portuguese, by the name of Desimees, in Algiers, a town situated on the opposite side of the river. A party of five, one an old shipmate of mine, hired a small shanty and kept bachelor's hall. We employed an old colored woman as housekeeper. On Saturdays we used to quit work early and go across the river to New Orleans and purchase our weekly supply of provisions. Although there was a United States mint in the city, there were at this time no cents in circulation. The smallest pieces of money were a five-cent piece, and a picayune,— six and a quarter cents,— and a Spanish coin called fourpence. It used to confuse Jack before the mast very much, that in Boston it was six shillings to the dollar, and in New York eight; that an eighth of a dollar, or twelve and a half cents, should be called ninepence in Boston, a shilling in New York, a long bit in New Orleans, and a levy in the Western States.

We got along splendidly keeping bachelor's hall, but we poor mortals were unable to endure so much prosperity, and, after remaining five weeks, surrendered the shanty to Miss Dinah, our aged colored landlady. The old lady was almost broken-hearted and wept bitterly when we left, saying, " I done feels drefful sorry fo' all my white chilens to go 'way and leave po' Dinah all 'lone." A few days afterward I shipped on board the steamboat *George Washington*, bound for Cincinnati.

On our third trip up the Ohio, one day a deck hand stepped up to me and said :

"Where were you raised, Charlie ? "

" Down east, in a little town near Boston, called Roxbury."

" Well, there is a man living in the town where I was raised whose name is the same as yours, and I'll bet two to one he is your father. He's got a family near Boston. He is now living in Spencer, Medina County, Ohio."

He then gave me directions as to how to find him.

After we had discharged the freight, I left the boat with all my earthly possessions, which were simply a change of clothing, in a bag hung over my shoulders, and a few shot in the locker (a little money). I followed my friend's direction to keep straight on until I came to the end of old Smith's road, which was eighty miles from Cincinnati, then turn to the left and inquire. He said that Spencer was about twenty miles toward the west. I had quite a pleasant walk across the State of Ohio. If I remember correctly, every team I saw on the road came from the opposite direction, so that I did not get a ride in the whole eighty miles. I was seven days in making the journey, and managed to put up at a tavern each evening. I enjoyed the walk much. I shall never forget one scene which occurred. It was on the fifth day, in the afternoon. Feeling somewhat weary, I sat down upon the brow of a hill, under a large, shady tree, nearly opposite which was an old farmhouse, the only one in sight. While resting here, I saw a tall, elderly man, with white hair reaching to his shoulders, leaning on a staff, come out of the house and go into a little cluster of bushes directly opposite where I was sitting. I saw him kneel, clasp his hands together, and look up toward heaven, then in hushed tones utter, "Our Father which art in heaven." I doffed my hat and bowed my head in reverence. It was a prayer of thanks—very brief, but one of the most fervent I have ever listened to. I have witnessed many touching scenes, but this one impressed itself upon my memory as the grandest of them all.

Arriving at the end of the road, which led into another that ran at right angles, I turned to the left, as directed, and soon came to a place called the "four corners," where there was a tavern, at which I remained over night. I arrived at the town of Spencer the following afternoon, and inquired if there was a gentleman living in that village by the name of Erskine. I was informed that there was, and that he boarded in a house about half a mile farther up the road, on the left. When I arrived at the house, I saw a very pleasant, elderly look-ing woman sitting at the window. I rapped on the door, and inquired if Mr. E —— resided there, and was told that he did. After a brief conversation I informed her who I was, when she invited me in and proceeded to relate my father's history from the date of his leaving Roxbury. Pointing to an old log-cabin on the opposite side of the road, she said I might find him at work there. I hesitated about calling there, and came very near turn-ing back, but the good woman talked to me very kindly and advised me to go. On entering the cabin I saw two old men sitting on a bench near the door. I made a few remarks to them about the weather, and passed along to where another old man was busily at work, bending over a currier's beam. It was some time before he looked up, but when he did, our eyes met and, for the first time in my life, I saw my father. I stepped up to him, saying,

"Haven't you seen me somewhere before?"

"Very likely, very likely," he replied. "I've often visited that town."

"That's the very place," I replied.

"Where?" said he.

"In the old town of Roxbury!" I exclaimed.

He was so overcome by this sudden disclosure he fell

prostrate upon the floor. The two elderly men referred to, lifted him up and tenderly laid him on the bench. It was some time before he regained his consciousness, but when he did, he wept like a child. The other men were also so much overcome that they retired from the cabin. The scene that followed within the cabin during the next half-hour is better imagined than described.

I remained at my father's boarding-house three days, during which time I learned from the good woman of the house more facts concerning the history of my father's life since he had left his home. She told me she had heard him say that about a year after his departure, while at work in Hartford, Conn., he drew nine thousand dollars in a lottery. He then stopped drinking, and fully resolved to return to his family and live a sober life the remainder of his days. For seven weeks he refrained from the use of intoxicating drinks. Then, receiving the money, he started for home, but thought he would just call at the tavern and take a parting glass with the boys. That glass aroused the old appetite. " More, more," cried the demon within him, drowning all nobler resolves. So resistless was this thirst that he spent a year in drunkenness, at the end of which time his money was gone. He did not return to his home as he really longed to do when he made that resolve, nor did he send a dollar to his family.

The third morning, after breakfast, I bade my father and the family in the house good-bye, and started for home, traveling a part of the way by the Erie Canal. When I arrived in Boston I found the family well, and astonished them by the story of my adventures in Ohio.

My father ultimately found his way back to Boston, but it was ten years after this time, and forty-two years and a half from the time he first left the town. While walking out from the Albany depot not a single building or landmark did he recognize until he reached the old Roxbury line. There, with bitter remorse, he

THE HOUSE WHERE I WAS BORN.

stood in front of the old mansion which had once been his happy and comfortable home.

A few days after my return I learned that able seamen were wanted for the navy, and thought quite strongly of shipping in it again, thinking I might possibly obtain a petty officer's berth. Calling one day at Jack Wright's boarding-house on Ann Street I found a number of old sailors who were discussing the brig *Somer's* tragedy, which had occurred a short time previous. One would have thought from the conversation that they were talking about bullies, tyrants, and brutes, instead of American naval officers.

" Why ! " growled out one old man-of-war's man, who had served in the navy over twenty years, " instead of making spread-eagles of us — tyin' the men up to the riggin' by their wrists with their arms extended — and lashin' 'em with the cats on their bare backs, now they'll put 'em in stocks, straight-jackets, or in double irons and gag 'em, and — "

" Jest look at the cowardly hangin' from the yard-arm o' them three young men on board o' the brig *Somers*, 'thout givin' 'em a chance to write a line to their fathers and mothers, or even say their prayers," interrupted another old weather-beaten sailor.

" Yes," spoke out a third, excitedly, " if you happen to cross an officer, let him be drunk or sober, you are counted a mutineer, and are strung up to the yard-arm or knocked down with a handspike or a belaying-pin ; and what are you going to do about it ? They seem to have forgotten the cowardly actions of the Portuguese boatswain's mate and other foreigners on board the unfortunate frigate *Chesapeake,* and keep right on promoting foreigners to petty officers' berths ; and I can't get promoted even to a Jimmy Duck's berth, or a captain of the afterguard. No more navy for me, shipmates."

The last speaker was a young American sailor who had

just returned from a three years' cruise on board the frigate *Potomac*.

I felt convinced that all these yarns were but too true, and said to myself, " No more navy for me, either." Thus ended my bright vision of procuring a petty officer's berth on board a man-of-war.

A few days after this I returned to my first love and shipped in a fore-and-after for Mobile. The schooner's crew consisted of the captain, and his father, — a very old sailor, — a young man, myself, and a small boy. The captain's wife and two daughters were also on board. We all bunked and messed in the cabin. The young ladies were very agreeable company.

The fifth day out, the captain's father — familiarly known as " Old Neptune" — died very suddenly, just at daybreak. It was a bright, beautiful day. About four o'clock in the afternoon we placed the dead body on a plank, one end of which rested on the lee rail of the schooner, the other on the head of a barrel. The remains were covered with a very old flag. The boy stood at the tiller, my shipmate and myself stood on either side of the foot of the plank, while the captain, his wife and two daughters were grouped together near the head of the body. The captain held a Bible in his hands, but was so overcome with grief he could neither read nor utter a word. He wept bitterly. His good wife and daughters made ineffectual efforts to comfort him in his bereavement. It was a sad funeral. Not a word was spoken, not even a whisper. Nothing broke the solemn silence but the sobs of the dead man's son, the rippling of the water under the schooner's bows, or the flapping of a sail.   After lingering some time the captain's wife gave the signal, when we raised the end of the plank and " Old Neptune's " body was consigned to a watery grave.

A SEA DIRGE.

Full fathom five thy father lies;
    Of his bones are coral made;
Those are pearls that were his eyes:
    Nothing of him that doth fade
But doth suffer a sea-change
Into something rich and strange.
Sea nymphs hourly ring his knell:
Hark! now I hear them,—Ding, dong, bell.
                                            —Shakespeare.

We made the passage to Mobile in seven days.   The captain, who owned two-thirds of the schooner, finding freights very dull, and wishing to lessen his expenses, discharged the young man, the boy, and myself.   The boy was indeed " a stranger in a strange land."   We all felt much sympathy for him.

Soon after leaving the schooner, I visited my uncle, Major Thomas Sturtevant, at Spring Hill, about six miles out from the city.   The few weeks that I remained with him I enjoyed much, the plantation hands giving me a great deal of amusement.

After leaving my uncle's home I passed over Lake Pontchartrain to New Orleans.   While there I fell in with an old shipmate by the name of Charlie Rugg, who was working at ship-painting in Algiers, opposite New Orleans.   I assisted him about painting the spars of the ship *Nathaniel Kimball.*   While at work on the fore-yard the foot rope parted, and I fell into the fore-rigging, which broke my fall, and thence onto the wharf, where I was taken up unconscious. Orders were at once given to carry me to Gritney Hospital. While on my way there I regained my consciousness, and, as soon as I understood the situation, told my friends to about-ship and leave me at John Gannoes', in New Orleans. After arriving there I lay on my beam-ends for over two months, during which time I had also a severe attack of cholera. The weather was very hot and the epidemic raged frightfully. After remaining quiet several weeks I felt improved, and gained considerable strength. While convalescing, I received the following lines :

DEAR CHARLIE.

He kissed me and then he said farewell
   While the tears rolled down his cheeks,
It seemed to me like his funeral knell
   And robbed my love of all its sweets.

      Oh! Charlie, dear Charlie, return to thy home,
      Thy Jennie is weeping, is weeping and lone.

O'er the ocean he's gone his fortune to seek,
   Oh! may he his fortune acquire;
Then hie to his home, where fond love shall complete
   His Jennie's most ardent desire.

      Oh! Charlie, dear Charlie, etc.

But if for dear Charlie no fortune is there,
   If strangers are heartless and cold,
Oh, may he return to his Jennie and share
   That love which is dearer than gold.

      Oh! Charlie, dear Charlie, etc.

> And whether dear Charlie gains fortune or no,
>   May love for his Jennie impart
> A wish to return to his home and bestow
>   Sweet peace to her wearisome heart.

These lines came from my bonnie lassie, my sweetheart Jennie. They took me between wind and water, and I at once made up my mind to return to Boston.

One of my former steamboat friends, Mr. Lane, mate of the *George Washington*, generously offered me a passage on his boat up the river to Cincinnati, which I accepted. When we arrived at Cincinnati I thanked my friend for his kindness, and took the steamer *Yorktown* for Wheeling, Va. From there I took a seat alongside the driver on a stage-coach over the Alleghany Mountains to Harrisburg, Pa. It was inconceivable to me how the driver managed to steer his four-in-hand clear of so many obstructions while his horses were going at full speed. The stage-coach keeled over many times where the road was steeper on one side than the other, and each time I thought surely we should be capsized. I enjoyed the ride intensely. The dense woods, the steep hills, the frequent villages, were indeed a novel scene. The whole trip, so full of variety, and so picturesque, greatly refreshed me. I think I must have been several pounds heavier when we arrived at Harrisburg than when I commenced the journey.

From Harrisburg I took the steam cars for Philadelphia. Arriving there I went directly to Chestnut Street, where my cousins resided. They gave me a very cordial welcome, and during my stay were untiring in their efforts to make my visit agreeable. I remained with them two weeks, then shipped in a full-rigged brig for Boston.

This craft reminded me much of one of my former sea-homes — the brig *Porpoise*. We left with the tide about four o'clock in the afternoon. While dropping down the Delaware we caught a large sturgeon, which proved to be delicious eating.

We had an extraordinarily long passage, not reaching Boston Light until early on the morning of the seventh day. By eight o'clock the brig was alongside of and made fast to Long Wharf. Bidding my shipmates adieu, I made sail for home. Soon after doubling the north-west corner of Canton Street, I fell in with and spoke " the girl I left behind me." One week later, at two bells, — seven o'clock in the evening, — we got under way, made all sail, and steered a direct course for North Bennett Street. Arriving directly off No. — we hove to, and hailed that godly man, Father Streeter, who tied the true lover's or matrimonial knot. Then, receiving his blessing and our clearance papers, we started off on the voyage of married life.

CONCLUSION.

IT has been truly said that it is not easy to do justice to the profession of the sailor. His noblest efforts are witnessed only by a few hardy spirits who are themselves actors with him. Not so in other professions. The words of the pulpit fall upon the ears of an attentive audience, whose human sympathies respond. The advocate, pleading in the court of justice, is surrounded by those who can pay homage to his eloquence. The judge records his opinions, and his name will be referred to in coming time. The senator, through the press, speaks to a listening nation. The artist, who imparts life to the canvas, leaves behind him the impress of his genius ; and the writer of romance keeps alive a world of ideal sympathy and passion.

The brave soldiers from all over our country parade the streets, and are cheered by their admiring fellow-citizens. But there is nothing of this inspiring nature to sustain the sailor in his conflict with the mighty deep. I have battled the ocean's storms for twenty years, and am aware that no language can give reality to the story of my experience. I have been swept from the vessel's deck and saved by a miracle, — none near to hear my despairing cry or witness my agony.

How often have my shipmates and myself faced death. The lightnings have flashed, the thunders have roared, the storms shrieked, and the whirling waters have threatened to engulf us ; but alone in mid-ocean we contended for mastery, and a line in the log-book is the only record of the peril we confronted.

As the sailor lives, so he dies. There is no audience but those who share his dangers. He lies down afar from home and friends, with no one to tell to the world the story of his battles, so bravely fought, though lost ; no one to witness his suffering, or note the courage with which he faced his last moment.

It is now sixty years since my dear mother gave me her parting blessing, and I sailed on my first voyage. Now on taking my bearings, overhauling a range of my log-book, taking an observation and working out my latitude, I find I am nearing the end of life's voyage. Soon I may expect to answer, " Aye, aye, Sir," when called higher up aloft, where there are no reefing top-sails, no Cape Horn, Cape of Good Hope, or storms of affliction, sorrow or grief, to double, but where we shall cruise in the Heavenly Seas above, among the Sunny Islands of the blest. All hands, rich and poor, high and low, ship owners and officers, and even Jack before the mast, will meet on a level there, on board of the Heav-enly Flag Ship, under one loving Lord High Admiral, who ruleth over all, and is no respecter of persons.

Shipmates, shall we meet together there?